Income Inequality

Income Inequality

Trends and International Comparisons

Edited by
John R. Moroney
Tulane University

LexingtonBooks
D.C. Heath and Company
Lexington, Massachusetts
Toronto

Library of Congress Cataloging in Publication Data

Charles Haywood Murphy Symposium in Political Economy, Tulane, 1978.
Economy, Tulane, 1978.
Income inequality.

1. Income distribution—Congresses. I. Moroney, John R. II. Title.
HC79.I5C46 1978 339.2 79-4726
ISBN 0-669-03058-9

Published simultaneously in Canada

Printed in the United States of America

International Standard Book Number: 0-669-03058-9

Library of Congress Catalog Card Number: 79-4726

To Joseph J. Spengler

Contents

List of Figures and Tables

Figures

Tables

Acknowledgments

A group of social scientists convened at Tulane, in New Orleans, Louisiana, April 6-8, 1978, to discuss issues concerning income distribution. As organizer of the conference, I was privileged to have worked with such an able group of scholars. The conference was a spirited one in every respect, and it encompassed a memorable blend of seasoned scholarship and social diversion—about four to one, just right to keep us alert and amiably critical.

Mrs. Omaya Wood handled the myriad administrative details with consummate cheerfulness and inspired efficiency, all the while serving as general administrative assistant to the Department of Economics. She flawlessly typed the repeated drafts of my manuscripts and major portions of other papers appearing in this volume. I welcome this opportunity to record my gratitude to her.

Most of the papers presented were designed for the conference. Two were subsequently published in journals. Edgar Browning's "The Burden of Taxation" appeared in the *Journal of Political Economy,* August 1978; a slightly shorter version of my paper "Do Women Earn Less under Capitalism?" appeared in the *Economic Journal,* September 1979. These papers are printed here with the kind permission of the editors of these journals.

Funding for the conference was generously provided through the Charles Haywood Murphy Program in Political Economy at Tulane.

1 Introduction

John R. Moroney

The Charles Haywood Murphy Symposium in Political Economy for 1978 addresses several important questions concerning the distribution of personal incomes. The questions fall into four groups, each presently under vigorous debate in the Western democracies. I shall not attempt to summarize the papers in this introduction; instead I shall outline the major themes of the conference.

The first question is central to any study of comparative economic systems: Is it possible to make meaningful international comparisons of income inequality; and if so, are there systematic differences in the degree of inequality according to alternative forms of economic organization? Harold Lydall (chapter 2) focuses squarely on the most vexing problems inherent in attempting international comparisons; and Janet Chapman (chapter 3) analyzes several difficulties encountered in comparing distributions in market and nonmarket economies.

A second question is of keen importance in mature economies with large and burgeoning government sectors: To what extent do fiscal variables affect income inequality?[1] To obtain a partial answer for market economies, Pechman and Okner (1974) followed a traditional methodology to estimate overall tax burdens (as a percentage of personal income) by income class in the United States. Using progressive incidence assumptions, they concluded that the overall tax system is mildly progressive over the lowest two income deciles, roughly proportional from the third decile (21.7 percent overall tax rate) through the ninth decile (23.1 percent) and steeply progressive within the highest decile (30.1 percent). Chapter 4, by Eugene Smolensky, Werner Pommerehne, and Robert Dalrymple, adheres to a "traditional" methodology of allocating tax burdens, and compares the pretax and posttax income distributions in the United States and West Germany. Edgar Browning (chapter 5) contends that the traditional methodology used by most scholars to allocate tax burdens is seriously flawed and that application of a correct procedure, devised in his chapter, produces a much steeper progression of tax burdens in the United States than has heretofore been recognized.

A third theme concerns inequality in the earnings of men and women. Solomon Polachek (chapter 6) presents a thorough statistical analysis of the demand- and supply-side determinants of women's earnings. His study, based on

I am pleased to acknowledge the helpful comments of Martin Bronfenbrenner on the first draft of this chapter.

U.S. data spanning the past twenty years, affirms the findings of others that women earn on the average considerably less than men in this country. Polachek goes further than other analysts, however, and applies a human capital framework to explain the persistently low relative earnings of women. Modern radical economists offer a different explanation. They attribute comparatively low women's earnings in the United States to fundamental institutions of capitalism that stultify opportunities for women in the marketplace. My own comparative study (chapter 7) reveals that during the past three decades or so women have earned less than men in a broad sample of capitalist as well as socialist economies. Yet if one sets aside the common law countries (Australia, Canada, the United Kingdom, and the United States), the earnings of women relative to those of men are practically identical within capitalist countries and the socialist countries of East Europe. This evidence plainly contravenes the radical thesis.

During the past twenty years or so much legislation in Western countries has aimed to improve the economic lot of certain ethnic, racial, sex, and age groups. The sting of differentiation in the marketplace or elsewhere, of course, is felt by individuals, not by collectives. Neoclassical economic tradition upholds the individual as the prime agent and suggests that redress for discrimination should be enacted on behalf of individuals, not groups. Lester Thurow, in chapter 8, contests the neoclassical view on empirical grounds. He demonstrates that in the United States average economic earnings have differed markedly across racial and other groups. This finding affirms, in his view, that individuals have in fact been perceived and rewarded partially on the basis of their noneconomic (group) characteristics. To permit members of such groups a justifiable opportunity to improve their relative position, he reasons that legislation should properly focus on groups rather than individuals.

International Comparisons of Income Inequality

The first problem encountered in making international comparisons is variation in the economic unit for which income is recorded. Several alternatives have been proposed, including the individual, the tax unit, the consumer unit, the spending unit, the household, and the family. The degree of measured inequality can be quite sensitive to the unit of observation. As Lydall shows, the greatest measured inequality (recorded by Gini coefficients) occurs among individuals. As a practical matter, measured inequality among consumer units on the one hand and households on the other is practically identical (see tables 2-2 and 2-3). But the distribution of incomes across families is substantially more equal than that across households.

Lydall emphasizes that most international comparisons are at root intended to describe disparities in the distribution of welfare rather than in the distribution of income per se. Of course there is no ideal scientific measure of the distribution of welfare, much less any such measure that would be suitable internationally. Lydall believes that the best surrogate is the distribution of household income, adjusted for differences in household size or composition. Making such adjustments with data recently published by the World Bank, he finds that household income inequality is reduced moderately in developed countries but is diminished sharply among rural households in India (see table 2-2, part B, and table 2-3).

A second important consideration is differences in pretax and posttax distributions. Most advanced market economies have tax systems that are nominally progressive but effectively less so. For example, the Gini coefficient for the distribution of pretax consumer unit income in Canada (1969) is 0.382 but is reduced to 0.354 for posttax income (table 2-2, part B). Using "normal" assumptions concerning the incidence of taxes, Smolensky, Pommerehne, and Dalrymple find even larger differences between pretax and posttax distributions: West German data for 1969 yield a pretax Gini coefficient of 0.364 but a posttax coefficient of 0.271. Applying similar tax incidence assumptions to 1970 U.S. data reduces the pretax Gini coefficient of 0.446 to a posttax value of 0.375. Indeed, the posttax distributions within a country are unsettlingly sensitive to assumptions concenring tax incidence. Using West German data and "regressive" tax assumptions, Smolensky and his colleagues compute a posttax (postgovernment expenditures) Gini coefficient of 0.282; however, under "progressive" assumptions the coefficient plummets to 0.161. These differences, attributable strictly to alternative assumptions concerning tax incidence, are considerably larger than the differences between Gini coefficients (based on pretax household incomes) for the United States, the United Kingdom, Pakistan, and India (rural households) presented by Lydall (table 2-3).

A third potential problem in the comparison of market and socialist economies is variation in nonearned services provided to individuals by the state. Timar (1978), for example, notes that in Hungary in 1975 roughly 72 percent of personal income was received by workers in the form of wages, approximately 15.5 percent as cash transfers, and approximately 12 percent as social benefits in kind. In the United States in 1975, on the other hand, 70 percent of personal income was received as wages and 14 percent as cash transfer payments; the balance consisted of property income, a significant portion consisting of proprietors' labor income (*Survey of Current Business,* July 1977, p. 27). There are of course noncash benefits in kind in the United States, which are not recorded in personal income distribution. What is not known in socialist countries, as emphasized by Chapman and Lydall, is the income in kind received by the hierarchical elites. But since the lion's share of personal income received in both capitalist and socialist countries consists of wages and cash transfers, the presumably stronger equalizing effects of income in kind within socialist economies may not create a serious problem vitiating international comparisons.[2]

A fourth problem, stressed by Lydall, is differences in the length of the income period. During any interval measured income consists of a systematic and a random component. In general, the longer the period over which income is measured, the smaller the random component and the smaller the dispersion in measured relative incomes. It thus appears that longer intervals of income measurement yield a truer picture of dispersion in systematic incomes. Yet the use of long periods introduces new problems, such as changes in the composition of the income earning unit. There appears to be no practical guideline for selecting an optimal income period. But for international or intertemporal comparisons, one should strive to use income periods of comparable length.

Bearing these caveats in mind, we may make some suggestive international comparisons. Lydall's preferred measure is inequality of household income standardized for household size. He presents evidence for such units, taken from the Royal Commission on the Distribution of Income and Wealth and from a recent study by Jan Michal (1977) that suggests that the distribution of posttax income is quite similar in the United Kingdom, Czechoslovakia, Hungary, and Poland: the Gini coefficients are 0.25 for the United Kingdom (1974), 0.21 for Czechoslovakia (1973), 0.24 for Hungary (1969), and 0.24 for Poland (1973).

Alternative evidence for eleven capitalist countries is available from the recent study by Sawyer (1976). Assuming that all countries have identical distributions of household size and making crude adjustments for taxes, Sawyer obtains the following Gini coefficients for the distribution of posttax income (p. 19):

Australia	(1966-1967)	0.35
Canada	(1972)	0.35
France	(1970)	0.42
Germany	(1973)	0.39
Japan	(1969)	0.34
Netherlands	(1967)	0.26
Norway	(1970)	0.30
Spain	(1971)	0.40
Sweden	(1972)	0.27
United Kingdom	(1973)	0.33
United States	(1972)	0.37

These estimates suggest that the greatest equality has been achieved in the Netherlands, Sweden, and Norway, an intermediate degree of equality in the United Kingdom, Australia, Canada, the United States, and Japan, and somewhat less equality in Germany, France, and Spain. Because of the crude adjustments used by Sawyer, these coefficients are not comparable to those presented by Lydall.

As a measure of income inequality the Gini coefficient is subject to well-known limitations (Wiles 1974, Michal 1973, 1975). Accordingly, it is useful to consider some alternatives. One widely used index that shows the spread between an upper income stratum and the median is the ratio of earnings at the upper tenth percentile to the median (P_{10}). Evidence on posttax per capita household incomes presented by Lydall suggests these distributions were practically identical in the United Kingdom in 1974 (P_{10} = 1.75), Czechoslovakia in 1973 (P_{10} = 1.67), Hungary in 1969 (P_{10} = 1.64), and Poland in 1973 (P_{10} = 1.81). (These numbers appear as P_{90} in table 2-4 but would be referred to by most other authors as P_{10}.)

Much more evidence is available concerning the distribution of earnings of full-time wage and salary earners. The P_{10} ratios for the pretax earnings of such individuals appear in table 1-1. Earnings inequality in the United States does not display any perceptible trend, and the average value of P_{10} is 1.86. The degree of inequality in Yugoslavia is quite comparable to that in the United States. The average value of P_{10} in Yugoslavia is 1.83, and there was no apparent trend between 1962 and 1971. An evidently greater degree of earnings equality has been achieved within the small socialist economies of Poland, Czechoslovakia, and Hungary, particularly the latter two. The average value of P_{10} for these three countries is 1.63.

Table 1-1
Ratios of Upper Tenth Percentile of Pretax Individual Earnings to Median Earnings of Individuals, Selected Countries

Country	*Year*	P_{10}	*Country*	*Year*	P_{10}
United States	1939	1.97	Hungary	1952	1.74
	1949	1.66	(state sector)	1955	1.68
	1959	1.67		1960	1.62
	1968	1.99		1964	1.60
	1972	2.12		1966	1.61
	1975	1.77		1968	1.61
Yugoslavia	1962	1.83	Poland	1960	1.74
(socialist sector)	1964	2.05	(socialist sector)	1964	1.77
	1967	1.75		1968	1.74
	1970	1.78		1972	1.83
	1971	1.75			
			Soviet Union	1946	2.7
Czechoslovakia	1959	1.52		1956	2.2
(socialist sector)	1962	1.51		1959	2.0
	1964	1.51		1961	2.0
	1966	1.52		1964	1.9
	1968	1.53		1966	1.8
	1970	1.56		1968	1.8
				1970	1.7

Source: United States: table 3-6, nonagricultural wage and salary earners; Yugoslavia and Poland: Michal, 1975, table 9.1; Czechoslovakia and Hungary: Michal, 1973, table 1; Soviet Union: table 3-5.

Inequality in the Soviet Union is a different story. Earnings differentials until the early 1960s were apparently larger than those in the United States. Wage differentials were of course used as crucial incentives throughout the Stalinist period. The economic and political liberalization initiated by Khrushchev and continued by his successors sparked a steady narrowing of earnings differentials, carefully documented by Janet Chapman. Nonetheless, with P_{10} as the yardstick, individual earnings differentials in the Soviet Union in 1968 or 1970 were comparable to those in the United States in 1975.

If one is willing to ignore the marked differences among the socialist economies and instead views them as representing a single prototypical system, there is practically no difference between average earnings inequality at the upper end of the scale in these countries and that in the United States.[3] The average value of P_{10} in the socialist countries for the post-World War II years is 1.7, that in the United States 1.8. These are measures of pretax earnings inequality. Since income taxes are both more important and more progressive in the United States than in the socialist economies, it is conceivable that greater equality of posttax earnings (measured by P_{10}) has been achieved in this country than in Yugoslavia, Poland, and the Soviet Union, although any differences would surely by negligible.

It is useful as well to consider differentiation at the lower end of the earnings scale. To do so, define P_{90} as the ratio of earnings at the lowest tenth percentile to median earnings. Consider first the inequality of posttax per capita household incomes, presented in table 2-4. Inequality in the United Kingdom in 1974 ($P_{90} = 0.56$) is equivalent to that in Czechoslovakia in 1973 ($P_{90} = 0.56$), Hungary in 1969 ($P_{90} = 0.58$), or Poland in 1973 ($P_{90} = 0.60$).

Next consider the P_{90} ratios for pretax earnings of individual full-time workers, presented in table 1-2. The P_{90} ratio in the United States has been stable at approximately 0.46 since 1968. Yugoslavia, Czechoslovakia, Hungary, and Poland display relatively homogeneous, trendless ratios; the average value in these four countries is 0.61.

The Soviet Union again manifests a trend toward greater equality. Relative inequality at the lower end of the Soviet earnings distribution until the early 1960s was comparable to that in the United States during the past decade. But by 1970 inequality of Soviet earnings was approaching that of the smaller European socialist countries. This elevation at the lower end of the Soviet earnings distribution is attributed by Chapman to increases in minimum wage rates, particularly to a sharp 50 percent increase in January 1968.

Czechoslovakia, Hungary, and Poland show greater overall equality of individual pretax earnings than the United States. Yugoslavia and, more recently, the Soviet Union also display somewhat greater equality, especially at the lower end of the earnings distribution. These findings accord with those of Pryor (1972), who found that wage incomes of men during the late 1950s and early 1960s were more equally distributed in European communist countries than in

Table 1-2
Ratios of Lower Tenth Percentile of Pretax Individual Earnings to Median Earnings of Individuals, Selected Countries

Country	*Year*	P_{90}
United States	1968	0.46
	1972	0.47
	1975	0.45
Yugoslavia (socialist sector)	1962	0.58
	1964	0.54
	1967	0.60
	1969	0.58[a]
	1970	0.60
	1971	0.57
Czechoslovakia (socialist sector)	1959	0.63
	1962	0.64
	1964	0.64
	1966	0.64
	1968	0.64
	1970	0.64
Hungary (state sector)	1952	0.60
	1955	0.61
	1960	0.62
	1964	0.64
	1966	0.62
	1968	0.61
	1970	0.62[b]
	1972	0.62[b]
Poland (socialist sector)	1960	0.57
	1964	0.59
	1968	0.55
	1972	0.62
Soviet Union	1946	0.38
	1956	0.46
	1959	0.49
	1961	0.50
	1964	0.53
	1966	0.55
	1968	0.56
	1970	0.58

Sources: United States: table 3-6, Nonagricultural wage and salary earners; Yugoslavia and Poland: Michal, 1975, table 9.1; Czechoslovakia and Hungary: Michal, 1973, table 1; Soviet Union: table 3-5.

[a]Michal, 1973, table 1.

[b]Michal, 1975, table 9.1.

Western nations. It is doubtful that these conclusions would be much modified by the use of posttax earnings data. However, the degree of inequality among posttax per capita household incomes in the United Kingdom is practically identical to that in Czechoslovakia, Hungary, and Poland. One thing is certain: the differences in income inequality across socialist countries and the evolutionary changes in the Soviet Union since World War II have been at least as great as the international differences between socialist countries (as a group) and the United States.

The Role of Fiscal Variables

Does the state induce greater equality through its capacity to tax, transfer, and spend income? It is widely held that modern governments, both democratic and totalitarian, promote greater equality, and this role is often used to justify the extension of government authority. A complete analysis calls for a two-pronged attack, one dealing with the general influence of governmental macroeconomic activity, the other with the specific instruments in the hands of the state. At the macroeconomic level we know that a high rate of employment, particularly during wartime, tends to reduce current earnings inequality. Members of the part-time and secondary labor market, especially women and racial minorities, are upgraded when full-time males are drafted for combat. Yet to focus on inequality of current earnings is to miss an important point. Those who die or are physically or psychologically maimed in war are drawn disproportionately from lower- and lower-middle-income groups. Their permanent income is destroyed or depleted more heavily than that of others as a consequence of active combat. It may be that greater inequality of permanent income is thereby induced. Apart from wars, a generally high level of economic activity exerts a modest influence in the direction of greater equality of current and permanent earnings. Statistical analysis of these macro influences is beyond the scope of the papers in this volume.[4]

The chapters by Smolensky, Pommerehne, and Dalrymple and by Browning focus on the specific influence of tax burdens by income class. Smolensky and his colleagues estimate the incidence of taxes, together with the benefits of public expenditures, on eleven size categories of household income in the United States and West Germany. Three alternative sets of tax incidence assumptions are used. The distribution of pretax factor income (excluding transfer payments) is somewhat less equal among households in the United States in 1970 (Gini coefficient = 0.45) than among households in Germany in 1969 (Gini coefficient = 0.36). If one excludes the redistributive effects of government spending and makes intermediate assumptions concerning tax incidence, posttax income inequality is reduced substantially; the Gini coefficient falls from 0.45 to 0.38 in the United States, and from 0.36 to 0.27 in Germany.[5] If the most progressive assumptions concerning tax incidence are applied and the redistributive effects of government spending are taken into account, aftertax inequality is reduced sharply; the Gini coefficient in the United States declines to 0.28, that in Germany to 0.16. Thus Smolensky and his colleagues show that aftertax income is distributed much more equally than pretax factor income and that the results are sensitive to alternative assumptions concerning tax incidence.

Browning's work reinforces this view. The main point of Browning's chapter is to show that the traditional method of allocating tax incidence according to income groups entails a crucial error if all income is not in the form of factor earnings. Consider a many-sector model in which initially there are no sales taxes and zero net savings for all household income categories. Now suppose that a uniform (say, 10 percent) sales tax is levied on all goods and services at the level of final demand, but that the money prices of all goods and services remain constant, say by reason of appropriate monetary policy. The real earnings of capital and labor thus decline by 10 percent.

If all income is indeed factor income (earnings of labor and capital), the burden of such a sales tax could be estimated correctly in proportion either to factor income or to consumption outlays. Traditionally, the tax burden has been estimated in proportion to consumption outlays. The justification for such an allocation is no longer correct, however, if some groups receive income in the form of transfer payments rather than factor earnings. Since posttax product prices are unchanged, a household that receives 100 percent of its income as transfer payments (whose real value remains unchanged following the imposition of the sales tax) would bear no tax burden whatsoever.

In trying to convey the essence of his discussion concerning sales tax incidence, I have grossly oversimplified Browning's analysis. After considering several complications, Browning suggests that the burden of a general sales tax should properly be allocated according to factor earnings rather than according to consumption. He argues in parallel fashion that the traditional method of allocating excise tax burdens in proportion to consumption of the taxed good is flawed. When some income is derived from transfer payments, he suggests that the correct procedure is to estimate the effects on the sources (income) and uses (expenditure) sides of the household budget and then to add them.

Browning reasons that moderate differences in consumption patterns by income level exert a minor influence on differential tax burdens across income classes. The crucial variable, then, is the percentage of income that each class receives as transfer payments. He estimates that in the United States this proportion varies from 65 percent for the lowest income quintile to 8 percent for the highest. Thus only 35 percent of total income received by the lowest quintile is subject to any burden attributable to sales and excise taxes, while 92 percent of income in the highest quintile is exposed to such taxes.

Browning's methodology is equally applicable in a setting of rising product prices if the monetary values of transfer payments and earnings from capital assets increase so that their real values remain constant. The political economy of transfer payments commends the workability of this hypothesis.

Browning's computations, based on the foregoing assumptions, yield a picture of tax burdens radically different from that portrayed by Pechman and Okner, who follow the traditional methodology. Indeed, they conclude that regardless of tax incidence assumptions, there is essentially no difference in effective tax rates between the tenth and ninety-seventh percentiles of family income units. They accordingly believe that the U.S. tax system exerts only a minor influence on the relative distribution of income. By contrast, Browning finds the overall tax system to be steeply progressive. Using competitive incidence assumptions for taxes other than sales and excise taxes, the effective overall rate rises continuously from 10.1 percent for the lowest income decile to 32.6 percent for the highest (table 5-3).

Further evidence on the equalizing role of government taxes and transfers is available from Sawyer (1976), who estimates the share of households, by income deciles, in pretax, pretransfer income and in posttax, posttransfer income in Canada, Sweden, and Spain. A partial reproduction of his findings appears in table 1-3. The disparities in pretax, pretransfer income between deciles 1 and 10 are strikingly similar for the three countries: households in the lowest two deciles have almost no earnings, while those in the highest decile earn between 28 percent and 30 percent of factor income. Taxes and transfers sharply reduce such inequalities, most dramatically in Sweden. Although the top decile has indefinably greater pretax, pretransfer income than the lowest decile in Sweden, it receives but five times as much posttax, posttransfer income as the lowest decile. Smaller but nonetheless substantial reductions in relative inequality occur in Canada and Spain.

This evidence reinforces the findings presented by Browning and by Smolensky and his colleagues. Taxes and transfers much reduce inequality in a range of capitalist economies. The comparative influence of fiscal instruments under capitalism and socialism has not been studied extensively, chiefly because the tax and transfer mechanisms are so different in the two systems.

Comparative Earnings of Women

Income disparity between men and women has received much attention in recent years. It is indisputable that, on the average, women earn less than men in

Table 1-3
Shares of Households, Ranked by Income Decile, in Pretax, Pretransfer Income and in Posttax, Posttransfer Income

	Share, by Decile, in		
Country	*Pretax, Pretransfer Income*	*Transfers*	*Posttax, Post-transfer Income*
Canada (1969)			
Decile 1	0.1	26.0	2.5
Decile 2	1.4	21.1	3.5
Decile 9	17.1	5.1	15.8
Decile 10	28.0	6.0	24.8
Sweden (1972)			
Decile 1	–0.2	17.0	4.1
Decile 2	0.3	20.3	5.3
Decile 9	18.4	5.5	15.3
Decile 10	28.8	5.2	20.3
Spain (1973-1974)			
Decile 1	0.0	33.1	4.4
Decile 2	1.0	17.8	3.2(?)
Decile 9	17.5	5.2	15.9
Decile 10	29.9	5.3	26.4

Source: Sawyer, 1976, appendix 3, p. 34.

the marketplace. This fact transcends all countries and all epochs in which earnings have been recorded. This fact, together with other proclaimed disenfranchisements, has sparked legislation to enhance the economic status of women, particularly in Western countries.

In the United States the comparatively lower earnings of women stem both from their lower wages within occupations (intraoccupational differentiation) and from their concentration in relatively lower-paying occupational groups (occupational differentiation). Polachek presents a thorough analysis of sex-based differentiation in this country. He emphasizes that sex-based earnings disparities could be primarily demand determined, primarily supply determined, or could result from some combination of these forces. Which remedial policies would be more effective depends crucially on whether supply-side or demand-size forces predominate. If the primary sources are rooted in demand and produce demand-based occupational segregation, then antidiscriminatory employment legislation is called for. If, however, the sources are found chiefly in supply, so that women acquire less capital (marketable skills) than men, an entirely different set of public policies is required: they should be designed to encourage continuous labor force participation and the acquisition of particular skills by women.

Polachek tackles this issue by first analyzing the occupational segregation thesis. Using nine broad occupational groups taken from the U.S. Census of Population for 1960 and 1970, he demonstrates large differences in the occupational structure of the male and female labor forces, with men being concentrated in the more remunerative occupations. Averaged over all occupations in 1970, the female hourly wage rate was but two-thirds that of men; and because a larger percentage of women worked part-time, their average annual earnings were only 46 percent of those of men. If pure occupational segregation were the only source of the overall wage differential, the gap could hypothetically be closed if either (1) males had precisely the female occupational distribution or (2) women had precisely the male occupational distribution. By computing the hypothetical earnings of men according to (1) and those of women according to (2), Polachek finds that occupational differentiation accounts for only about 20 percent of the actual wage gap. He thus concludes that the major sources of earnings disparities must be sought elsewhere.

Turning to the supply side, Polachek finds systematic differences between men and women in continuity and length of labor force participation and in college educational choices. For men and women of a given age, the ranking by years of labor market experience is married males, never-married males, never-married females, and married females. Thus among workers in a given age bracket, men on the average have acquired more human capital in the form of work experience and on-the-job training. Men also tend to major in different types of undergraduate college training than women. From a sample of 718 undergraduates in 1959, Polachek reports that men specialized more in business, engineering, and physical sciences; women more in home economics, education, and nursing. College preparation thus tends to provide different foundations for further training and work experience for men than for women.

What crucial economic and sociological variables affect earnings and occupational choice? Using the 1967 National Longitudinal Survey sample of 933 white, married women who were working in 1966, Polachek finds that both years of schooling and years of work experience significantly increased their hourly wage rates. By contrast, periods spent out of the labor force, as well as labor force intermittency, depressed wages. Polachek recognizes that the years of work experience and periods spent out of the labor force may be partially determined by, as well as determinants of, women's wages. For example, low wages may be a source of discouragement and may thereby inhibit labor force participation. He therefore obtains first-stage estimates of work experience and time spent out of the labor force, then uses these instrumental variables to reestimate the earnings equations. The instrumental variables remain highly significant. From this evidence he concludes that the period of a married woman's life spent out of the labor force is governed mainly by home responsibilities, not by low market earnings.

Differences in labor force experience and intermittency account for much of the earnings gap between married men and married women. Indeed, the total life-cycle incomes of never-married men and never-married women are similar, although the patterns of annual earnings differ. Using average earnings based on the 1960 U.S. Census, one can see that the annual earnings of never-married men rise sharply between the ages of twenty and thirty, peak when these men reach their mid thirties, and decline steadily thereafter. Earnings of never-married women rise to a peak when they reach their late forties, beyond which they decline but remain above the earnings of never-married men of comparable age (figure 6-1).

A person's occupational choice is critically influenced by his acquired human capital; and one's incentives to acquire human capital are partly determined by available occupational choices. This two-way path is widely recognized. But the lanes may be narrower and steeper for women than for men. Polachek investigates this question with a simultaneous equations model that permits identification of the primary sources of occupational differentiation. The idea is straightforward. If the acquisition of human capital by women is not rewarded by better jobs, demand-based occupational discrimination exists. By contrast, if aspirations toward high occupational goals do not motivate women to acquire as much human capital as men, even though their skills, if acquired, would be equally rewarded, then observed differences in occupational distributions are attributable chiefly to behavioral differences on the supply side.

Polachek uses the National Opinion Research Center occupational prestige scores as indexes of occupational attainment, and level of schooling as the index of purchased human capital. The model is estimated by applying three-stage least squares to two independent samples: 8,963 working women and 27,021 men sampled from the 1960 Census of Population.

The results are striking. For equivalent increases in schooling, the proportionate increase in occupational prestige is much higher for women (+0.37) than for men (+0.21), and the difference is significant at the 99.9 percent confidence level. But for equivalent perceived payoffs in occupational prestige, men apparently acquire far more schooling than women (table 6-9). If one accepts Polachek's model as valid, the findings are revolutionary. The occupational carrot is larger for women, but men acquire more schooling in pursuit of equal or smaller expected occupational advancement. This model so strongly contradicts prevailing views concerning occupational discrimination that it should be tested with other measures of occupational prestige and other samples, in this country and abroad.

On the other hand, certain modern radicals have ascribed the comparatively low earnings of women in the United States to allegedly "capitalistic" institutions (see Davies and Reich 1972). The contemptible instruments of oppression, in their view are (1) the nuclear family and woman's specialized role therein; (2) the separation between marketplace and household production activities; and (3) a wage-labor market primarily for the benefit of men. Their reasoning is specious, for all these institutions characterize modern socialist economies as well.[6] And none of the radicals has yet performed a comparative study of women's relative earnings.

My chapter does just that. The predominantly capitalist economies include Australia, Canada, the United Kingdom, and the United States, as well as several non-English-speaking countries: Austria, Belgium, Chile, Finland, France, Germany, Israel, Japan, the Netherlands, and Norway. Separate earnings of men and women could be obtained in only three socialist countries: Czechoslovakia, Hungary, and Poland. However, I also review some information concerning sectoral employment of men and women in Communist China, Cuba, and the Soviet Union.

Consider initially the economy wide ratios of median pretax earnings of full-time, year-round workers (table 7-1). The ratio of women's earnings to men's earnings in Czechoslovakia, Hungary, and Poland in the postwar period shows little variance and has a mean value of 0.676. The earnings ratio shows much greater variation across capitalist countries, in which the arithmetic mean is 0.613. This average, however, conceals major differences within the capitalist economies. The average earnings ratio in the English-speaking nations is 0.582, but a significantly higher average of 0.688 is obtained for Belgium, Finland, France, and Israel. For the purpose of classifying relative earnings of women, a simple division of economic systems as capitalistic and socialistic is not very meaningful.

The same is true if we focus on earnings ratios of full-time manual workers (table 7-2). The average ratio in Hungary and Poland is 0.657, a figure consistent with two sample surveys in Soviet cities in the mid 1960s that reported ratios of 0.64 and 0.69.[7] By contrast, the average ratio in eleven capitalistic economies is 0.600. Among these, however, the English-speaking countries have a mean ratio of 0.551, the others a significantly higher ratio of 0.648. Aside from the English-speaking societies, there is simply no difference between the relative earnings of women under capitalism and European-style communism.

Although sex-specific earnings are not available for communist countries outside the Soviet Bloc, there is evidence that women were concentrated in the low-wage sectors of Communist China (1955) and Cuba (1970), as well as in the Soviet Union (1973). The relative economic position of women has almost certainly improved in these countries in recent years. But whether women are economically better off under socialist than under capitalist institutions remains essentially an article of faith.

I should perhaps emphasize that my chapter focuses strictly on the narrow question of women's relative earnings. The broader question of economic well-being is of course a closely related but distinct issue that would require a comparative study of social security, inheritance, and claims by family and society on men's and women's energies outside the marketplace. It is widely believed, for example, that societal tolls on women are particularly acute in Communist China and Cuba, where much "volunteer" work is in fact mandatory. On the other hand, the economic benefits of social security, as well as the inheritance of property, are more favorable to women than to men in the United States and other Western countries.

A Theory of Groups

Throughout the history of Western civilization, particularly during the past hundred years or so, much sociological analysis has centered on groups. Thus Marx spoke of alienated workers, execrated the bourgeoisie, and heralded a class struggle in which the proletariat would triumph. On the other hand, American political and legal philosophy have traditionally concentrated on individuals as the prime agents and have upheld the values of rugged individualism. Yet the economic legitimacy of groups as groups has become more firmly embedded in our political and legal thinking during the past twenty or thirty years. For example, class action suits were practically unheard of in this country twenty years ago but are now commonplace. And although many American colleges in the early 1960s maintained admissions policies prohibiting the disclosure of racial identity of applicants, the affirmative action programs of the 1970s either encourage or require racial identification. Seldom, however, are the root questions posed: To what extent is the economic analysis of groups a valid procedure, and what characteristics may be used to define a legitimate group? The analysis of these questions is the central purpose of Thurow's chapter.

His starting point is that we live in a highly stochastic economic world in which the economic and other identifiable characteristics of individuals typically explain only 20 percent to 30 percent of the interpersonal variation in earnings. The greatest share of the variation is attributable to chance and to psychological traits such as ambition and learned habits of work.[8] Because most of the variation in individual earnings is unexplained in the statistical sense, it is impossible to know whether any individual has been treated fairly or unfairly in society. There are in fact great differences in the observed earnings of individuals having equal intrinsic abilities and who have played the same economic lottery. Yet if we consider the earnings of a large group of individuals sharing some common observable characteristic such as race or sex, it may well be possible to tell whether this group as an aggregate has played the same economic lottery as some other group. And since it is possible to identify only group discrimination, compensatory measures must necessarily be focused on groups, not individuals.

Having established the necessity of group analysis, Thurow asks, What criteria can be used to distinguish between legitimate and illegitimate economic groups? Thurow suggests two: groups should be large enough to contain individuals with the same distribution of innate abilities and the same potential distribution of economic characteristics; there must also be significant differences between the mean economic reward of one group and that of others. If such groups can be properly identified, then how can equality of opportunity practicably be achieved? Thurow suggests that in order to create equality of economic opportunity among groups (and presumably their constituents) in the long run, members of groups disadvantaged in the past must be given special privileges (reverse discrimination) until their average income is equal to that of other groups. In Thurow's view the members of various groups, on the average, would then have equal odds in the economic lottery. An amusing consequence follows: If such equality of opportunity were ever achieved, economically legitimate groups would vanish, according to his second criterion.

Thurow then presents some interesting evidence concerning differences in average earnings of different groups classified according to race, sex, age, and region. He shows that legislation in the United States has often been based on an acceptance of the political legitimacy of certain groups, such as farmers and the aged, but not of others such as racial or religious minorities. As a matter of practical politics this is understandable. The aged may be a politically acceptable group because most voters will one day belong; racial or religious minorities may be politically less acceptable because their membership is obviously more restricted.

Summary and Conclusions

The papers presented at the Murphy Symposium for 1978 provide firm answers to several important questions. Perhaps equally important, they bring into focus other questions that cry out for analysis.

The principle of inequality is well established in both primarily capitalistic and modern socialist economies. It is not often rigorously defended in capitalist societies because it is a well-understood consequence of market processes; but it is carefully rationalized by communist theoreticians. The apologetics of the Soviet sociologists cited in my chapter underscore the need for totalitarian regimes, whose predecessors led a revolution under a different banner, to justify inequalities within their system. The principle of Christian communism, "from each according to his talents, to each according to his needs," worked well in the intimate Christian communes of the first and second centuries. Yet throughout history this principle has been proven practicable only within nuclear or extended families in which the bonds of love and kinship supplant the instincts of greed and envy.

Inequality of wage incomes is an essential characteristic of modern capitalistic and socialist economies. With P_{10} ratios as the yardstick, inequality of pretax earnings is roughly comparable in the United States, Yugoslavia, and the Soviet Union. A greater degree of earnings equality has been achieved in Czechoslovakia and Hungary. Using P_{90} ratios as an alternative measure, however, indicates that all European socialist economies recently manifested greater equality of earnings than the United States. Formal statistical study of wage dispersions, based on a broad range of capitalistic and socialist economies, stands as a fruitful avenue for future research.[9] It would be enriched if the governments of Cuba and Communist China would publish the relevant statistics for their economies.

Income inequality is of course a much broader issue than inequality of wages alone. The dispersion in the distribution of wealth typifying capitalistic economies causes a greater dispersion of incomes, particularly at the extreme upper end of the distribution, than in socialist countries where property is both more equally distributed and less important as a source of income. Regrettably, the Gini coefficient is the only statistic characterizing overall income distributions about which we have much international information. Using the Gini coefficient computed from posttax per capita household incomes, Lydall demonstrates that recent income distributions in the United Kingdom, Czechoslovakia, Hungary, and Poland are indistinguishable. Sawyer's (1976) related (but not completely comparable) evidence places the Netherlands, Sweden, and Norway in this group as well but suggests that Australia, Canada, France, Germany, Spain, and the United States are marked by greater income inequality. The still broader, more complex questions concerning inequality in the distribution of personal well-being remain to be carefully posed and analyzed.

Aftertax earnings of capital and labor are distributed much more equally than pretax earnings in the United States. If the redistributive effects of government spending and transfer payments are accounted for, Smolensky and his colleagues estimate that a further reduction in personal income inequality is realized in the United States and in Germany. As nonearned transfer payments become a more important source of income to lower-income groups, Browning's methodology for allocating tax burdens takes on greater quantitative significance. And the trade-off between greater equality of posttax, posttransfer income and intensity of individual productive work effort becomes sharper.

Women earn, on the average, less than men in capitalistic and socialist economies alike. Polachek proposes some salient reasons for this fact; and although his analysis is confined to the United States, his methods are applicable to other countries and should certainly be followed up. If we gauge the position of women in the marketplace by overall earnings ratios, there is no meaningful difference between socialist economies and non-English-speaking capitalist societies. The statistically relevant distinction is between English-speaking and non-English-speaking countries. We do not yet know why women earn less, relative to men, in English-speaking societies than in societies that speak other languages. This important subject requires much further study.

Notes

1. Evidence concerning the growth of government in advanced capitalistic countries is presented in the recent study by Nutter (1978).

2. Pryor (1968), for example, finds that certain types of public expenditures vary more widely within the groups of communist and capitalist countries than they do across countries typified by different economic systems.

3. I do not advocate that one disregard such differences as size and level of economic development that distinguish the Soviet Union from the smaller communist countries. Pryor (1972) has shown that such differences are significant determinants of (nonagricultural) income inequality and cannot properly be ignored.

4. Some empirical evidence of macroeconomic influences is found in Anderson (1964) and Batchelder (1964).

5. This posttax Gini coefficient suggests that Germany displays very nearly the same equality of posttax household incomes as the United Kingdom; but this estimate is inexplicably smaller than the posttax estimate of 0.39 obtained for the year 1973 by Sawyer (1976).

6. Much more carefully reasoned critiques of the position of women, which recognize explicitly that the nuclear family and patriarchal value systems predate the evolution of capitalism, are presented by Rowbotham (1974), Zaretsky (1976), and Rubin (1978).

7. Swafford (1978) presents the most complete analysis to date of female and male earnings in the Soviet Union. Using an unpublished sample covering 1,284 women and 1,890 men in Soviet Armenia for the year 1963, he finds the ratio of mean earnings to be 0.648.

8. The importance of "learned habits of work" as a determinant of individual earnings is stressed by Lydall (1968, pp. 83 ff). Mental health itself

appears to be the most crucial determinant of an individual's performance. For fascinating documentation, see Menninger (1938). See also Bergler (1949).

9. Pryor's paper (1972) is a landmark in this respect.

References

Anderson, W.H. Locke. 1964. "Trickling Down: The Relationship between Economic Growth and the Extent of Poverty among American Families." *Quarterly Journal of Economics* 78 (November):511-524.

Batchelder, Alan B. 1964. "Decline in the Relative Income of Negro Men." *Quarterly Journal of Economics* 78 (November):525-548.

Bergler, Edmund. 1949. *The Basic Neurosis.* New York: Grune and Stratton.

Davies, Margery, and Reich, Michael. 1972. "On the Relationship between Sexism and Capitalism." In Richard C. Edwards, Michael Reich, and Thomas E. Weisskopf, eds., *The Capitalist System: A Radical Analysis of American Society.* Englewood Cliffs, N.J.: Prentice-Hall.

Lydall, Harold F. 1968. *The Structure of Earnings.* London: Oxford University Press.

Menninger, Karl A. 1938. *Man against Himself.* New York: Harcourt, Brace and Company.

Michal, Jan. 1973. "Size Distribution of Earnings and Household Incomes in Small Socialist Countries." *Review of Income and Wealth,* Series 19 (December):407-427.

_______. 1975. "An Alternative Approach to Measuring Income Inequality in Eastern Europe." In Z. Fallenbuchl, ed., *Economic Development in the Soviet Union and Eastern Europe,* vol. 1: *Reforms, Technology, and Income Distribution.* New York: Praeger.

_______. 1977. "Size Distribution of Household Incomes and Earnings in Developed Socialist Countries: With a Proposed Marginal Utility-Weighted Gini Coefficient." Mimeographed.

Nutter, G. Warren. 1978. *Growth of Government in the West.* Washington, D.C.: American Enterprise Institute for Public Policy Research.

Pechman, Joseph A., and Okner, Benjamin A. 1974. *Who Bears the Tax Burden?* Washington, D.C.: Brookings Institution.

Pryor, Frederic. 1968. *Public Expenditures in Communist and Capitalist Nations.* Homewood, Ill.: Richard D. Irwin.

_______. 1972. "The Distribution of Nonagricultural Labor Incomes in Communist and Capitalist Nations." *Slavic Review* 31 (September):639-650.

Rowbotham, Sheila. 1974. *Woman's Consciousness, Man's World.* Baltimore, Md.: Penguine Books.

Rubin, Gayle. 1978. "The Social Nature of Sexism." In Richard C. Edwards, Michael Reich, and Thomas E. Weisskopf, eds., *The Capitalist System: A*

Radical Analysis of American Society, 2d ed. Englewood Cliffs, N.J.: Prentice-Hall.

Sawyer, Malcolm. 1976. *Income Distribution in OECD Countries.* Paris: Organization for Economic Cooperation and Development.

Swafford, Michael. 1978. "Sex Differences in Soviet Earnings." *American Sociological Review* 43 (October):657-673.

Timar, Janos. 1978. "Income Distribution and Incomes Policy in Hungary."

Wiles, Peter. 1974. *Distribution of Income: East and West.* Amsterdam: North-Holland.

Zaretsky, Eli. 1976. *Capitalism, the Family, and Personal Life.* New York: Harper and Row.

2 Some Problems in Making International Comparisons of Inequality

Harold F. Lydall

It is essential for meaningful comparisons that the objects to be compared are measured in standard units. No one doubts the need for standardization in measuring physical objects. But economic entities are not always so carefully defined and measured. In no department of economics, to my knowledge, is there such inadequate standardization of measurement techniques as in the study of size distributions of income.

If two classes of objects are to be compared, we must be able to determine, first, which objects should be members of the two classes and, second, precisely which characteristics of the objects are to be compared. If we apply these criteria to size distributions of income, they tell us that we need to decide what we mean by an income unit and what flow of income is to be measured. Moreover, since income is a flow per unit of time, this second question has two aspects: What categories of income are to be included? What is the appropriate period of measurement?[1]

The Income Unit

There is a wide choice of possible units: they include the individual, the tax unit, the consumer unit, the spending unit, and the household. Under each category we may include all possible units of that description, or we may restrict the population. For example, individuals may be limited to economically active persons, to those in receipt of a separate money income, or to those with a money income above some threshold. Alternatively, we may exclude all individuals who are only partly economically active, for example, because they usually work part-time or because they have worked for only part of the period of measurement. Each of these decisions yields a different distribution of income. If we include people with zero incomes, we shall have a highly skewed distribution with a large degree of inequality. If we include part-time or part-period workers, the distribution will be more unequal than if we exclude them. If we include men, women, and children, the distribution will usually be more unequal than one confined to one of these categories.

While the incomes of individuals are of interest for some purposes, international comparisons of inequality are more often concerned with the problem of the distribution of welfare. Since individuals usually share their incomes with members of their family, or at least with those members with whom they live, and to some degree with other members of the same household, the distribution of welfare depends on the distribution of income between and within these units. We know very little about the distribution of welfare within families or households, and economists have hitherto contracted out of that question. Perhaps it is partly for that reason that there has been a tendency to accept uncritically income distributions in which families or households are the ultimate units. It would be difficult otherwise to account for the equal weights usually given to units of completely different size and composition in such distributions.

If equality is the standard, the income standard for households of different size and composition needs to be unequal. It makes no sense, therefore, to measure inequality of incomes across households or other heterogeneous units and to treat such measures as indexes of inequality of welfare. If we try to cover ourselves by saying "subject of course to a given distribution of households by size and composition," we are agreeing to renounce the use of our inequality measures for international comparisons, and even for comparisons within a single country over any period of more than a few years.

Each type of income unit yields a different estimate of the degree of inequality. In general, the smaller the unit, the greater the apparent degree of inequality. This rule–which is not without exceptions–is a consequence of the partly endogenous process of clustering people into income-sharing units. In poorer countries this clustering is inevitable; the completely impoverished must cling to their relations and form extended families. But in advanced industrialized countries the extended family is breaking up, partly as a result of the welfare state, and even the nuclear family is beginning to disintegrate in some cases. The effects of these trends are almost certainly to increase measured inequality, although the fragmentation of income units is in large part voluntary.

Tax units are usually defined as single adults and married couples–the smallest of the composite units. If there were no tax exemption limit, which truncates a distribution of tax units, we might expect the inequality of tax units to be greater than the inequality of larger units. Even with some degree of truncation, this seems to be the usual case.

The term *consumer unit* is used to describe the families and unrelated individuals who form the ultimate income units of the Current Population Survey in the United States and the corresponding survey in Canada. This unit is wider than the tax unit in many cases, for example, for families containing more than one nuclear family. But the inclusion of a large number of unrelated individuals makes the degree of inequality of income of consumer units almost as great as the degree of inequality of a distribution of tax units. Separate analysis of families may seem to be a sensible compromise. But if the proportion of unrelated individuals in the population is growing, as it has been in recent years, it is difficult to argue that the distribution of family incomes tells the whole story.

The spending unit, which has not been widely used, is intermediate between the family and the household. The household is the largest of the units employed, and it generally yields the smallest degree of measured inequality.

If we are interested primarily in the distribution of welfare, none of these income units is satisfactory. We should be choosing a unit within which there is a large degree of income pooling and then adjusting the measured income of that unit for its size and composition. If we choose the household as our pooling unit, which may be as good a choice as any, we should at least divide household income by the number of persons in the household, to obtain per capita household income. We can then count either the number of households or the number of persons who are in each range of per capita income. This very simple adjustment surely makes more sense than taking a crude distribution of any of the previously listed income units.

To be more sophisticated, we may give each type of household a weight dependent on its size and composition. If we have an "equivalence scale," it will tell us how many "equivalent units" there are in each type of household. The number of equivalent units is supposed to measure the relative cost of achieving an equal level of welfare in households of different types. If we divide each household income by its number of equivalent units, we obtain a measure of the welfare level of the members of that household. As before, we may construct alternative frequency distributions, after ranking households by their income per equivalent unit: a distribution of households, of persons, or of equivalent units.

In making comparisons of income distributions, whether across countries or over time, I believe that we shall come closer to the truth about the distribution of welfare if we rank households either by per capita income or by per equivalent unit income than if we use the crude distributions of income units that are commonly available. Even if we were to use the same income units in each country or over time the socioeconomic significance of that unit is likely to differ or change. It is even worse, of course, if we use different units in different countries. Yet this is frequently done. Even when we rank households by per capita income or by equivalent unit income, we cannot be sure that the results are strictly comparable in different distributions for the socioeconomic meaning of a household may be different, or may change, and this will affect the degree of aggregation of income in the original units from which the per capita or per equivalent unit distributions are derived.

Income Coverage

Measured personal income may include a wide range of different items: money income from factor services, cash transfers, private income in kind, public income in kind, capital gains, investment income of life insurance and pension funds, and so on. In most cases inclusion of cash transfers and income in kind reduces measured inequality in market-economy countries. It is often claimed that income in kind, such as public education and health services, has a strongly equalizing effect in socialist countries; but no estimates are ever given of the income in kind (or fringe benefits) of the hierarchy.

It is questionable whether social benefits should be valued at cost, as is the normal practice, since rationed goods and services have less utility to the consumer than goods and services purchased on a free market for the same total outlay. A society in which all goods were rationed equally, and exchange were forbidden, would be both very unequal and very dreary.

Inclusion of capital gains usually increases measured inequality, but not in a period of rapid inflation, if only real gains are included.

A notable example of the serious distortion of inequality measurement resulting from inadequate income coverage is given by the distributions of household incomes in France quoted in a United Nations report (1967). Household incomes were obtained by aggregating tax assessments on all persons apparently living in the same dwelling. But French tax assessments exclude most kinds of social transfers and, at least in the period to which the distributions refer, greatly underestimate the incomes of the self-employed, especially the numerous peasants. Statistics derived from these data show the bottom 10 percent of French households receiving 0.7 percent of total income in 1956 and 0.5 percent in 1962—one-fourteenth and one-twentieth of population averages (Jain 1975). These figures have been widely quoted and used to demonstrate that French inequality is exceptionally large. From other evidence it seems that the conclusion is correct, but these figures greatly exaggerate the degree of French inequality.

In almost all advanced market economies there are highly progressive income taxes. In the less developed countries income taxes are often nominally progressive but not very effective. In socialist countries income taxes are low and only very slightly progressive. Hence it is misleading to compare pretax income distributions across all three groups of countries. Yet this is regularly done, without apology. It would be better to use posttax distributions for the countries with highly progressive tax structures, and preferably for all.

Should we also allow for differences in indirect taxes? This is a more difficult question. If one country has high taxes on necessities and low taxes on luxuries, while in another country it is the other way about, it seems that inequality of money income underestimates real inequality in the first country and overestimates it in the second. But this conclusion depends on an implicit assumption that personal utility levels are independent of the degree of scarcity of luxury goods. In a country where luxuries are heavily taxed, relatively few people with high money incomes buy luxuries. But those few have a greater sense of distinction and perhaps arouse a greater feeling of envy than those with high incomes in a country where luxuries are more widely distributed. I do not think that we know enough about the factors influencing cardinal welfare to be able to say that the structure of indirect taxes works unambiguously in one direction rather than another. In any case, of course, it is not the structure of indirect taxes that matters but the structure of relative prices, which may be influenced by factors besides taxes.

In principle, some adjustment should be made for different levels of prices in different parts of a country, such as in different regions or in urban and rural areas.[2] If price levels vary appreciably, the inequality of money incomes exaggerates the degree of inequality of real incomes. Unfortunately, for lack of suitable data, this correction is practically never made. Consideration of the problem suggests that large and geographically diversified countries are likely to have greater measured inequality of money incomes than smaller and more homogeneous countries, even when their real degree of inequality is the same.

The Income Period

A fundamental characteristic of income flows is that they fluctuate over time. On the one hand, there are systematic changes, such as the growth of earnings in early years of work experience and the decline in earnings in years close to retirement. On the other hand, there are random fluctuations. Random fluctuations have definite causes, such as illness, overtime work, changes in piecework conditions, industrial disputes, unexpected promotion, change of job; but the occurrence of these causes is largely unpredictable. For the self-employed there are additional causes of random fluctuations, which are often large.

In general, both in the case of life-cycle variations and in the case of random fluctuations, the longer the period of measurement of income, the smaller the degree of relative dispersion of individual incomes. From a practical point of view, however, it is random fluctuations that are most likely to affect comparability, since life-cycle variations extend over a span of time too wide to be used as a period of measurement in any normal circumstances. Actual statistics of income are sometimes collected for a period as short as a week, more often for a month, and frequently—at least in some countries—for as much as a year. It is obvious that an individual's income for a week is likely to vary to a greater degree, in proportion to the mean income of his group or to his own trend income, than a month's income, and it is likely to vary even more than a year's income. Indeed, for some kinds of income, such as investment income or entrepreneurial income, income in a given week or month may vary from zero to a large positive (or negative) amount.

Since random fluctuations in income (Friedman's "transitory" income) add a misleading component to income inequality, and since their pattern and probability of occurrence may vary from one country to another, it might seem advantageous to have all income periods as long as possible. But when we consider the practical implications of such a rule for data collection, it becomes clear that the rule needs to be modified. There are three practical objections to the use of very long periods of measurement. First, long periods of measurement reduce the degree of sensitivity of the system of measurement to change. Second, long periods may be more difficult to measure accurately than shorter periods. Third, since the composition of the population changes over long periods, it becomes more difficult as the time period extends to identify income units that have been in existence throughout the period and to decide what to do with those that have been in existence for only part of the period.

This last point is of considerable practical importance. Suppose, for example, that the source of data on income distribution is the income tax administration. From their point of view, an income unit (a tax unit) begins to exist if a separate tax file is created; and a new file is started for any individual (except perhaps the wife of an already taxed husband) who starts to receive an income at any time during the year. The number of tax units in a given year is equal to the number of tax files active in that year. But many of those tax units have received income for only part of the year. Part-year incomes occur for young people who start work during the year, for spouses who divorce or separate and start receiving a separately taxed income, and for people who emigrate or die during the year; the numbers involved are substantial. In the United Kingdom, for example, the proportion of part-year tax units is estimated to be about 8 percent of all tax units (including in tax units those persons who would be counted as such if they were not exempted from tax). Their income distribution has a very low mode and is highly skewed; their exclusion from the population of tax units significantly reduces the degree of inequality. In 1974-1975 the effect was to reduce the Gini coefficient from 0.371 to 0.349, to reduce the share of the top 10 percent from 26.6 percent to 25.9 percent, and to raise the share of the bottom 10 percent of tax units from 2.6 percent to 3.3 percent.[3]

A similar problem arises, probably in a more acute form, in the collection of survey income data in the United States and Canada.[4] For example, in the U.S. Current Population Surveys consumer units (families and unrelated persons) are classified by their status at the time of interview in March. But their incomes are reported for the preceding calendar year. The consequences of this "income-composition lag" are very strange. For example, a young single adult who was living with his parents during the calendar year but is living separately in March (and presumably has an independent income at that time) may be recorded as having zero income during the calendar year. To the uncritical analyst, who assumes that the reported statistics relate to current flows of income, such a person appears to be living in absolute poverty. Another case that produces a similar effect is that of a wife who has recently (or at any time during the previous fifteen months) separated from her husband, or whose husband has died, and whose independent income is now larger than it was during the preceding calendar year. There are also people whose measured incomes move in the opposite direction: for example, a woman who gave up work after marriage. But these errors do not compensate for each other. Both types of error tend to increase measured dispersion in comparison with the dispersion that would be measured if the income flow were related to income unit composition in a more consistent manner. But the first type of error has an especially serious effect, because it increases significantly the number of persons apparently (but not really) living in poverty.

On this problem of the income period there is a difficult choice to be made. Random fluctuations in income can be reduced (proportionately) if the income period is extended; but the problem of matching income to the composition of the income unit is thereby increased. I cannot see any ideal solution to this difficulty; but it would at least be helpful to analyze separately income units whose income level has been significantly affected by a change in their personal composition. It is probable that the removal of such units from the usual U.S. and Canadian distributions would significantly reduce the measured level of inequality in those countries, and especially reduce the proportion of incomes at the bottom of the distribution.[5]

Reporting Errors

Even when all definitions are the same in two distributions, the results may be affected by differences in the nature of the reporting errors. These errors divide into biases and random errors. Survey data are usually biased downward by underreporting of income, especially investment income, entrepreneurial income, and subsidiary sources such as pensions and transfers. The net effect is probably to understate the shares of both the rich and the poor. The Gini coefficient may not be greatly affected, but the measured Lorenz curve may intersect the true Lorenz curve. Biases also occur in tax assessments and may well be similarly concentrated at the two ends of the distribution.

Random errors are often very large, especially but not exclusively in voluntary data derived from censuses and surveys (see, for example, Sirken, Maynes, and Frechtling 1958). Unless these errors are sufficiently negatively correlated with true income, the variance of measured income overstates the true variance of income. I suspect that this is a significant factor in accounting for the level of measured inequality of income in the U.S. Current Population Surveys and in the corresponding Canadian surveys. Income data collected in Eastern European countries suffer from some bias arising from underreporting of subsidiary earnings, but reports of major sources of income are probably made with greater care for accuracy than in Western countries.

Effects on Inequality of Variations in Definitions

Since different countries use different definitions of the income unit, income coverage, and the income period (and use different techniques of data collection), it is important to estimate the effects of such variations in definitions on the measured degree of inequality.[6] It is impossible at this stage to give a comprehensive answer to that question. But we have some information about the effects of certain changes in definition. The effects are often large in relation to the differences found in a crude comparison of two distributions, and it may be useful to give a few examples.

The World Bank has recently published a collection of processed income distributions from eighty-one countries, in many cases including several distributions for the same country (Jain 1975). This is a valuable collection, but it needs to be used with great caution. The authors have drawn attention to some of the main differences in the definitions used, but they have not, in my opinion, given a sufficiently strong warning against treating the various distributions as comparable.

There is perhaps not much danger that users will try to compare distributions that have a different type of geographical coverage, for example, urban and rural areas. But they may too easily be led to compare distributions that have the same geographical coverage but are based on different income units. Four main types of income unit are distinguished in the report: economically active persons, income recipients, households, and workers.[7] When the same population is measured in each of these ways, the degree of inequality that emerges is largest for economically active persons, smaller for income recipients, usually smaller still for households, and, if only full-time workers are included, smallest for workers.

The last of these four definitions occurs only in published distributions for the countries of Eastern Europe, namely, Bulgaria, Czechoslovakia, Poland, and Yugoslavia; only in the first three of these is it the only type of distribution included in the collection. Das (1977) has used the World Bank data for an analysis of differences in the degree of inequality in countries at different levels of per capita income. He regressed measures of inequality and income shares on the logarithm of per capita income and on the logarithm squared, and he included dummy variables for different definitions of the income unit and for some aspects of coverage (mainly urban, rural, and national). He omitted the three Eastern European countries, for which only earnings distributions were given, but he allocated dummy variables to economically active persons and income recipients. Some of his results, based on a regression across 118 distributions from seventy-one countries, are given in table 2-1.

The table shows that when economically active persons are used instead of households, the Gini coefficient is increased on the average by 0.13. This is a very large change in a Gini coefficient. When income recipients are used, the

Table 2-1
Estimates of the Effects on Selected Parameters of an Income Distribution of Employing Income Units Other than Households

Parameter	*Economically Active Persons*	*Income Recipients*
Gini coefficient	+0.130 (0.021)	+0.050 (0.016)
Share of bottom 20 percent	−2.48 (0.45)	−1.19 (0.35)
Share of second 20 percent	−2.71 (0.53)	−0.84 (0.42)
Share of top 5 percent	+10.35 (1.83)	+4.33 (1.43)

Source: Das, 1977, table 2.1A.
Note: Standard errors in parentheses.

difference is as much as 0.05, which is also large. The effects on income shares of using either of these definitions are to reduce the shares of the bottom 95 percent of income units and to increase the share of the top 5 percent. The proportionate reduction in shares is larger for economically active persons than for income recipients and larger, by both definitions, for the lowest income groups.

Ahluwalia (1976) has used a similar method of analysis, covering approximately the same sample of countries. But he included the three Eastern European countries for which only "worker" distributions are given. Adding to these a Yugoslav household distribution and an East German distribution of worker-households, he allocated to these five distributions a "socialist" dummy variable. His regression results showed that socialist countries are much more equal than nonsocialist countries. For example, the top 20 percent of socialist income units receive about 20 percent less of total income than is received by the same group in other countries, and the bottom 20 percent about 5.5 percent more (Ahluwalia 1976, table 1).

But it is clear that Ahluwalia's dummy variable measures two different effects: the socialist effect and the income unit effect. Some indication of the importance of the latter effect, taken separately, can be obtained by comparing two Yugoslav distributions, both referring to 1968, and both published in the World Bank report. These show that the income share of the top 20 percent in the worker distribution was 35.0 percent and in the household distribution 41.4 percent, while the corresponding shares of the bottom 20 percent were 10.5 percent and 6.6 percent. The Gini coefficient for workers was 0.25, for households 0.35. We may conclude that a change of income unit can have an even greater effect on the measured degree of equality than a change of economic system. (For a similar failure to distinguish these two effects see Cromwell, 1977.) In practice, when socialist countries publish income distribution data, they almost invariably choose methods that yield the smallest possible measures of inequality, while nonsocialist countries generally choose methods that yield higher measures of inequality.

The distributions in the World Bank collection are almost all pretax distributions, and the great majority refer to composite units such as households or tax units. Unless one allows for differential systems of taxation and for differences in the size and composition of units, these distributions are strictly noncomparable on these grounds, independently of the type of income unit used. (The tax effect was ignored in Ahluwalia, 1976, and in Cromwell, 1977.)

Even the most superficial scrutiny of the World Bank distributions reveals that some of them are inherently suspect. For example, a 1966-1967 Bangladesh national distribution of "population" shows the top 5 percent of persons receiving only 10.1 percent of income. A 1970 Brazilian distribution of salaried employees shows the bottom 10 percent receiving 1.1 percent of the total. A 1966 Cyprus distribution shows the top 5 percent of urban households receiving 12.1 percent of urban income. West German distributions for 1955, 1960, and 1964 show the top 5 percent of income recipients receiving about 35 percent of income.[8] A 1962 distribution for Tripoli Town in Libya shows the top 5 percent of households receiving 13.3 percent of income, and the bottom 10 percent receiving 4.6 percent. A 1968-1969 distribution for Sierra Leone (excluding the Western Province) shows the bottom 10 percent of households receiving zero income.

Further Effects of Alternative Definitions

In the World Bank collection different types of income unit are classified under the heading of households. These include, besides households in the normal sense, families of related persons forming part of a household and consumer units, which are families and unrelated individuals counted equally. The distinction between households, families, and consumer units is standard in the United States and Canada but not much (or at all) used elsewhere. For the United States and Canada abundant and widely quoted data are available; thus it is desirable to examine the effects of changing these definitions of the income unit. Some evidence on this question for four Western countries is given in table 2-2, part A. It is also necessary to consider the effects on measured inequality of replacing pretax by posttax incomes and converting household or other composite unit incomes to per capita incomes. Evidence on these effects, for the same four countries, is given in part B of the table.[9]

The lessons that can be drawn from part A are quite consistent, so far as the data permit. Distributions of individual incomes are very unequal; distributions

Table 2-2
Definition Effects on Measured Inequality
(Gini coefficients)

Income Unit	*Canada*	*Sweden*	*United Kingdom*	*United States*
A. *Pretax incomes*				
Individuals	0.467	0.520	0.462[a]	0.506
Consumer units	0.390	–	0.358	0.418
Households	–	0.373	0.350	0.412
Families	0.325	–	0.300	0.371[b]
B. *Households (HH) or consumer units (CU)*	*CU*	*HH*	*HH*	*CU*
Pretax HH or CU	0.382	0.346	0.344	0.404
Pretax per capita[c]	0.363	–	0.307	0.376
Posttax HH or CU	0.354	0.302	0.318	0.381
Posttax per capita[c]	–	0.254	–	–

Sources: Section A: Stark, 1977, tables 132, 133, 139, and 142; section B: Sawyer, 1976, tables 3-7.
[a]1972-1973
[b]1975
[c]Calculated from data in Sawyer, 1976, table 7.

of consumer units are much less unequal; distributions of households are slightly less unequal than distributions of consumer units; and distributions of families are significantly less unequal than distributions of households. If we leave aside distributions of individual incomes, we can reduce the Gini coefficient by about 0.05-0.06 by moving from consumer units to families.

From part B we can see that there are considerable further opportunities for reducing the Gini coefficient. If we switch from pretax to posttax income, we can reduce the coefficient by 0.023-0.028 in Canada, the United Kingdom, and the United States and by as much as 0.044 in Sweden. On the other hand, if we convert a pretax distribution of households or consumer units to a per capita distribution, the Gini coefficient is reduced by 0.037 in the United Kingdom, 0.028 in the United States, and 0.019 in Canada. A similar conversion to a per capita basis in Sweden, but starting from posttax income, reduces the Gini coefficient by 0.048.

Sweden is the only country for which we have an estimate of the effects of combining both the switch to posttax income and the per capita adjustment. The results in this case are remarkable, producing a fall in the Gini coefficient from 0.35 to 0.25. If we assume that changes in the Gini coefficient for the two types of adjustment are additive, we find that the joint effect in Canada is to reduce the coefficient by 0.047, in United Kingdom by 0.063, and in United States by 0.051. These may well be minimum estimates.[10]

Evidence on the effects of converting pretax distributions from a composite income unit basis to an equivalent unit basis are given in table 2-3.[11] The effects

Table 2-3
Gini Coefficients for Income Units and Equivalent Units, Pretax Incomes

Country	*Income Units*	*Equivalent Units*
United States (1974)		
Consumer units	0.410	0.374
Households	0.386	0.361
Families	0.357	0.360
United Kingdom (1975)		
Consumer units	0.355[a]	–
Households	0.343	0.295
Families	0.287	0.283
Sri Lanka (1973)		
Households	0.469	0.445
Pakistan (1970)		
Households	0.352	0.314
India (1960)		
Rural households	0.332	0.263

Source: Das, 1977.
[a]Stark, 1977, table 23.

of changing from a household to an equivalent unit basis are substantial in India, Pakistan, and the United Kingdom but less so in Sri Lanka and the United States. The change from a family basis to an equivalent unit basis, however, is of negligible importance in the two cases for which data are available, namely, the United States and the United Kingdom. The major effect of switching to an equivalent unit basis, at least in industrialized countries, seems to be to reduce the influence of one-person households or consumer units on the measured degree of inequality. This suggests that in the absence of more refined measures the inequality of family incomes in industrialized countries may be taken as an approximate estimate of the inequality of equivalent unit incomes.

An East-West Comparison

The most difficult international comparisons of inequality are those between socialist and nonsocialist countries. The principal reason is not the difference of system, of taxation methods, of social security provisions, or of any other "real" differences but the fact that socialist countries publish so little relevant information. Indeed, the dominant socialist countries–the Soviet Union and China–publish nothing about income distribution. This is a curious paradox if we assume that a major goal of socialism is equality.

Recent estimates for three "state socialist" countries of Eastern Europe—Czechoslovakia, Hungary, and Poland—have been made by Michal (1977). In Czechoslovakia and Poland the published data refer to households classified by per capita income; in Hungary some distributions of households by household income have also been published. Michal has analyzed the per capita household distributions for these three countries; and a selection of his figures is given in the lower half of table 2-4. The upper half of the table contains estimates from two different sources for the United Kingdom. Since the socialist country figures relate to per capita income after tax, the nearest equivalent figures for the United Kingdom are those in the fourth line. A comparison of this line with the estimates for the socialist countries suggest that there is little difference between the United Kingdom and this group of countries.[12]

Can anything be said about other countries in the two groups? Our previous tables suggest that inequality in the United States and Canada is somewhat greater than inequality in the United Kingdom. But a final judgment about the degree of inequality in North America cannot be made until we have an estimate of the effect on measured inequality of the income composition lag in the annual surveys. On the other hand, inequality in Sweden (per capita and posttax) appears to be about the same as in the United Kingdom. The Gini coefficient for Sweden in 1972 on this basis was shown in table 2-2 to be 0.254, effectively the same as the coefficient for United Kingdom posttax equivalent unit income in 1974 (table 2-4). But what about the Soviet Union. No one

Table 2-4
United Kingdom and Eastern Europe: Comparison of Income Inequality

Country	P_{10}	P_{25}	P_{90}	S_1	S_{10}	G
United Kingdom (1974)						
Household pretax	30	57	196	2.2	24.3	0.348
Household posttax	34	62	189	2.6	23.3	0.323
Equivalent units, pretax	50	70	186	3.4	22.5	0.29
Equivalent units, posttax	56	74	175	4.2	20.8	0.25
Eastern Europe (per capita posttax)						
Czechoslovakia (1965)	53	72	167	–	–	0.240
Czechoslovakia (1973)	56	72	167	–	–	0.207
Hungary (1969)	58	74	164	–	–	0.236
Poland (1973)	60	74	181	–	–	0.240

Sources: United Kingdom: Lines 1 and 2 from Royal Commission on the Distribution of Income and Wealth, 1977, tables D9, D10. The percentile ratios in lines 3 and 4 are from Lansley, 1977, and the other measures are estimates based on Lansley's original distributions, communicated privately. Eastern Europe: Michal, 1977.

Note: P_i = ith percentile expressed as a percentage of the median; S_j = jth interdecile share; G = Gini coefficient.

outside the Soviet Union's statistics office knows. According to Wiles (1974, p. 48) the Soviet Union in 1966 was slightly more unequal (per capita, posttax) than Sweden and the United Kingdom and much more unequal than Bulgaria, Czechoslovakia, and Hungary. But, on the same basis, the Soviet Union was much more equal than the United States. This result, however, makes no allowance for the income-composition lag effect in raising measured inequality in the United States.

Conclusions

It is possible to make large changes in measured inequality by changing the definition of the income unit, income coverage, and the income period. By moving from a distribution of households by household pretax income to a distribution of per capita (or per equivalent unit) posttax income, one may reduce the Gini coefficient in industrialized countries by between 0.05 and 0.10. Removal of the income-composition lag effect on U.S. and Canadian distributions could reduce the corresponding Gini coefficients by as much as 0.03, perhaps by more.

Most of the small socialist countries of Eastern Europe publish income distributions. These are usually on a posttax per capita basis, which yields a low estimate of inequality. If Western country distributions were adjusted to the same definition, they would probably show Sweden as very slightly more unequal than the small socialist countries, followed by the United Kingdom. Of the other major Western countries, France seems to be the most unequal, while Germany, the United States, and Canada are probably more unequal than the United Kingdom. On the socialist side, however, the Soviet Union is substantially more unequal than the smaller socialist countries. Since the United States, Canada, and the Soviet Union are all continental countries, their measured degree of inequality is probably overstated in comparison with smaller and more homogeneous countries.

All these comparisons are made on a relatively narrow data base. They take no account of capital gains, fringe benefits, social benefits in kind, ownership of capital, or economic power. No allowance is made for noneconomic variables such as freedom of choice, movement, organization, thought and expression, availability of open and impartial justice, national independence, and other rights. If the peoples of Eastern Europe were free to choose between their present combination of liberty and equality and a Western alternative combination, we might learn something about the trade-offs between these objectives from people who have had wide experience with different alternatives. It seems unlikely that many people in the West would freely choose Eastern Europe's combination of moderate economic inequality with its high degree of political inequality and national subordination. This is not a sufficient reason, however, for being complacent about our existing situation.

Notes

1. These questions have been discussed many times before, going back at least to the well-known article by Dorothy Brady (1951). My excuse for rehearsing them here is that they seem to be somewhat neglected in international comparisons.

2. Welfare differences between urban and rural areas are affected not only by differential prices but also by differential needs. It costs more to live and work in a big city than in the country, although there may be some compensating satisfactions.

3. See Royal Commission on the Distribution of Income and Wealth (1977, table 8). The numbers of tax units and their distribution are given in table E3.

4. My attention was first drawn to this point by Peter Wiles.

5. The extent of this bias is impossible to estimate accurately without special tabulations from the surveys. The effect may be to increase the Gini coefficient by at least 0.03, probably more. The British data cited before show a reduction of 0.022 when part-year tax units are removed. But this does not allow for the effect on the U.S. and Canadian survey statistics of attribution of zero incomes to a number of individuals who would not have appeared at all in a distribution of tax units in the preceding year. A possible guide to the importance of this effect would be to compare the posttax Gini coefficient from the U.S. Consumer Expenditure Survey of 0.338 (from Stark 1977, table 114) with the posttax Gini from the Current Population Survey (table 2-2) of 0.381.

6. In my view, it is more important to solve this problem than to construct new value-weighted inequality indexes. Atkinson (1970) has suggested that if only we had a proper value-weighted index of inequality, then correct comparisons of inequality could be made. But the introduction of value weights cannot correct for biases arising from different systems of definition and measurement.

7. Three other categories–population, per capita, and per capita household–are not income units but methods of ranking income units. They occur less frequently in the collection and may be neglected in this discussion.

8. These figures are derived from estimates made by the Deutsches Institut für Wirtschaftsforschung and reported by the United Nations (1967). According to notes in the latter source, private companies were added as independent units the distribution of persons, so that the top 5 percent of "persons" includes a large proportion of private-company undivided profits. These distributions for West Germany have been quoted widely in the literature.

9. Previous estimates of the effects on measured inequality of changing the definition of the income unit can be found in Cole and Utting (1957) and Benus and Morgan (1975).

10. As shown in table 2-4 a move from household pretax income to equivalent unit posttax income in the United Kingdom (in 1974) reduces the

Gini coefficient by approximately 0.1, the same as the fall in Sweden from household pretax income to per capita posttax income.

11. Slightly different equivalence scales were used in the United States, the United Kingdom, and the other three countries, but the use of alternative scales was not found to make a great deal of difference to the results.

12. Wiles (1974, p. 48) gives significantly higher estimates of the upper percentiles for a 1969 United Kingdom distribution to posttax per capita income. His results do not, however, seem to be consistent with official estimates of the dispersion of posttax household incomes, for example, in *Report No. 5* of the Royal Commission on the Distribution of Income and Wealth (1977). Lansley's (1977) use of equivalent units instead of number of persons as the household income divisor may produce a slightly reduced degree of dispersion. But it is difficult to believe that this is the major explanation for the discrepancies between his results, even in earlier years, and those of Wiles.

References

Atkinson, A.B. 1970. "On the Measurement of Inequality," *Journal of Economic Theory* 2:244-63.

Ahluwalia, M.S. 1976. "Inequality, Poverty and Development." *Journal of Development Economics* 3:307-342.

Benus, J., and Morgan, J.N. 1975. "Time Period, Unit of Analysis, and Income Concept in the Analysis of Income Distribution." In J.D. Smith, ed., *The Personal Distribution of Income and Wealth*. New York: National Bureau of Research, distributed by Columbia University Press.

Brady, D.S. 1951. "Research on the Size Distribution of Income." In *Studies in Income and Wealth, vol. 13.* New York: National Bureau of Economic Research, pp. 1-55.

Cole, D., and Utting, J.E.G. 1957. "The Distribution of Household and Individual Income." In M. Gilbert and R. Stone, eds., *Income and Wealth, Series VI.* London: Bowes and Bowes.

Cromwell, J. 1977. "The Size Distribution of Income: An International Comparison." *Review of Income and Wealth,* Series 23:291-308.

Das, T. 1977. "Effects of Demographic Change and Choice of Income Unit on the Size Distribution of Income." Ph.D. thesis, University of East Anglia.

Jain, S. 1975. *Size Distribution of Income: A compilation of Data.* Washington, D.C.: World Bank.

Lansley, S. 1977. "Changes in the Inequality of Household Incomes in the U.K. 1971-1975." University of Reading Discussion Paper in Economics Series A, No. 98. Mimeographed.

Michael, J.M. 1977. "Size-Distribution of Household Incomes and Earnings in Developed Socialist Countries: With a Proposed Marginal-Utility-Weighted

Gini coefficient." Mimeographed. State University of New York at Binghamton.

Sawyer, M. 1976. *Income Distribution in OECD Countries.* Paris: Organization for Economic Cooperation and Development.

Sirkin, M.G., Maynes, E.S., and Frechtling, J.A. 1958. "The Survey of Consumer Finances and the Census Quality Check." In *An Apparisal of the 1950 Census Income Data.* Princeton: Princeton University Press.

Stark, T. 1977. *The Distribution of Income in Eight Countries.* Background Paper No. 4, Royal Commission on the Distribution of Income and Wealth. London: Her Majesty's Stationery Office.

United Kingdom, Royal Commission on the Distribution of Income and Wealth. 1977. *Report No. 5, Third Report on the Standing Reference.* London: HMSO.

United Nations. 1967. *Incomes in Postwar Europe: A Study of Policies, Growth, and Distribution.* Geneva.

Wiles, P. 1974. *Distribution of Income: East and West.* Amsterdam: North-Holland.

Commentary

Joseph A. Pechman

Harold Lydall has admirably summarized the many pitfalls in making international comparisons of the distribution of income. There is no question that differences in the definition of the income unit, the income concept, and the income period generate large differences in the degree of income unequality for one country, let alone for several. Hence, as Lydall points out, it is important to be sure that international comparisons are based on comparable sets of figures; otherwise the comparisons are not only meaningless but also misleading. Since I find virtually nothing to quarrel with in Lydall's paper, my remarks are supplements to, or emphasis of, some of his major points.

The Income Unit. Income distribution data are often based on administrative records and therefore may not provide information on the welfare of the basic economic decision-making unit. For example, social security and tax records provide data on earnings of individuals or taxpayer units, which are of interest for some purposes but not for comparisons of economic welfare. For this purpose, a family or household unit is appropriate, since individuals in such units can share income and consumption. I prefer the household unit, although it is often difficult to decide how much beyond the nuclear family one should go.

With the household unit as a basis of measurement, it is essential to put households of various sizes on an equivalent basis. Lydall is quite right in chiding income distribution experts on their failure to correct for equivalence, and I believe that U.S. analysts should take his admonition seriously. It will be difficult to work out a consensus on a scale of equivalence, but even a per capita basis would be an improvement over present procedures.

The Income Concept. Since many distributions of income came from administrative records, the concept of income depends heavily on the source of the data. Thus tax records provide information on the tax definition of income, while social security records produce distributions of earnings. Field surveys seem to have a variety of concepts, depending on the preconceptions of the managers of the surveys and what they regard as feasible for data collection through personal interviews.

My preference is to try to obtain data on the basis of an economic definition of income, which includes the ordinary sources of income (wages, interest, dividends), transfer payments, and capital gains. In practice, all income items other than wages and salaries are seriously understated in field surveys, and most of them do not attempt to collect data on capital gains.

To overcome these difficulties, my colleagues and I at Brookings have been preparing distributions of economic income by merging the data we obtain from field surveys and from a large sample of federal tax returns.[1] The resulting distributions add up to the national income totals. So far, we have completed files for the years 1966 and 1970, and we expect to complete the 1973 file shortly. The microdata are available for use by research workers at marginal cost.

To show what effect different concepts of income have on the distribution of income, I have calculated the Gini coefficients for all U.S. households excluding unrelated individuals for the year 1970. The results are shown in table 2C-1. As might be expected, the distribution of money income is much more equal than the distribution of income reported on tax returns and of total economic income. The income tax is much more equalizing than all taxes, so that the distribution of income appears much more equal (relative to the distribution before taxes) when only the income tax is taken into account than when all taxes are included.

The Brookings file will provide income distributions for the different years for these and other income concepts. Hence it will be possible to trace the changes in income distributions over time on the basis of consistent definitions of income. In this way we hope to avoid the errors introduced in comparative analysis by changing definitions of income.

The Income Period. The use of a one-year accounting period is arbitrary and undoubtedly understates the degree of inequality. It would be useful to measure this understatement for recent years.[2] However, I think it is unrealistic to expect the regular surveys to provide income distributions for more than one year. It will be possible to expand the income horizon for data collection purposes only

Table 2C-1
Comparison of Gini Coefficients, 1970

Tax or Transfer Treatment	*Money Income*[a]	*Adjusted Gross Income*[b]	*Expanded Adjusted Gross Income*[c]	*Adjusted Family Income*[d]
Before taxes, including transfers	0.360	–	–	0.411
Before taxes, excluding transfers	–	0.427	0.429	–
After federal income tax, excluding transfers	–	0.411	0.405[e]	–
After all taxes, including transfers	0.353	–	–	0.399

Source: Brookings 1970 MERGE file. Excludes unrelated individuals.

[a]Census money income concept.

[b]Federal tax concept.

[c]Federal tax concept plus exclusions for capital gains, sick pay, dividends, and moving expenses.

[d]Economic definition of income.

[e]Assuming 1970 federal income tax law applied to expanded adjusted gross income.

when governments begin to collect multiyear data from households for their own purposes (say, for tax or social security purposes), but that day is a long way off.

Notes

1. The methods are described by Joseph A. Pechman and Benjamin A. Okner, in *Who Bears the Tax Burden* (Washington, D.C.: Brookings Institution, 1974), appendix A, pp. 84-92.

2. For an analysis based on incomes in the 1930s, see Frank A. Hanna, Sidney M. Lerner, and Joseph A. Pechman, *Analysis of Wisconsin Income* (New York: National Bureau of Economic Research, 1948), pp. 209-215.

3 Are Earnings More Equal under Socialism: The Soviet Case, with Some United States Comparisons

Janet G. Chapman

While the ultimate goal of communism is distribution according to need, the operative principle under Soviet socialism is distribution according to contribution. The centrally established system of wage and salary rates, supplements for conditions of work, and incentives is intended to serve as a major allocative mechanism in getting people to acquire the skills and take the jobs in the occupations, industries, and regions where there is planned demand for labor and to provide the material incentives necessary to induce people to work effectively. Egalitarianism in wage determination is frowned on. In principle, any distribution according to need is to be done through the social welfare system in the form of free education and health care, pensions for the old and those unable to work, stipends for students, and, more recently, allowances for young children (to age eight) for families with a per capita income below the poverty norm of 50 rubles a month. In practice, this distinction is not so clear.

There is evidence that Soviet wage differentials were wide and increasing from the early 1930s through the Second World War (Bergson 1946; Yanowitch 1963; Chapman 1970, pp. 7-14). In the postwar period, in contrast, there has been a sharp decrease in differentiation in earnings. I shall deal mainly with earnings, as the information on income distribution is scanty and ambiguous.

Soviet Wage Policy Since 1956

Trends in wage differentials between the end of World War II and 1956 are not entirely clear, but at least one measure shows that interpersonal differentiation in earnings decreased substantially. This decrease may have been primarily the result of a bread allowance increment in lower-level wages granted to compensate for the increased price of bread and other basic necessities in late 1947 which accompanied the abolition of rationing. Beginning in 1956, a wage reform was put into effect in industry and other material branches of production between 1956 and 1960 and in the services in 1964-1965. During 1972-1975 a second wage reform was affected in the material branches, and this reform was begun in the services in 1976 and is still in process.

One feature of the reforms was the introduction of a minimum wage in 1957 (the first since 1937) and subsequent substantial increases in the minimum wage. A minimum wage of 27-35 rubles per month was established in 1957 for wage earners and salaried workers in industry, construction, transportation, and communications (about 55 percent of all Soviet wage and salary earners). In 1959 a minimum wage of 40 rubles a month was introduced, along with the first wage reform in the material branches between 1959 and 1960 and in the services in 1964-1965 (Chapman 1964). In January 1968 the minimum wage was raised for all wage earners and salaried workers simultaneously by 50 percent to 60 rubles. The minimum wage introduced during the second wage reform is 70 rubles and had been put into effect in all sectors of the economy by the end of 1977, although other aspects of the wage reform in services had not been completed in all regions (Report on 1977 Plan Fulfillment 1978).

A second feature of these wage reforms was a freeze on upper-level salaries. During the first reform at least some of the highest salary rates were cut, and apparently few, if any, were raised.[1] During the second wage reform only those with basic wage or salary rates up to 200-230 rubles were to receive pay increases. This ceiling refers to increases in basic rates. Persons with wage or salary rates above the ceiling could still increase their earnings through bonuses, author's royalties, honoraria, consulting fees, and the like.

The reforms have generally reduced differentials in rates based on skill differentials. Table 3-1 shows the changes in the range of the basic wage rates for wage earners in several industries. Differentials between industries have been reduced, but the basic rates are still higher in the producer goods industries than in the consumer goods industries. The policy has been to increase and make more uniform differentials for conditions of work and for geographical place of work.

Provisions for incentive payments and bonuses were restricted in the first reform, while the limits were made more liberal in the second reform.

The effect of these reforms on the structure of basic wage and salary rates in 1960 and 1975 may be seen in table 3-2. (This table covers a broad range of occupations but not the entire spread, as some of the highest-paying jobs are excluded and some of the rates in the services that were below the minimum wage effective in the material branches are excluded.) In industry, for example, the rate for the most skilled underground coal miner (the highest-paid industrial wage earner) exceeded the minimum wage by 5.75 times in 1960 and by 3.28 times in 1975. Similarly, the basic salary of a director of a large coal-mining combine exceeded the minimum wage by 11 times in 1960 and by only 6.4 times in 1975. If a similar ratio prevailed in the United States, the director of one of the largest factories would have a salary of a little over $35,000![2]

In studying Soviet earnings distribution one must remember that a pervasive "second economy," or parallel market, provides many sources for legal and illegal incomes that go unrecorded in any Soviet statistics. In spite of widespread

Table 3-1
Basic Wage Scales for Soviet Industrial Wage Earners

	Ratio of Rate for Highest Skill Grade to Rate for Lowest Skill Grade		
Industry	*1955*	*1960*	*1975*
Coal mining, underground	3.1-3.8	3.75	1.86
Ferrous metallurgy	3.3-4.1	3.20	2.10
Chemicals	2.0-3.2	2.30	1.92
Machinery	1.9-3.6	2.00	1.71
Paper	2.1-2.6	2.00	1.71
Textiles and leather	2.4-2.6	1.80	1.71
Light industries (except textiles and leather)	2.4-2.6	1.80	1.58
Food industries	1.9-2.6	1.80	1.58

Sources: Aganbegian and Maier, 1959, p. 135; Chapman, 1970; Osborn, 1970, p. 172; Maier, 1963, p. 148; Kostin, 1973, p. 15; Shkurko, 1975, pp. 7-18; Volkov, 1974; Gurianov and Kostin, 1973, pp. 221-229.

problems of alleged bribery and white-collar embezzlement in this country, the prevalence of extralegal earnings under Soviet conditions is probably wider. We do not know how seriously they affect income distribution (Grossman 1977; Smith 1976, chap. 3).

The Interoccupational Distribution of Earnings

The Soviet data presented so far suggest that there has been a decrease in differentials in earnings. There has been a continuous tendency for a narrowing of the differential between wage earners (*rabochie*) and managerial and professional personnel (*inzhenerno-tekhnicheskie rabotniki*). In industry, in the prewar and war years, earnings of managerial and professional personnel were over twice the earnings of wage earners; since 1945 the difference has been steadily narrowing, so that in 1976 managerial and professional people earned on average only 22 percent more than wage earners. The trend was even more pronounced in construction (table 3-3). The American differential is considerably higher; the average earnings of managerial-professional personnel exceeded average earnings of workers by 74 percent in 1968 and by 69 percent in 1975 (table 3-4). In the Soviet case increases in wages of manual workers have been greater than for professional and managerial personnel, while salaries of those at upper levels have been frozen. Many workers earn more than technicians (the lowest-paid of the professional group) and the top basic wage rate in several industries is above the starting salary for engineers, economists, norm setters, and dispatchers (table 3-2). At the same time there has undoubtedly been a larger expansion in

Table 3-2
Structure of Basic Wage and Salary Scales in Selected Sectors of the Soviet Economy, 1960 and 1975

Branch and Category of Worker	*Basic Monthly Rate in Rubles* 1960	1975
Minimum wage	40[b]	60-70[c]
Industry		
Wage earners, machinery industry	48-96	72-124
Wage earners, highest (underground coal)	230	230
Clerical personnel		
Light industry	45-90	–
Heavy industry	50-105	–
Technicians, machinery industry	75-90	90-115
Engineers, economists, norm setters, machinery	85-120	105-150
Foremen, machinery	90-125	120-155
Managers, food industry	80-200	–
Machinery	100-330	150-330
Highest paid (coal)	450	450
Medicine		
Hospital attendants	35-45	–
Nurses, doctor's assistants	45-98	60-110
Doctors	72-151	90-170
Education		
Teachers with higher education	52-131	100-145
Assistant to full professor, with degree[d]	175-450	175-450
Assistants and instructors, without degree	105-165	125-185
Average actual earnings, all wage earners and salaried employees[e]	80.6	145.8

Sources: Chapman, 1964, 1970, 1979; *Izvestiia*, July 14, 1964 (*Current Digest of the Soviet Press* 16 (19):14-16); *Trud*, September 7, 1972 (*Current Digest of the Soviet Press* 25 (19):16; Hoffberg, 1969, pp. 38-39; TsSU, 1977, p. 472; Dolgopolova and Shakhmagon, 1963, pp. 148, 152-53.

[a]Excluding regional supplements, supplements for conditions of work, incentive and bonus payments.

[b]The 40-ruble minimum was in effect in the material branches, but there was no minimum wage in services until 1964-1965 when the 40-ruble minimum was extended to services.

[c]The 70-ruble minimum was in effect in the material branches but is still in the process of being put into effect in the service branches.

[d]Doctor of sciences degree for full professors, candidate of sciences degree for other ranks.

[e]Including regional supplements, supplements for conditions of work, incentive and bonus payments.

employment of the lower-paid managerial and professional–technicians, foremen, ordinary engineers–than of managers and chief engineers.[3] This would tend to lower average earnings for the group as a whole.

Table 3-3
Relations between Earnings of Wage Earners and Earnings of Managerial-Professional Personnel and Office Workers, Soviet Union 1940-1976

	Average Earnings of Managerial-Professional Personnel		*Average Earnings of Office Workers*	
Year	*Industry*	*Construction*	*Industry*	*Construction*
1940	213	242	111	147
1945	230	311	101	166
1950	176	212	93	127
1955	166	196	89	114
1960	148	156	81	94
1965	146	148	84	94
1970	136	135	85	92
1975	123	115	82	81
1976	122	111	83	79

Sources: TsSU, 1968, pp. 138-139, 145; TsSU, 1977, pp. 472-473.
Note: Average earnings of wage earners = 100.

Soviet office workers during and prior to the war earned more than manual workers, especially in construction, but they have since lost this advantage. In

Table 3-4
Relationship between Earnings of Wage Earners, Office Workers, and Professional-Managerial Personnel in U.S. Manufacturing

	Average Annual Earnings (dollars per year)			*Index*[a]		
Occupation	*Male*	*Female*	*Both*	*Male*	*Female*	*Both*
1968						
Wage earners	7,402	4,141	6,725	100	100	100
Clerical and sales workers	8,636	5,088	6,901	117	123	103
Professional-managerial	12,093	6,663	11,716	163	161	174
1975						
Wage earners	12,047	6,700	10,908	100	100	100
Clerical and sales workers	13,886	8,292	10,699	115	124	98
Professional-managerial	19,164	10,917	18,398	156	163	169

Sources: U.S. Department of Commerce, *Current Population Reports, Consumer Income*, Series P-60, no. 66, 1969, table 45; no. 105, 1977, table 54.
Note: Full-time, year-round workers.
[a]Earnings of wage earners = 100.

industry clerical workers have earned about 81 percent to 85 percent as much as wage earners since 1960, and no definite trend is apparent. In construction the trend has been downward, with clerical workers earning about 94 percent as much as wage earners in the 1960s and only 79 percent as much in 1976 (table 3-3). This is explained primarily by a greater increase in wages in construction than in industry, for average earnings of clerical workers are higher in construction than in industry (TsSU 1977, pp. 472-473). The premium for a level of literacy adequate to perform clerical work of the prewar years has been eroded by the general rise in the level of education as well as by the willingness of women to work for relatively low wages at a desk in an office rather than on the factory floor or assembly line. The relative backwardness of Soviet clerical work–much hand writing and calculating on the abacus is apparently still done–may be another factor. Clerical work has evidently been given a low priority. The number of clerical workers per thousand wage earners declined between 1940 and 1966 from ninety-one to forty-nine in industry and from sixty-one to thirty-nine in construction (TsSU 1968, pp. 84, 123). Probably some of the general types of work formerly done by clerical workers are now performed on a more sophisticated level by people in the managerial-professional category.

To judge from figures for only two years, a similar trend may be occurring in the United States. Among full-time year-round American workers, clerical workers earned 3 percent more than manual workers in 1968 and 2 percent less than manual workers in 1975. American clerical workers in recent years have earned more than manual workers only when men and women are considered separately (table 3-4).[4]

The Interpersonal Distribution of Earnings

While information on basic wage and salary rates and on average earnings for the economy as a whole and by sector is reasonably extensive, information on the distribution of earnings among individuals is far less complete. The basic sources of information on the distribution of individual earnings are periodic censuses carried out by the Central Statistical Administration since 1956. These require detailed reporting by all state enterprises and institutions on the number of wage earners and salaried workers employed and the total wage fund. In addition, for those who worked the full month of the census, their distribution by wage and salary grade and their distribution by total earnings, including all bonuses, are reported. Wage earners and salaried workers in all state enterprises and institutions include most of the civilian labor force, including those employed on state farms. Excluded are the military, members of collective farms, members of cooperatives, domestic servants, and (probably) employees of the Communist party. The censuses are for the month of March and have apparently been made in 1956, 1959, 1961, 1964, 1968, 1970, and 1972 (Chapman 1977; McAuley 1977; Rabkina and Rimashevskaia 1972). Data for 1946 are sometimes cited in comparison, but they may not be comparable.[5]

Unfortunately, although these data clearly exist, very little has been published. What has been published are a few useful summary measures, such as decile ratios, some details for selected parts of the census, and curves of the distributions without numbers or any clues as to scale. Wiles and Markowski (1971), Wiles (1974), and McAuley (1977) tackled the problem by careful measurement of the areas under the curves to arrive at distributions for some of the years for which the curves have been published. Rabkina and Rimashevskaia (1972) also provide equations for the mean and decile ratio of the earnings distributions for the period 1946-1968 and indicate that the distributions are very close to log-normal. That is, they present the two basic parameters—the mean and the standard deviation (which can be computed from the decile ratio)—that are necessary, given the log-normal shape, to calculate estimated ruble distributions for these years. I followed this clue in Chapman (1977).

Soviet economists seem to use these data with considerable confidence and have not subjected these censuses to the kinds of criticism that they have made of the sample surveys of household budgets. The more important questions about the reliability of the data are as follows.

1. The data include earnings of an individual only as reported by his main place of work. It is not clear whether such establishment reports include additional earnings from the state sector, such as wages paid in a second part-time job, or for author's royalties and honoraria when paid by an institution other than the institution from which the individual receives his regular salary. I have been told that employees are supposed to report such extra earnings to the primary employer for calculation of income tax and union dues (D.N. Karpukhin, director of the Research Institute for Labor, personal communication, May 1978). It is possible also that while only workers employed the full month are covered, some of these are part-time workers.[6]

2. While the instructions for reporting earnings indicate that payments in kind where provided for by law are to be included, it is widely assumed that this does not include the "perks" of office provided to the industrial, Party, governmental, and intellectual elites—the chauffered car, a summer dacha or a good apartment, free or half-price monthly food allowances, as well as access to shops where scarce high-quality products can be obtained.

3. No earnings, legal or illegal, from the private sector are included. The opportunities for private income are probably quite unevenly distributed among individuals and occupations, but this distribution may well not parallel the distribution by level of earnings from the job in state enterprises and institutions. Thus the distribution of total actual earnings may differ significantly from

the distribution of earnings as reported by the state enterprises and institutions. Unfortunately, there is no way to take the additional legal and illegal private income into account.

The available measures of earnings differentiation reported in Soviet publications and some of the measures of differentiation based on the McAuley and Chapman computations are shown in table 3-5. If the 1946 figure is reasonably reliable, it shows an extremely high degree of differentiation of earnings by any standard.[7] Wartime rationing was still in effect at this time, so the differences in purchasing power were smaller than the differences in money earnings. Since 1946, there has been a sharp drop in differentiation of earnings, particularly to 1968. Between 1956 and 1959 the drop in the ratio of the average earnings of the highest-paid 10 percent to the average earnings of the lowest-paid 10 percent was much sharper than the drop in the decile ratio. This must reflect the reductions in top salaries, which is said to have taken place in 1957; those affected would almost certainly have been above the tenth percentile. Average earnings of those in the lowest 10 percentile probably also increased as the new minimum wage (then 27-35 rubles) was put into effect. It

Table 3-5
Measures of Differentiation of Earnings of Soviet Wage Earners and Salaried Employees, 1946-1975

	Ratio of Average Earnings of 10 Percent Highest Paid to 10 Percent Lowest Paid (reported)		*Ratio between Earnings at Indicated Percentiles of Distribution*[a]				
			P_{10}/P_{90}	P_{10}/P_{50}		P_{90}/P_{50}	
Year	*USSR*	*Leningrad*	*Reported*	*Computed*[b]		*Computed*[b]	
				M	*C*	*M*	*C*
1946	–	–	7.24	–	2.7	–	.38
1956	8	–	4.4	2.0	2.2	.41	.46
1959	5.8	4.6	4.2	2.0	2.0	.47	.49
1961	–	4.0	4.02	2.0	2.0	.46	.50
1964	–	3.7	3.69	1.8	1.9	.54	.53
1966	–	3.6	3.26	1.9	1.8	.58	.55
1968	5	3.3	2.7	1.7	1.8	.61	.56
1970	–	–	3.2	–	1.7	–	.58
1972	–	3.3	3.10	–	–	–	–
P1975[c]	4	–	2.9	–	–	–	–
1976	–	–	3.35	–	–	–	–

Sources: Sarkisian, 1972, pp. 125-126, 132; Loznevaia, 1968, p. 129; Rimashevskaia, 1965, p. 43; McAuley, 1977, p. 225; Chapman, 1977, p. 261; Yanowitch, 1977, p. 25; Rabkina and Rimashevskaia, 1978.

[a]Measured from the top of the distribution.

[b]M refers to McAuley's computations, C refers to Chapman's.

[c]Anticipated rather than planned.

was reported that at the beginning of the wage reform (probably 1956) the number with earnings below 30 rubles was slightly above 10 percent of all wage earners and salaried workers, and by 1961 the number with earnings below 30 rubles was about 3.2 percent of all (Chapman 1977, p. 275). The drop in 1968 is attributable to the 50 percent increase in the minimum wage for everyone on January 1 and some adjustments in wage rates of those close to the new minimum wage. There has been a tendency for differentials to increase since 1968 as a result of adjustments in middle-level wage rates. The figures shown for 1975 are those anticipated in 1972 as a result of the second wage reform, which was at that time apparently expected to be completed in 1975. In fact, it was completed only in the material sectors by 1975 and is still being put into effect in the service sectors.

The sharp reduction in inequality in the Soviet Union has reduced it to the degree of equality that had earlier been achieved in Poland and Yugoslavia, though differentiation of Soviet earnings is still somewhat more unequal than in Bulgaria, Czechoslovakia, and Hungary.

There are a number of problems in comparing the Soviet distribution with the distribution of earnings in the United States. First is the group of workers to be covered. The Soviet data include workers on state farms but exclude members of collective farms, while in the American case one can either include all in agriculture or exclude all. The Soviet data relate only to wage earners and salaried workers, but these are almost the entire labor force, while self-employment in the United States is not insignificant, particularly among professionals, such as doctors and lawyers, who would be state employees in the Soviet Union. Because of these problems, I have calculated two sets of measures for the United States. Both are confined to full-time, year-round civilians aged fourteen or over, since the Soviet data refer to full-month workers. The first covers all with earnings and the second nonagricultural wage earners and salaried workers. The U.S. data are based on surveys of a sample of families and cover all earnings, while the Soviet data are based on establishment reports and cover only earnings from the reporting establishment.

The American data are shown in table 3-6. These show a decrease in inequality in earnings between 1939 and 1949, which persisted at least until 1959. The inequality had increased by 1968. The 1975 figures suggest that we may be in a new trend toward decreasing differentiation except for the lowest-paid nonagricultural wage earners and salaried workers (P_{90}/P_{50} decreases between 1972 and 1975.) Henle's (1972) study of the trend among male workers over the period 1958-1970 found little change in the differentiation of earnings among all male full-time earners but an increase in inequality for male full-time wage and salary income and also for all male workers for either earnings or wage and salary income. A major factor was a faster increase in full-time male earnings in several of the higher-paid occupations (professional and technical, managers and supervisors, sales workers) as well as a greater expansion of

Table 3-6
Measures of Differentiation of Total Money Earnings in the United States, Full-time, Year-round Civilians Aged Fourteen and Over, Selected Years

Year	P_{10}/P_{90}	P_{10}/P_{50}	P_{90}/P_{50}	P_{85}/P_{50}
All with Money Earnings				
1939	–	2.05	–	0.45
1949	–	1.73	–	0.56
1959	–	1.76	–	0.52
1968	4.92	2.06	0.42	0.51
1969	5.75	2.07	0.36	–
1972	5.04	2.22	0.44	–
1975	4.35	1.97	0.45	0.53
Nonagricultural Wage and Salary Earners				
1939	–	1.97	–	0.54
1949	–	1.66	–	0.63
1959	–	1.67	–	0.60
1968	4.30	1.99	0.46	0.54
1972	4.48	2.12	0.47	–
1975	3.95	1.77	0.45	0.51

Sources: 1939-1959: Lydall, 1968, pp. 359, 361, as calculated from U.S. census data; 1968-1975: computed from data in U.S. Department of Commerce, *Current Population Reports: Consumer Income,* Series P-60, no. 66, 1969, table 46; no. 90, 1973, tables 53 and 60; no. 105, 1977, table 52; U.S. Bureau of the Census, *Census of the Population,* 1970, *Detailed Characteristics,* U.S. Summary, table 247.

employment in these occupations. Another factor that was probably significant was the increase in the inflow of young people into the labor force (the postwar baby boom) which may have depressed wages for those who had less education and took manual jobs at the bottom of the economic ladder. This is quite a different pattern from that observed in the Soviet Union in approximately the same period, with a large rise in the minimum wage and a freeze of upper-level salary rates. The minimum wage in the Soviet Union during the postwar years has played a significant role, since the entire structure of wage and salary rates is built around it.

The Soviet distribution for 1946 (if it reflects reality) was considerably more unequal than any distribution shown here for the United States. By the 1950s, in contrast, the degree of inequality among Soviet wage and salary earners had been reduced to roughly the level prevailing among American nonagricultural wage and salary earners in the early 1970s. In the 1970s, the Soviet earnings distribution has been considerably more equal than the American.

The Problem of Soviet Income Distribution

In the November 1977 anniversary issues of Two Soviet journals, two Soviet labor economists give conflicting statements about the trend in the distribution of Soviet income. Sarkisian (1977), the source of most of the decile ratios of the distribution of earnings, presents the following decile ratios of the distribution of income for wage earner and salaried worker families (probably on a per capita basis): 1958, 3.6; 1967, 3.3; 1976, below 3. In the following paragraph he says that the gap between real per capita incomes of *kolkhozniki* (members of collective farms) and wage earners and salaried employees has been substantially reduced.[8] Maier (1977), on the other hand, reports that analysis of data for the past fifteen to twenty years (since 1957 or 1962) shows that differentiation of incomes has not narrowed. His study refers to the population as a whole and to the two main social groups (wage earners and salaried employees, and *kolkhozniki*), especially to *kolkhozniki*. He points to the role of the size and composition of the family, particularly the number of earners and number of dependents, as well as to the difference in earnings as determinants of per capita family income distribution.

He points out that the threefold increase in the minimum wage between 1957 and 1968 led to a decrease in differentiation of wages and salary earnings but that this decrease was insufficient to overcome the influence of other factors and to lead to a decrease in differentiation of total incomes of wage earner and salaried worker families. After 1968, earnings differentials began to increase, in turn leading to an increase in differentiation of income for wage earners and salaried employees.

Among *kolkhozniki,* Maier continues, the rapid increase in the average pay received by *kolkhozniki* was not accompanied by any minimum wage. As a result, the differentials in pay increased, and thus there was an increase in the differentiation of income between *kolkhozniki* and the population as a whole.

During this period the number of students on stipends increased, the number of pensioners increased, and pensions were extended to collective farmers. The size of the pension was increased, but not enough to significantly affect the distribution of income. The introduction of children's allowances in 1974 also did not significantly change the distribution of income (Maier 1977, pp. 51-53).

What is going on here? Sarkisian is evidently reporting the results of studies that have been made. The figures for 1958 and 1967 and, probably, 1976 apparently refer to the special sample surveys of income among wage earner and salaried worker families and, for more recent years, *kolkhozniki* families. The results may be true of the group surveyed, but apparently there are serious deficiencies in the representativeness of the surveys. For the group surveyed there is evidence that in 1958 and 1967 per capita family income was less equally distributed than earnings but that the difference was smaller in 1967 than in 1958.[9]

Maier, on the other hand, no doubt has in mind the serious deficiencies in these surveys and possibly additional information on the incomes of those excluded from the income and budget surveys.[10] The family budget surveys have been seriously criticized by Soviet writers, and economists find it impossible to use them to obtain an accurate picture of income distribution. The sample for the family budget survey is chosen from employees at their place of work, a procedure that automatically excludes anyone not working and probably increases the chances of selecting families with two earners. Not all sectors are covered, and some of the lowest-paying sectors, such as trade and services, are not covered or are underrepresented. The special sample income surveys were an attempt at improvement, but apparently they suffer from many biases due to underrepresentation of some groups and areas and the complete exclusion of pure pensioner and pure student families.[11]

Given these reservations about the data—and to this one might add the problem of how illegal earnings affect the distribution—I shall attempt to explain the Soviet earnings revolution.

Explanations for the Soviet Revolution in Earnings

The Soviet government as primary employer, educator, and setter of wage and salary rates has considerably more power over the distribution of earnings than a nonsocialist government. A major function of the Soviet wage system is the allocation and motivation of labor. As Western scholars have found, there are many similarities between the principles on which Soviet wages are set and the principles of wage determination in a market economy (Bergson 1946; Kirsch 1972). Thus, as in a market economy, there are inevitably conflicts between allocative efficiency and equity. However, the Soviet government's control over the structure of the demand for labor through planning of output and its control over the structure of the supply of labor through planning the structure of education reduce the importance of the structure of wages as the allocative device (Zielinski 1977). While there is considerable freedom of occupational choice, graduates of vocational schools, specialized secondary schools, and institutions of higher education are assigned to their first jobs, and the Party has considerable control over appointments to all the most important jobs. This control gives some extra degrees of freedom to take into account principles of equity or political pressures and economic and political constraints in setting wage differentials. The sharp reduction in inequality in earnings that has taken place seems to reflect a mixture of economic, ideological, and social considerations.

Some purely economic developments would tend to make reduced wage differentials appropriate. The first is the great increase in the level of education, which has made the highly educated less scarce and raised the level of education among the less skilled workers, reducing differentials in skills. Between 1955 and 1976 the total number of wage earners and salaried workers slightly more than doubled, the number with specialized secondary education increased by 2.67 times, while the number with higher education increased by 4.58 times (TsSU 1977, pp. 461, 477). Most young people enter the labor force today with at least a secondary education, which has raised the level of their skills or trainability well above that of most of the people they are replacing.[12]

Second, what Soviet economists like to call the scientific-technological revolution has led to narrower differentials in the nature and conditions of work. The grade 1 (lowest grade) manual worker today has to know considerably more than a grade 1 worker of twenty or thirty years ago and, with the help of vastly increased and modernized equipment, is considerably more productive.

Third, a shortage of labor is developing, as almost all persons of working age have already been brought into the labor force. Thus those reaching working age are virtually the sole source of additional labor. While the postwar baby boom has caused a bulge in the number reaching working age in the 1970s, there will be a sharp decline in the 1980s.[13]

Certain contrary tendencies are the perceived need to increase differentials to induce people to take jobs in unpleasant conditions or places or to compensate them for such conditions. Another is the effort to tailor individual rewards, through the incentive provisions, more closely to individual effort and results on the job. While the equalizing factors have been stronger to date, Maier estimates that in the future the general result of the two contradictory tendencies will stabilize the level of differentiation of earnings (Maier 1977, p. 53).

A number of factors, market-type and extramarket, seem to explain the large increase in the minimum wage and the freeze on upper-level salaries. The explanation offered by Soviet economists for the sharp increase in the minimum wage is that it must cover the "cost of production and reproduction of labor power." "This requires a minimum level of compensation for all employed individuals, 'independent of the share of their labor contribution to the creation of the social product.' Such a level would not only meet the needs of sheer physical subsistence but would provide the minimum amenities required for cultural growth, work morale and the 'normal' reproduction of the work force" (Yanowitch 1977, p. 27; see also Rabkina and Rimashevskaia 1972, pp. 24-33). Such a minimum is also seen as a historical matter, rising with technological progress and the growth of the material and cultural needs of the population (Rabkina and Rimashevskaia 1972, p. 32).

It was apparently decided that it was necessary and possible to make a real effort to raise real wages. Given the history of Soviet real wages, this decision is not surprising. By the mid 1950s real wages had recovered from the wartime low and exceeded the level of the late 1930s, but the average Soviet worker in 1954 earned at best only a little more than he had in 1928 and at worst even less than in 1928.[14] In 1956, 10 percent of all wage earners and salaried employees were earning less than 30 rubles a month. In terms of consumer purchasing power in 1954 dollars, this amounted to only $30 a month and the average wage was approximately $74 a month (Chapman 1970, p. 108). In 1958 the average Soviet nonagricultural wage was, in 1954 dollars, less than one-quarter of the corresponding American figure (Chapman 1963a, p. 252). Somewhat later, Soviet economists worked out a minimum subsistence-level budget for a family of four, taking the cheapest foods, clothing, and so on, which required a family money income of 50 rubles per capita for 1965.[15] At that time the average per capita money income of the Soviet population, as estimated by Schroeder and Severin (1976, pp. 627, 652), was something over 45 rubles a month, less than the estimated minimum subsistence level. Equity as well as the efficiency and morale of the work force seemed to require an increase in real wages, especially for those at the lower end. Warned by the Poznan worker uprising over living conditions in June 1956 which led to the fall of Boleslaw Bierut, the head of the Polish United Workers (Communist) Party and his replacement by Wladyslaw Gomulka, the Soviet Party leadership may also have worried about the stability of their own power.[16]

In the Soviet Union, as in the United States, the minimum wage falls far short of the official definition of a minimum level of well-being for a family of four, even in the Soviet case if both parents work at the minimum wage.[17]

Another factor that must have had a strong influence on the policy of raising lower-level wages was the developing mismatch between aspirations, particularly among young people, and available jobs. The scientific-technological revolution and the revolution in education did not move closely in step. While much work has been automated and made less arduous and unpleasant—or more interesting—a large proportion of the available jobs are still in manual labor, and many of these jobs are arduous and some are dangerous.[18] The high level of education, particularly of the young, has apparently created a scorn for the many nasty jobs available to them and a level of aspiration beyond the level of the occupations available to most of them. The "overeducated American" evidently has a Soviet counterpart.[19] Various Soviet sociological surveys indicate that Soviet youths' plans for further education and careers are more ambitious than many are able to fulfill (Yanowitch 1977, chap. 3). Their problem has become more acute as the number who finish secondary education has increased much faster than the number of places in universities. The proportion of secondary school graduates able to continue full-time study at college level has fallen from about two-thirds in the early 1950s to one-fifth in the early 1970s (Yanowitch 1977, p. 80), leading to fierce competition for places in the universities and other higher educatonal institutions. There appears to be a form of queuing for the more attractive jobs, but with the queuing taking place at the university gate rather than at the employer's gate.

Given a more than adequate queue for the professional jobs requiring a higher education and shortages of labor for the still technologically backward manual jobs, it would make sense to reduce the differentials in wages between them.[20] There is also increasing recognition, especially among sociologists, that some kinds of work are rewarding in themselves and may not need such high pay while those in unrewarding work should be compensated for this (Yanowitch 1977, p. 28). That all education is free and that students in specialized secondary schools and institutions of higher education receive stipends should, of course, mean that the pay differentials for occupations requiring a specialized or higher education could be less than in countries where this is not true.

Another aspect of the same problem is the high turnover among young people. Much of the turnover is among youths who have failed the college entrance examination in one discipline and institution and take a job only until they may take another examination for entrance to a college-level institution.[21] Many have completed the general secondary education (the traditional route to the university) and are not trained for any specific occupation. Thus although they are generally more ambitious and more likely to have come from professional families, they are less well equipped for most jobs than those who have been to the vocational or the specialized secondary schools. Raising the lower-level wages may have done much to alleviate the frustration of such youths, to lure more into taking jobs immediately after secondary school, and to encourage them to stay with the jobs even though they dislike them. Indeed, a 1973 study by the Institute of Labor found that dissatisfaction with wages had previously been the most important cause of labor turnover in industry but that this had fallen to the third or fourth cause since the measures taken between 1965 and 1970 to raise wages.[22]

Freezing upper-level salary rates for over twenty years would surely not be possible in a market economy. In part, the freezing of upper-level salary rates may be attributed to the constraints of inflationary pressure. If so much additional purchasing power went to the low paid, there would not be room, given the limits on consumer goods to be made available, to allow pay increases for the better off. In addition, as Wiles points out, Stalin set differentials for upper-level salaries much too high and Khrushchev lowered the inequality substantially without obvious trouble (1974, Lecture IV). It is true, though, that under Stalin the risks associated with being a manager, for example, were considerably greater than under subsequent leaders, and Stalin may also have felt it necessary to try to buy the allegiance of the elite. Brezhnev has evidently counted on being able to further reduce the differentials without trouble.

How has the Soviet leadership gotten away with this? They clearly have more control over those in the upper-level jobs than over the masses of workers. One is the Party's control over all important job assignments. Second, where else would these people go? They are still in the jobs with the highest pay and status, even though relatively their pay advantage has been reduced. A third is the fear of losing the "perks" of office which, unlike salary, cannot be saved and taken when the job is left. A fourth is the extreme difficulty of emigrating. With this degree of control, the leadership has evidently felt it safe enough to assume that managers and professors and others in the more responsible positions will continue to work as hard as before even though their salary rates remain frozen. They may even work harder to earn bonuses or other extra earnings in the effort to maintain their accustomed standard (Chapman, 1979).

McAuley concludes that the sharp reduction in inequality in earnings "is no mean achievement and one that I doubt could have occurred in the absence of centralized wage setting" (1977, p. 227). Wiles argues that the Soviet and other East European experience suggests that we too could go much farther toward equality (or cutting top salaries) without obvious trouble (1974, Lecture IV). The sharp reduction in earnings differentials in the United States during World War II is an example of what can be done. However, the power of the federal government to use its wartime wage controls to reduce earnings differentials depended on the widespread consensus of the population that the burdens of the war should be borne relatively equally. The reduced differentials evidently changed popular notions of what "fair" differentials were. But, as Thurow points out, "no one knows how to engineer such changes in less extreme situations. Indeed, some sociologists have concluded that only wars can cause changes in norms of relative deprivation (1975, p. 111; see also pp. 58-59, 110-111, 191-193).

Perhaps the best hope to achieve greater equality in market economies is in measures designed to decrease inequalities in opportunities at the premarket level. As Phelps Brown concludes, "We have found that the main cause of inequality of pay is the inequality of abilities to work. There are great difficulties in the way of breaking the link between pay and ability, and prescribing equal pay for unequal work. The best way to reduce the inequality of the effect is to reduce that of the cause" (1977, p. 332).

Notes

1. Salaries of rectors with professional rank of the largest institutions of higher education were reduced from 800 to 600 rubles a month, and salaries of full professors with doctor of sciences degrees and ten or more years of service were cut from 550 rubles to 450 rubles in 1957 (Hoffberg 1969, pp. 38-39).

2. This is 6.4 times the minimum U.S. wage effective January 1978 of \$5,512 (\$2.65 per hour for 40 hours a week, 52 weeks). Presumably a factory director would not be the highest executive in a large corporation, who should more properly be compared with the head of an industrial ministry in the Soviet Union.

3. The number of managerial-professional personnel per thousand wage earners increased in industry from 99 in 1940 to 132 in 1966 and in construction from 69 in 1940 to 120 in 1966. The number of specialists with specialized secondary education increased more than the number with higher education between 1955 and 1966 (TsSU 1968, pp. 84, 123, 251).

4. The persistence of a differential for lower-level white-collar workers above manual workers in the nonsocialist countries noted by Phelps Brown may in part be due to looking at male and female earnings separately (1977, pp. 40-42, 65-66). Data are not available for Soviet male and female earnings separately.

5. McAuley (1977) suggests that the 1946 figure may be derived from the family budget data which are, by Soviet admission, very faulty. It is possible, however, that a special earnings survey was made in 1946. In 1947 rationing was abolished and the former ration prices were, on the whole, raised; at the same time lower-level wages and salaries were raised to compensate for the increase in prices of bread and other basic necessities. An earnings survey would have been a logical step in preparation for this. If it was, it does not, of course, mean that the 1946 survey was comparable to those starting in 1956.

6. N.E. Rabkina suggested this as a possible explanation for the relatively large numbers in the lowest class interval, with earnings below the minimum wage (personal communication, May 1974). An alternative explanation at least for some years might be that these were largely people for whom the current "minimum wage" was not yet in effect. For further discussion of the reliability of these data, see Chapman, 1977, pp. 261-264, 274-278; McAuley, 1977.

7. There are very few P_{10}/P_{50} ratios as high as this in Lydall's comparisons of a number of countries in the late 1950s and 1960s (1968, table 5.2, p. 143).

8. Sarkisian, 1977, p. 58. In an earlier work (Sarkisian 1973, cited in Yanowitch 1977, p. 25) he cites the following decile ratios: 1965, 3.8; 1970, 3.2. These are probably based on the family budget studies which are viewed as even more unreliable.

9. Rabkina and Rimashevskaia (1972, p. 215) show the relationship between the decile values for earnings and for per capita income for 1958 and 1967.

10. He presents no figures relating to earnings or income distribution other than those readily available elsewhere, such as the ratio of average earnings to the minimum wage.

11. See McAuley, 1977, for a discussion of these problems and also for reconstructions of income distributions based on the income surveys.

12. In the early 1970s some 85 percent of Soviet youngsters continued their education beyond the eighth grade, with perhaps three-fourths doing so in institutions that provided a complete secondary education (Yanowitch 1977, p. 62).

13. In 1970 the labor force was 89.9 percent (90.8 percent for males and 89.1 percent for females) of the population of working age (age sixteen to fifty-nine for men and sixteen to fifty-four for women). Increments to those of working age are estimated at over 2 million a year during the 1970s and only a little over 500,000 a year in the 1980s (Rapawy 1976, pp. 5-7).

14. With 1928 taken as 100, the index of the real net nonagricultural wage in 1954 was 83 at 1937 prices and 129 when the index is calculated using 1928 prices for the period 1928 to 1937 and 1954 prices for the period 1937 to 1954 (Chapman 1963b, p. 145).

15. G.S. Sarkisian and N.P. Kuznetsova, *Potrebnosti i dokhodov semyi* (Moscow: 1967); D.N. Karpukhin and N.P. Kuznetsova, "Dokhody i potreblenie trudiashchikhsia," in *Trud i zarabotnaia plata v SSSR* (Moscow, 1968); both as cited in Vinokur, 1979.

16. Quite possibly there had been protests by workers in the Soviet Union itself. There have been rumors but little if any firm evidence concerning such events.

17. For the period 1971-1975, when the minimum wage was 60 or 70 rubles, the Soviet normative budget of minimum well-being for a family of four was 265.8 rubles a month, of which about 199 rubles was assumed to be met by wage and salary income (Soviet data as cited in Vinokur 1979; Kunel′skii 1968, pp. 20-21).

18. If we exclude workers who set and adjust machinery by hand, 42 percent of Soviet industrial wage earners were engaged in purely manual labor in 1975 (Sonin 1977, p. 97).

19. A study of the National Assessment of Educational Progress found that 44 percent of American seventeen-year olds appear to aspire to professional jobs while only 14 percent of the jobs in the economy are classified by the Department of Labor as professional (Gene Maeroff, *New York Times,* November 11, 1976).

20. L. Bliakhman of the Economics Department of Leningrad University informed me (personal communication, June 1974) that among young Leningrad women there were ten applicants for each place in the Library School but less than one applicant per available job in the textile mills, although earnings of textile workers were higher than earnings of librarians.

21. Soviet institutions of higher education are much more specialized than American, and entry is to a specific specialty or discipline. A student may take the entrance exam in only one discipline at a time.

22. Nauchno-issledovatel′skii institut truda, 1973, p. 154.

References

Aganbegian, A.G., and Maier, V.F. 1959. *Zarabotnaia plata v SSSR* (Wages in the USSR). Moscow: Gosplanizdat.

Bergson, Abram. 1946. *The Structure of Soviet Wages.* Cambridge, Mass.: Harvard University Press.

Chapman, Janet. 1963a. "Consumption." In A. Bergson and Simon Kuznets, eds., *Economic Trends in the Soviet Union.* Cambridge, Mass.: Harvard University Press.

_______. 1963b. *Real Wages in Soviet Russia Since 1928.* Cambridge, Mass.: Harvard University Press.

_______. 1964. "The Minimum Wage in the USSR." *Problems of Communism,* September-October, pp. 76-79.

_______. 1970. *Wage Variation in Soviet Industry: The Impact of the 1956-1960 Wage Reform.* Santa Monica, Calif.: RAND Corporation.

_______. 1977. "Soviet Wages under Socialism." In Alan Abouchar, ed., *The Socialist Price Mechanism.* Durham, N.C.: Duke University Press.

_______. 1979. "Recent Trends in the Soviet Industrial Wage Structure." In Arcadius Kahan and Blair Ruble, eds., *Industrial Labor in the USSR.* Elmsford, N.Y.: Pergamon Press (forthcoming).

Dolgopolova, A., and Shakhmagon, A. 1963. *Oplata truda na predpriiatiiakh pishchevoi i rybnoi promyshlennosti* (Payment of Labor in Enterprises of the Food and Fish Industries). Moscow: VTsSPS Profizdat.

Grossman, Gregory. 1977. "The 'Second Economy' of the USSR." *Problems of Communism,* September-October, pp. 25-40.

Gurianov, S. Kh., and Kostin, L.A. 1973. *Trud i zarabotnaia plata na predpriiatii* (Labor and Wages in the Enterprise), 2d ed. Moscow: Ekonomika.

Henle, Peter. 1972. "Exploring the Distribution of Earned Income." *Monthly Labor Review,* December, pp. 16-27.

Hoffberg, George. 1969. *Wages in the USSR, 1950-1967: Education.* Washington, D.C.: U.S. Department of Commerce, Bureau of the Census, Foreign Demographic Analysis Division, International Population Reports Series P-95, No. 66.

Kirsch, Leonard J. 1972. *Soviet Wages: Changes in Structure and Administration since 1956.* Cambridge, Mass.: MIT Press.

Kostin, Leonid. 1973. *Organizatsiia oplaty truda* (The Organization of Labor Payment). Moscow: Profizdat.

Kunel'skii, L. 1968. "Sotsial'no-ekonomicheskoe znachenie povysheniia minimal'nykh razmerov zarabotnoi platy" (The Socioeconomic Significance of Raising the Minimum Wage). *Sotsialisticheskii trud,* No. 12, pp. 14-22.

_______. 1972. *Sotsial'no-ekonomicheskie problemy zarabotnoi platy* (Socioeconomic Problems of Wages). Moscow: Ekonomika.

Loznevaia, M. 1968. "Matematicheskie metody v planirovanii zarabotnoi platy" (Mathematical Methods in Planning Wages). *Sotsialisticheskii trud,* No. 10, pp. 125-136.

Lydall, Harold. 1968. *The Structure of Earnings.* Oxford: Oxford University Press.

Maier, V.F. 1963. *Zarobotnaia plata v period perekhoda k kommunizmu* (Wages in the Period of the Transition to Communism). Moscow: Izd. ekonomicheskoi literatury.

_______. 1977. "Aktual'nye problemy povysheniia narodnogo blagosostoianiia" (Current Problems of Raising the Level of Well-being). *Voprosy ekonomiki* (Problems of Economics), No. 11, pp. 47-56.

McAuley, Alastair. 1977. "The Distribution of Earnings and Incomes in the USSR." *Soviet Studies* 29, no. 2 (April):214-237.

Nauchno-issledovatel'skii institut truda (Research Institute for Labor). 1973. *Dvizhenie rabochikh kadrov v promyshlennosti* (The Movement of Workers in Industry). Moscow: Statistika.

Osborn, Robert J. 1970. *Soviet Social Policies: Welfare, Equality, and Community.* Homewood, Ill.: Dorsey Press.

Phelps Brown, Henry. 1977. *The Inequality of Pay.* Oxford: Oxford University Press.

Rabkina, N.E., and Rimashevskaia, N.M. 1972. *Osnovy differentsiatsii zarabotnoi platy i dokhodov naseleniia* (Principles of the Differentiation of Wages and Incomes of the Population). Moscow: Ekonomika.

_______. 1978. "Distributive Relations and Social Development." *Ekonomika i organizatsiia promyshlennogo proizvodstva* (Economics and Organization of Industrial Production), No. 5 (translated in *Current Digest of the Soviet Press* 30 no. 47 (December 20):1-4).

Rapawy, Stephen. 1976. *Estimates and Projections of the Labor Force and Civilian Employment in the USSR, 1950-1990.* Washington, D.C.: U.S. Department of Commerce, Bureau of Economic Analysis, Foreign Economic Report No. 10.

"Report of 1977 Plan Fulfillments." 1978. *Pravda* and *Izvestiia,* 28 January (*Current Digest of the Soviet Press* 34, no. 4, p. 13).

Rimashevskaia, N.M. 1965. *Ekonomicheskii analiz dokhodov rabochikh i sluzhashchikh* (The Economic Analysis of the Incomes of Wage Earners and Salaried Employees). Moscow: Ekonomika.

Sarkisian, G.S. 1972. *Uroven', tempy, i proportsii rosta real'nykh dokhodov pri sotsializme* (The Level, Rate, and Proportions of Growth of Real Incomes under Socialism). Moscow: Ekonomika.

_______. 1977. "Razvitoi sotsializme i blagosostoianie mass" (Developed Socialism and the Well-being of the Masses). *Sotsialisticheskii trud,* No. 11, pp. 52-64.

Schroeder, Gertrude E., and Severin, Barbara S. 1976. "Soviet Consumption and Income Policies in Perspective." In Joint Economic Committee, *Soviet Economy in a New Perspective.* Washington, D.C.: U.S. Government Printing Office.

Shkurko, S. 1975. "Tarifnaia sistema v promyshlennosti na sovremennom etape razvitiia ekonomiki" (The Wage System in Industry in the Current Stage of Development of the Economy). *Sotsialisticheskii trud,* No. 1, pp. 7-18.

Smith, Hedrick. 1976. *The Russians.* New York: Quadrangle.

Sonin, M. 1977. "Problemy raspredeleniia i izpol zovaniia trudovykh resursov" (Problems of the Distribution and Utilization of Labor Resources). *Sotsialisticheskii trud,* No. 3, pp. 94-103.

Thurow, Lester C. 1975. *Generating Inequality: Mechanisms of Distribution in the U.S. Economy.* New York: Basic Books.

TsSU. Tsentral'noe statisticheskoe upravlenie (Central Statistical Administration). *Narodnoe khoziaistvo SSSR v——g.* (The National Economy of the USSR in (year). Moscow: Statistika. (annual).

_______. 1977. *Narodnoe khoziaistvo SSR za 60 let* (The National Economy of the USSR during sixty Years). Moscow: Statistika.

_______. 1968. *Trud v SSSR* (Labor in the USSR). Moscow: Statistika.

Vinokur, Aaron. 1979. "Income of Families of Soviet Workers: Economic, Normative, and Sociological Aspects." In Arcadius Kahan and Blair Ruble, eds., *Industrial Labor in the USSR.* Elmsford, N.Y.: Pergamon Press (forthcoming).

Volkov, A.P., ed. 1974. *Trud i zarabotnaia plata v SSSR* (Labor and Wages in the USSR), 2d rev. ed. Moscow: Ekonomika.

Wiles, Peter. 1974. *Distribution of Income: East and West.* Amsterdam and Oxford: North Holland; New York: American Elsevier.

Wiles, Peter, and Markowski, Stefan. 1971. "Income Distribution under Communism and Capitalism: Some Facts about Poland, the U.K., the USA and the USSR." *Soviet Studies* 22, no. 3:344-369; no. 4:487-511.

Yanowitch, Murray. 1963. "The Soviet Income Revolution." *Slavic Review* 22:683-697.

_______. 1977. *Social and Economic Inequality in the Soviet Union.* White Plains, N.Y.: M.E. Sharpe.

Zielinski, Janusz. 1977. "Wages: Comments and Extensions." In Alan Abouchar, ed., *The Socialist Price Mechanism.* Durham, N.C.: Duke University Press.

Commentary

Evsey D. Domar

From the point of view of a discussant, Janet Chapman's paper is far from ideal: it is reasonable, it contains no conclusions unsupported by the evidence presented, and it lacks internal contradictions. I really have no quarrels with it. Hence I shall limit myself to a few comments on issues that the paper raised.

Soviet Income Inequality. Chapman confirms Kuznets' findings that early industrialization is likely to increase income inequality.[1] Indeed it should. The demand for engineers, executives, and skilled workers in general rises faster than the supply; and the state of disequilibrium produced by the industrialization itself creates opportunities for high profits. In time the supply of qualified personnel increases and, as things settle down, fewer "killings" are made. In the Soviet Union the latter are not supposed to exist; nevertheless, the Soviet performance fits nicely into this pattern: inequality increased in the 1930s and decreased in recent years. As a matter of fact, judging by the excess supply of Soviet would-be professionals (as shown by intense competition for university seats) and an excess demand for manual workers, Soviet planners might be able to reduce income inequality even more.

I must confess that when I find the Soviet government, or any government for that matter, behaving in such a rational manner, that is, doing exactly what we prescribe, I become rather uneasy and begin to wonder about the correctness of our prescriptions. It is just too good to be true.

Comparisons with the United States. The pitfalls of international comparisons of income inequality are too well known to warrant extended comments here.[2] Chapman correctly notes that under Soviet statistical methods a person holding more than one job may distort the measure of inequality. (It need not necessarily be reduced.) She also suggests that various job perquisites (not only in the Soviet Union, by the way) should be taken into account. I do not know whether special stores for the elite charge lower prices than ordinary stores, but the former are reported to be better stocked with goods (thus reducing the uncertainty and time needed for shopping); the goods are reported to be of higher quality and of greater variety. This last characteristic–greater variety–has its cost and, of course, benefits as well.[3] But unfortunately, we have no method for quantifying its effect and incorporating it into the real value of consumer expenditures. If we did, perhaps Soviet income inequality might be found to be a bit higher. On the other hand, if the expenditures of each class were deflated by its own price index, Soviet measure of inequality would decrease compared with the American because in the Soviet Union necessities are cheap (food and rent are subsidized) and luxuries are expensive. (Education is free, but which income class is more likely to benefit from it?)

In the last decade or two a number of changes have been taking place in the United States. I wonder what effect they have had and will have on our income distribution. The greater opportunities for blacks, for instance, should make it more equal.[4] What about the entrance of large numbers of women into the labor force? What are the effects of lower birth rates? of increasing numbers of professionals? How are measures of inequality affected by changes in the composition of the labor force in general?

It is usually agreed that the distribution of permanent incomes should show less inequality than that of annual ones. Because of greater volatility of profits and greater incidence of unemployment, I expect that the divergence between annual and permanent incomes in this country should be greater than in the Soviet Union. Hence the use of permanent incomes would reduce the difference in inequality between the two countries.

Should American income distribution be made more equal? The demand and the supply of skills in the Soviet Union suggest the possibility of further decreases in income inequality. It seems, at least at first glance, that the opposite may be true in this country. We have an excess supply of unskilled labor (judging by unemployment statistics) and a shortage of some professionals. Is it true then, as the radicals charge, that a capitalist system cannot function effectively without a good deal of income inequality? Should we increase it?

Other Heretical Thoughts. Chapman remarked that the control exercised by Soviet planners over the demand and supply of different kinds of skills reduces the importance of wage differentiation. To carry this idea a bit further, direct allocation of labor by compulsion might make wage differentiation completely unnecessary and thus result in equal incomes, or at least, wage rates. (One hopes that the planners, by estimating shadow wages, will know how to allocate labor.) Thus we find a certain trade-off between personal freedom and income inequality.[5] It follows that a reduction in income inequality is not necessarily a blessing, even for egalitarians.

Indeed there is also a trade-off between equality and power. Imagine an academic department containing one professor who is immensely better (and more famous) than all the rest. On the basis of actual performance, he should be paid, perhaps, four times as much as any of his colleagues. But such a difference is against academic tradition, which limits the difference to, perhaps, some 50 percent. As a result, the famous professor can wield great power over his colleagues, because his departure would be an irreplaceable loss. But if he were paid his due, four others could be hired instead, and his resignation would not be such a great threat. It is too bad that distribution of power cannot be measured, but is inequality of power any better than inequality of income?

Sometimes I ask my undergraduates the following question: assuming that your lifetime income is given and that no part of it can be saved, would you prefer a falling, constant, or rising annual income? Economic theory asserts that a dollar today is better than a dollar tomorrow (even in the absence of saving), but my students invariably choose a smaller income today and a larger one tomorrow. As they put it, they want to have something to look forward to. I think they are right: old age has so many disadvantages (as I myself can testify) that, with a falling income, the future would look dismal indeed. Yet a rising annual income, compared with a constant one, would result in a greater measure of inequality at a point of time.

If our incomes were solely sources of living, many distributional problems would be simplified. Unfortunately, one's income has a large element of achievement and reward in it; hence an attempt to make the distribution more equal can and undoubtedly will damage the achievement element. In this respect the Soviets and the Chinese (at least under Mao) have had an advantage over us in their use of nonmonetary awards; and so have the British with their knighthoods and titles. But are we absolutely sure that an unequal distribution of nonmonetary rewards (otherwise they lose all meaning) is necessarily better, in some sense, than an unequal distribution of incomes?

Notes

1. Simon Kuznets, "Economic Growth and Income Inequality," *American Economic Review* 45 (March 1955):1-28.
2. See chapter 2, this volume.
3. Imagine the savings our economy could make if, for instance, we produced only three kinds of shoes for men and five for women.
4. According to Michael Reich, the discrimination against blacks creates greater inequality even among whites because the concentration of blacks in low-skill occupations reduces white earnings in them. See his "Economics of Racism," in Richard C. Edwards, Michael Reich, and Thomas E. Weisskopf, eds., *The Capitalist System: A Radical Analysis of American Society* (Englewood Cliffs, N.J.: Prentice-Hall, 1972).
5. See chapter 2, this volume.

4 Postfisc Income Inequality: A Comparison of the United States and West Germany

Eugene Smolensky, Werner W. Pommerehne, and *Robert E. Dalrymple*

Comparing income distributions across countries is full of traps. One can only be appalled at the cavalier way in which comparisons are often made from a grab bag of country-specific studies, even by distinguished scholars.[1] The wide variation in results reported for the same country in the same year is illustrated in table 4-1. The range is 73 Gini points (17 percent of the mean).[2] These differences arise from differences in the definition of income, the unit of observation, the collection of the data, and the calculation of the Gini coefficient. However, even in two sources for which the only major difference is the sample (the Current Population Survey and the Survey of Consumer Finances), Gini coefficients differ by 7 percent.

In this intercountry study a concerted effort was made to make the income definitions, the reporting unit, and the computational procedures comparable. West Germany in 1969 and the United States in 1970 were also in roughly the same stage of the business cycle.[3] Nevertheless, incomparabilities undoubtedly remain. Sampling and reporting error surely remains, and all the differences that we report between the two countries may be in the sample data but not in the universes. We think, however, that while the remaining incomparabilities are probably somewhat greater than for different data sources in the same country in the same year, they are not much larger than among data sets for one country in widely separated years. That is, differences in the same measures have to be 20 percent or so before they can be taken seriously.

Inequality, measured by the Gini coefficient, can be calculated for various income concepts. The basic concept of this chapter is the distribution of factor income (employee compensation, proprietor's income, dividends, and other

The research reported here received support from funds granted to the Institute for Research on Poverty at the University of Wisconsin-Madison by the Department of Health, Education, and Welfare pursuant to the Economic Opportunity Act of 1964. We are indebted to Guenter Schmaus and Manfred Euler for providing yet unpublished data. We would also like to thank Sheldon Danziger, Knut Gerlach, and Alva Myrdal for helpful comments on an earlier draft presented at the Annual Meeting of the Southern Economic Association, New Orleans, November 4, 1977.

Table 4-1
Gini Concentration Ratios in the United States, 1970

Basic Data Source	*Gini Coefficient (X 1,000)*
Survey of Consumer Finances	380
Office of Business Economics	402
Current Population Survey	409
Reynolds and Smolensky, 1977	446
Internal Revenue Service	453

Source: Reynolds and Smolensky, 1977, p. 35.

market payments to owners of factors of production but not public transfers or taxes) among households. That is, households are first sorted according to their factor incomes, and aggregate factor income in each class is calculated. The benefits of public expenditures less the burdens of taxes, at all levels of government, are then added to aggregate factor income in each income class under alternative incidence assumptions. Incidence assumptions are grouped to produce a regressive, progressive, or normal income distribution. Collectively these income concepts will be referred to as final income. Conceptually this measure presumes that all the behavioral adjustments to the fisc that affect the size distribution (for example, reduced work effort because of high marginal tax rates) are accounted for in the factor income distribution. Since the fisc affects both the factor and the final distribution, the difference between inequality in the final and factor income distributions is not a measure of redistribution due to public budgets. Final income is simply an unusually broad definition of income appropriately viewed as generated in a simultaneous interplay of both public and private activity in each country. To measure redistribution due to public budgets requires data on a counterfactual state in a world of zero government (such as a Lindahl equilibrium) which could then be compared with final income. Of course we do not contemplate calculating the distribution of income in the United States and West Germany in Lindahl equilibrium.

An important additional assumption is that recipients value the benefits of public expenditures at cost and hence that total benefits equal expenditures.[4] No distributional consequences are computed for any deadweight burdens in the system.

Incidence Assumptions

The Gini coefficients for factor income and for four measures of final income, each derived from one of the four sets of incidence assumptions, are presented in table 4-2. Underlying the normal income concept are conventional incidence assumptions. Personal income taxes are assumed not to be shifted, estate and gift taxes fall entirely in the highest income class, the corporate income tax is divided equally between dividend recipients and consumers, excise and sales taxes are borne entirely by consumers, employer as well as employee social security contributions are borne entirely by employees, and the residential property tax is paid by consumers of housing, while consumers of general output pay commercial property taxes. The incidence of expenditures is assumed to fall entirely on recipients directly identified, for example, children under eighteen for elementary and secondary school expenditures. The expenditures of government for which direct beneficiaries cannot be readily identified (called general expenditures) are distributed one-half by the distribution of households and one-half by the share of factor income. Because this, or any other, incidence assumption about general expenditures is hard to justify, general expenditures are also distributed like factor income so that general expenditures do not affect the Gini coefficient. When the distributive effects of general expenditures have been neutralized in this way, the distribution is labeled "Without General Expenditures."

In the two remaining income concepts, incidence assumptions that are more regressive and more progressive, respectively, are employed. The regressive assumptions are that general government expenditures are distributed by factor income, corporate income taxes are entirely shifted forward to consumption, and property taxes are slightly more regressively distributed. The progressive assumptions are that general government expenditures are distributed as are households, and the corporate income tax, sales and excise taxes, social security contributions and the property tax are all slightly more progressively distributed than in the normal case.

Accounting for Differences in Final Income Inequality

Factor income inequality in West Germany is 82 Gini points less than in the United States. The results for final income are fairly insensitive to the incidence assumptions: differences between the two countries vary between 99 and 123 Gini points.[5] In general, however, adopting any of the final definitions of income increases the measured difference in inequality between the two countries by about 25 percent.[6]

Final income consists of factor income plus the benefits of public expenditures less the cost of taxes. The differences in final income inequality between West Germany and the United States is about 105 Gini points. By far the largest source of difference in final income inequality between the two countries is accounted for by differences in factor income inequality.[7]

Factor income is more equally distributed in West Germany than in the United States because the sum of employee compensation (which includes the

Table 4-2
Gini Coefficients for Selected Definitions of Income: West Germany 1969; United States 1970

	Gini Coefficient (X 1,000)	
Income Concept	*West Germany*	*United States*
Factor income	364	446
Final		
Normal	240	339
Without general expenditures	271	375
Regressive	282	384
Progressive	161	284

employer share of social security contributions) and proprietor's income is dramatically more equally distributed. (The Gini coefficients are 0.373 and 0.452 respectively.)[8] In principle this difference could be a consequence of the fisc, in particular to the backward shifting of the social security contribution. However, the social security contribution, which we assume is fully borne by employees, is both larger and more regressive in West Germany. Employee compensation would therefore be more equally distributed, all else equal, in the United States than in West Germany if the difference in the wage distribution was due only to the backward shifting of the social security contribution.

Why wages are more equally distributed in West Germany we cannot say. Many hypotheses come readily to mind, but none has been tested.[9] That the difference is attributable to the fisc cannot be ruled out. The bottom 15 percent of U.S. households receives almost no employee compensation and subsists almost entirely on transfer income. Paradoxically, the relatively high transfer levels to nonelderly, primarily female household heads in the United States may increase inequality in two ways (Kuznets 1975). First, the number of poor households may increase. Large transfer payments make it possible to maintain a separate household. For example, mothers of illegitimate children who would otherwise live with their parents may maintain their own households. Had they lived with their parents all the factor income of the unit would have been attributed to one household. By living in two households their factor income is divided between them and inequality as measured here increases. Second, transfer recipients may reduce their work effort. Both effects reduce the amount of wage income accruing to the lowest percentiles of the distribution and increase the measured inequality of employee compensation, factor income, and final income.

The quantitative importance of these induced effects of the transfer system is still to be determined. Danziger and Plotnick (1977) find that the growing proportion of aged and women family heads and the growing number of individuals living alone raised the Gini coefficient by 15 to 20 Gini points between 1965 and 1975. What role the transfer system played in this large shift is not clear. Ross and Sawhill (1975) find a very small effect of welfare payments on female headship rates in 1974. Reynolds and Smolensky (1977) report that the Gini coefficient of employee compensation in the United States increased by only 5 points between 1950 and 1970. Transfers, female, and aged headship ratios all grew very rapidly during these two decades. It seems reasonable to conclude, quite tentatively, that the major difference in inequality in earnings is not accounted for by the fisc and therefore that the major difference in inequality in final income between the two countries is also not accounted for by the fisc.

Accounting for Sources of Difference

The direct effect on income inequality (without implying any behavioral response) of including any particular tax or expenditure program in the definition of final income can be calculated. If all programs except the one of interest are distributed as is factor income, and if the program of interest is distributed by its normal incidence assumption, then any difference between the Gini coefficients for factor income and the resulting distribution can be accounted for by this program. This procedure can be used to partition the total differences between the factor income and normal income Gini coefficients into an exhaustive, additive set. (We must reemphasize that this algebraic exercise abstracts from the behavioral responses to the various programs.)

The results of partitioning the differences between factor and final income are listed in table 4-3 (see also appendix 4A). Comparing the two columns shows the direct effect of total taxes to be very similar—slightly regressive—in the two countries. This similarity occurs largely because social security contributions in West Germany are more regressive even though the personal income tax is more progressive. Two startling differences, however, are revealed on the expenditure side. First, social security benefits are, all else equal, far more equalizing in West Germany than in the United States. Even though other transfer payments are substantially more equalizing in the United States, the effect of the West German social security system is so large that the effect of all transfer payments is nearly one and one-half times more equalizing in Germany. Second, state and local expenditures in the United States are substantially more redistributive than in West Germany. The larger equalizing effect of state and local expenditures in the United States is attributable mainly to primary and secondary school expenditures.[10]

A Hypothesis

The relative significance of social security and public education in the two countries may reflect politics at work. In the United States children (under age

Table 4-3
Accounting for Sources of Change in the Gini Coefficient, Normal Incidence: West Germany 1969, United States 1970

Income Concept	*Gini Coefficient (X 1,000)*	
	West Germany	*United States*
Factor income	364	446
Normal	240	339
Difference	124	107
Percentage of difference attributable to		
General expenditures	*24.5*	*33.6*
Taxes	*–4.9*[a]	*–7.5*[a]
Personal income	13.8	7.5
Social security contributions	–10.7[a]	–5.6[a]
All other[b]	–8.1[a]	–9.3[a]
All transfer payments	*78.0*	*49.5*
Social security	70.9	31.8
All other[c]	7.1	18.7
Other specific expenditures	*2.3*	*24.3*
Federal[d]	2.2	8.4
State and local	0.1	15.9
Education	0.1	11.2
Other[e]	–0.1[a]	3.7

Note: Italic items may not add to 100% due to rounding.

[a]A negative sign indicates that the item raises rather than lowers the normal Gini coefficient relative to initial inequality.

[b]Sales, excises and customs, estate and gift taxes, property taxes, corporate income taxes, other taxes.

[c]Public assistance, other welfare, unemployment compensation, and other transfers.

[d]Veterans' benefits; net interest paid; agriculture; elementary, secondary, and other education; higher education; highways; labor; and housing and community development.

[e]Veterans' benefits; net interest paid; agriculture; highways; and labor.

twenty) are a one-third larger proportion of the population than in West Germany, 38.1 percent versus 29.9 percent in 1970 (Institute of Developing Economies 1976, pp. 182, 235). The proportion of the population over age sixty-five, on the other hand, is about one-third larger in West Germany than in the United States, 10.1 percent versus 13.5 percent (pp. 182, 235). Perhaps for these reasons per child expenditure on education in the United States is approximately 2.7 times that of West Germany, at the September 1969 exchange rate (Federal Reserve Board 1970, p. A89), while in West Germany social security benefits, as measured by the transfer ratio, are 2.5 times the expenditure in the United States.[11] Relatively large groups may be able to secure relatively larger per capita benefits.

Wilensky (1975) concluded that demographics were the most important single factor determining differences in welfare expenditures among countries.

"If there is one source of welfare spending that is most powerful–a single proximate cause–it is the proportion of old people in the population" (p. 47).[12] The aged as a proportion of the population is growing in the United States. If the aged use their growing political influence to move the social security system of the United States toward a replacement rate similar to that in West Germany, then the conventionally measured distributional impact of the fisc will be increased. If the current U.S. "transfer ratio" was the same as in West Germany in 1970, and taxes were raised proportionately, then assuming incidence unchanged, the Gini coefficient would have been 45 points lower.[13]

The difference in inequality in final income between the United States and West Germany is large, but that difference is not accounted for, at least in any obvious way, by the role of the state as manifested by the fisc. Attention is clearly directed toward further analysis of the labor markets of the two countries.

Postscript: Canada

As table 4-4 reveals, Canada stands in a similar relation to the United States as West Germany. The difference in inequality in final income between the United States and Canada is also large and, once again, accounted for by differences between factor income distributions. Unlike the case for West Germany, however, the lesser inequality in factor income in Canada is not attributable to a single kind of functional income. Employee income is more equally distributed in Canada than in the United States (414 versus 452 Gini points), but the difference is not nearly so dramatic. Our general conclusion is sustained: that the difference in final income between the United States and other countries is not accounted for, at least in any obvious way, by the fisc.

Table 4-4
Gini Coefficients for Selected Definitions of Income: Canada 1970, United States 1970

	Gini Coefficient (X 1,000)	
Income Concept	*Canada*	*United States*
Factor income	391	446
Final: normal	291	339

Notes

1. See Tinbergen, 1975, for example. Schnitzer (1974), on the other hand, explicitly avoids intercountry comparisons.

2. It is convenient to multiply the Gini coefficient by 1,000, and to speak of the difference in terms of Gini points. Thus the 73 Gini points referred to here mean that for the Internal Revenue Service data the Gini coefficient as conventionally expressed is 0.453 while for the Survey of Consumer Finances it is 0.380. The difference 0.073 we shall refer to as "73 Gini points."

3. Both countries are near cyclical peaks, but the United States is on the downside while West Germany is on the upside. See Organization for Economic Cooperation and Development, 1973, p. 15, and National Bureau of Economic Research, 1973, p. 15.

4. For evidence that this assumption is not very misleading see Smolensky et al., 1977, and Pommerehne, 1977.

5. Several factors account for the progressive income concept's having a much larger difference than the other final income concepts. Eliminating factor income as a distributor for general expenditures makes the net effect *more* progressive in the United States, since factor income is more unequally distributed in the United States. The change in incidence assumptions for two of the tax categories (social security contributions and excise, customs, sales, and other taxes) offsets the general expenditure effect and accounts for almost all the relatively larger difference. Both of these tax categories are approximately twice as large a share of factor income in West Germany as in the United States. Although these taxes are more regressively distributed in West Germany in both the normal and progressive cases than in the United States, the Gini coefficient for these taxes rises substantially more for West Germany than for the United States when progressive assumptions are used. A larger effect on the distributors combines with a larger share of these taxes in total taxes to produce the observed result.

6. The Lorenz curve for the West Germany factor distribution probably lies within that for the United States throughout. When plotted they appear to cross at about the ninety-sixth percentile, but that crossing is undoubtedly due to the small number (eleven) of income classes. The Lorenz curves for West Germany lie almost entirely within that for the United States under the normal incidence assumptions, and the picture is only very slightly altered with general expenditures neutrally distributed. On the whole, therefore, the Gini coefficients are reasonable descriptive statistics.

7. The significance of less inequality in factor income for inequality in final income is even larger than this comparison implies. Factor income is a component of final income. Factor income inequality further affects final income indirectly, since it generally serves as all or part of the distributor of general government. Comparing the normal and without-general-expenditures

coefficients in table 4-2 suggests that the inequality in factor income indirectly accounts for an additional 12 Gini points of the difference between the two countries. Thus almost 90 percent of the difference is approximately attributable to inequality in factor income.

8. These data are not shown in the tables. They refer to the distribution of wage income across income classes formed on the basis of total household money income.

9. One possibility is that German wage data is biased toward equality, since the data are from a consumer expenditure survey. However, the U.S. data are also from a household survey. The data for West Germany used in this paper are from EVS 1969 (Statistisches Bundesamt, 1970-1973) weighted to match the 1969 population, including guest workers. We preferred these data to the SPES data, which may be more accurate in the aggregate, for two reasons. First, the uncorrected survey data are more consistent with the uncorrected Current Population Survey (CPS) data. (The SPES data are conceptually comparable to Budd's (Budd 1970; Budd, Radner, and Hinrichs 1973) reworking of the CPS data.) Second, we did not have enough detail on the components of factor income from SPES. While we know the SPES distributions of wages, social security contributions, and proprietor's income, we do not know the separate distributions of dividends, interest income, and net rental income.

If property income is combined into one category and distributed according to the distribution of wealth, it is then possible to make most of the the calculations reported for the EVS sample data. The resulting Gini coefficient for factor income is 7 percent (25 points) greater, and the Gini coefficients for the final income concepts are around 17 percent (45 points) greater. The single distribution for income from wealth accounts for 78 percent (19 points) of the change in the factor income Gini coefficient. Due to the large impact of the change to a single wealth distribution, and because the qualitative conclusions of the paper are unaffected by these quantitatively different results, we prefer the EVS data.

10. Benefits for education were distributed according to the number of children under age eighteen in each income class. It has been alleged, sometimes, that education expenditures per student are lower for poor children in the United States.

11. The transfer ratio is the product of the ratio of social security benefits per recipient and the reciprocal of the participation rate in the program (OECD 1976, pp. 19-22).

12. Wilensky did not look at education expenditures per se and therefore missed the apparently powerful influence of parents.

13. On the other hand, if the growing young population of West Germany received the educational benefits that American children receive, the effect would not be dramatic because the distribution of children across income classes is similar to the distribution of factor income in West Germany.

References

Budd, E.C. 1970. "Postwar Changes in the Size Distribution of Income in the U.S." *American Economic Review* 60:247-260.

Budd, E.C., Radner, D.B., and Hinrichs, J.C. 1973. *Size Distribution of Family Personal Income: Methodology and Estimates for 1964.* Bureau of Economic Analysis Staff Paper No. 21. Washington, D.C.: U.S. Department of Commerce.

Danziger, Sheldon, and Plotnick, Robert. 1977. "Demographic Change, Government Transfers, and Income Distribution." *Monthly Labor Review,* April, pp. 7-11.

Federal Reserve Board. 1970. *Federal Reserve Bulletin,* 56, no. 9. Washington, D.C.: Board of Governors, Federal Reserve System.

Institute of Developing Economies. 1976. *Age Pyramids of the World Population, 1950-1970.* Tokyo: Hommura-cho, Ichigaya, Shinjuku-ku.

Kuznets, Simon. 1975. "Demographic Aspect of the Distribution of Income among Families: Recent Trends in the United States." In Willy Selekaerts, ed., *Econometrics and Economic Theory: Essays in Honor of Jan Tinbergen.* New York: International Arts and Sciences Press.

National Bureau of Economic Research. 1973. *Fifty-third Annual Report.* New York: National Bureau of Economic Research.

Organization for Economic Cooperation and Development. 1973. *OECD Economic Surveys: Germany.* Paris.

_______. 1976. *Public Expenditures on Income Maintenance Programs.* Paris.

Pommerehne, Werner W. 1977. "Trasferimenti Non Monetari contro Trasferimenti Monetari: Una Favola di Scienza Finanziaria." *Revista di Diritto Finanziario e Scienza delle Finanze* 36:121-133.

Reynolds, Morgan, and Smolensky, Eugene. 1977. *Public Expenditures, Taxes, and the Distribution of Income.* New York: Academic Press.

Ross, Heather L., and Sawhill, Isabel V. 1975. *Time of Transition.* Washington, D.C.: Urban Institute.

Schnitzer, Martin. 1974. *Income Distribution.* New York: Praeger.

Smolensky, Eugene, Stiefel, Leanna, Schmundt, Maria, and Plotnick, Robert. 1977. "Adding In-Kind Transfers to the Personal Income and Outlay Account: Implications for the Size Distribution of Income." In F. Thomas Juster, ed., *Distribution of Economic Well-being.* New York: Conference of Income and Wealth, National Bureau of Economic Research.

Tinbergen, Jan. 1975. *Income Distribution.* New York: North Holland.

Wilensky, Harold L. 1975. *The Welfare State and Equality.* Berkeley and Los Angeles: University of California Press.

U.S. Data Source

Reynolds, Morgan, and Smolensky, Eugene. 1977. *Public Expenditures, Taxes, and the Distribution of Income: The United States, 1950, 1961, 1970.* New York: Academic Press, pp. 108-109, 114, 18, 121, 128-129, 132; appendix tables B.3, C.3, D.3, D.6, E.3, E.6.

Canada Data Sources

Dodge, David A. 1975. "Impact of Tax, Transfer, and Expenditure Policies of Government on the Distribution of Personal Income in Canada." *Review of Income and Wealth,* Series 21, no. 1, pp. 1-52.

_______. 1973. Appendixes to "Impact of Tax, Transfer, and Expenditure Policies on the Distribution of Personal Incomes in Canada." Supplied by the author on request.

West Germany Data Sources

Bundesanstalt fuer Arbeit. 1970. *Amtliche Nachrichten der Bundesanstalt fuer Arbeit.* Arbeitsstatistik 1969-Jahreszahlen, 18 (special number), pp. 259-260.

Euler, Manfred. 1973. "Einkommensverwendung in privaten Haushalten 1969." *Wirtschaft und Statistik,* February, pp. 88-97.

_______. 1973. "Ausgewaehlte Aufwendungen fuer den privaten Verbauch." *Wirtschaft und Statistik,* February, pp. 264-273.

_______. 1973. "Die Verteilung des Geld- und Grundvermoegens der privaten Haushalte nach sozialen Gruppen:Versuch einer statistischen Analyse." *Allgemeines Statistisches Archiv* 57:255-294, tables 6, 8.

Hanusch, Horst. *Personale Verteilung Oeffentlicher Leistungen. Eine Analytische und Empirische Studie* forthcoming, appendix tables 2, 3.

Integriertes Mikrodatenfile 1969 fuer die Bundesrepublik Deutschland des SPES:Projektes, December 1977. Frankfurt: University of Frankfurt.

Krupp, Hans Juergen. 1975. *Moeglichkeiten der Verbesserung der Einkommens–und Vermoegensstatistik.* Goettingen: Otto Schwartz.

Kunz, Dieter. 1973. "Die Einkommen der Haushalte aus Sozial-versicherungsrenten." *Wirtschaft und Statistik*, December, pp. 706-711.

Sachverstaendigenrat. 1975. *Jahresgutachten 1975 des Sachverstaendigenrates zur Begutachtung der gesamtwirtschaftlichen Entwicklung.* Bonn: Deutscher Bundestag, Drucksache 7/4326, p. 232.

Statistisches Bundesamt. 1970. *Fachserie M, Reihe 18, Einkommens–und Verbrauchsstichproben,* no. 1. Wiesbaden: St. B., pp. 10-19.

_______. 1970. *Fachserie A, Reihe 5, Haushalt und Familien, 1969* no. 1. Wiesbaden: St. B., pp. 34-35, 40-43.

_______. *Statistisches Jahrbuch fuer die Bundesrepublik Deutschland.* Wiesbaden: St. B., several years.

_______. 1971. *Fachserie M, Reihe 18, Einkommens–und Verbrauchsstichproben,* no. 2, Wiesbaden: St. B., pp. 15-20, 147-151.

_______. 1972. *Fachserie L, Finanzen und Steuern, Reihe 1, Haushaltswirtschaft von Bund, Laendern und Gemeinde.* II: *Jahresabschluesse, Oeffentliche Finanzwirtschaft 1969.* Stuttgart.

_______. 1973. *Fachserie M, Reihe 18, Einkommens–und Verbrauchsstichproben* no. 4. Wiesbaden: St. B., pp. 34-42.

_______. 1973. *Fachserie M, Reihe 18, Einkommens–und Verbrauchsstichproben,* no. 5. Wiesbaden: St. B., pp. 26-35.

_______. 1973. *Volkswirtschaftliche Gesamtrechnungen.* Wiesbaden: St. B.

Wicke, Lutz. 1975. "Die personelle Vermoegensverteilung in der Bundesrepublik Deutschland am Jahresende 1969." *Finanzarchiv* 34:39-65, tables 7-10.

Appendix 4A

Table 4A-1
Background Data: West Germany 1969, United States 1970

Income Concept	*West Germany*	*United States*
Factor income (NNP, millions)	541,250 DM	$886,542
Final income (millions)	539,566 DM	$899,650
Difference[a] (millions)	−1,684 DM	$ 13,108
Percentage of factor income		
General Expenditures	*16.7*	*16.4*
Taxes	*44.3*	*33.9*
Personal income	8.5	11.2
Social security contributions	11.7	6.5
All other[b]	24.1	16.2
All transfer payments	*18.3*	*7.3*
Social security	15.5	4.7
All other[c]	2.8	2.7
Other specific expenditures	*9.0*	*11.7*
Federal[d]	3.6	3.5
State and local	5.3	8.1
Education	3.9	6.1
Other[e]	1.4	2.0

Note: Subtotal of italic items may not add to totals for italicized items due to rounding. Total expenditures do not equal total taxes because of government surpluses or deficits.

[a]A negative difference indicates a government surplus.

[b]Sales, excises and customs, estate and gift taxes, property taxes, corporate income taxes, other taxes.

[c]Public assistance, other welfare, unemployment compensation, and other transfers.

[d]Veterans' benefits; net interest paid; agriculture; elementary, secondary, and other education; higher education; highways; labor; and housing and community development.

[e]Veterans' benefits; net interest paid; agriculture; highways; and labor.

Commentary

G. Randolph Rice

It has become a ritual within the economics profession for discussants to aggressively take the offensive in their appointed task. The chapter by Eugene Smolensky and his colleagues does not tempt me into that approach to reviewing their work. However, there are a few questions and some corroborating suggestions with regard to their conclusions that I would like to offer.

The question posed by the paper is, Do the respective fiscs in the United States and West Germany have notably different effects on the inequality of final incomes? The conclusion is that the difference between inequality in final incomes between the United States and West Germany is large but that this difference is not attributable to the fisc per country. Hence, as the authors suggest, the extension of this work falls to the labor economist and not the public finance researcher.

The problems of comparable data across countries are outlined at the beginning of the chapter, and attempts have been made to deal with this issue in a straightforward manner. The solutions seem reasonable. There is one concern, however, that could be important. The point is made in note 3 that the annual data (the use of annual data for meaningfully gauging income inequality is an issue in itself) for both countries are from similar phases of the business cycle. Currently available research papers provide information about how the pretax income in the United States changes over the business cycle; for example, Metcalf's (1972) macroeconometric model of the United States incorporates the size distribution of income as an endogenous variable, and Mirer's (1973) simulation of the economy in various business cycle "states" begins with a benchmark of full employment incomes for respective income classes and notes their changes through the respective "states." But lack of information on what happens to the postfisc income distribution in the United States over the business cycle and lack of a comparable postfisc cyclical model for West Germany may be sidestepping an important issue with a rather simple assumption. To say that both countries are near cyclical peaks implies that we are holding constant the cyclical effects; this may not be true.

The use of the Gini coefficients as the measures of inequality should not pose any problems inasmuch as the West Germany Lorenz curve lies within that for the United States. I do not have a feel for whether the conclusion that "on the whole, therefore, the Gini coefficients are reasonable descriptive statistics" is too general. Specifically, what degree of confidence should we impute to "on the whole" and "reasonable descriptive statistic"? Perhaps an alternative index could substantiate the conclusion. But this is a minor point.

The ultimate conclusion of the paper is that the difference in inequality in final income between the two countries is not attributable, at least in any obvious way, to the role of the state as manifested by the fisc. Perhaps the qualifier, "at least in any obvious way," was made with a recent study by Sawers and Wachtel (1975) in mind. A synopsis of their theory suggests some possibilities that would have been accounted for in the factor incomes but would not have been recognized as fisc factors with the current methodology. For example, Sawers and Wachtel suggest that government purchases and taxes, apart from their direct effects, can alter several determinants of prefisc income distributions in the private sector. They specifically indicate that industrial concentration, capital structure, and the character of labor markets can be substantially modified by government taxation and purchasing policy.

In line with this suggestion and with the proposals for further analysis of the labor markets in the current paper, it is my feeling that a very basic problem with understanding earnings inequality has not been adequately dealt with in the literature. Specifically, many of the earnings models, whether from the human capital approach or otherwise, have relied on some poor proxies or indirect descriptive techniques for identifying important variables. It may be that we cannot currently do better in measuring the characteristics that truly "matter" in the labor force. Moreover, our attempts to account for all factors, presuming that we have adequately captured the proper variable, may have been incorrectly specified if we impute simultaneously to all facets of the labor market an earnings function of homogenous structure. Of course, different specifications can be accommodated provided the data are accurate (in the conceptual sense), but this mending of the model is not fully adequate given today's data. My proposal for this type research is away from the typical mold of regression-type models and earnings functions and toward an indirect distribution model that takes account of basic economic decisions by producers (including capital-labor substitutability), takes account of institutional characteristics that may differ across income classes, explicitly notes occupational structures that do in fact present different within- and across-earnings arrays (not a homogenous income), and more aptly takes account of the "true" factors that theory implies are important in the earnings matrix. Only then can we be sure that some of the less obvious factors, public and private, have been identified. But these suggestions merely corroborate Smolensky and his colleagues' feelings about a need for greater understanding of the labor markets. My closing concerns, therefore, are that we not overlook the "at least in any obvious way" caveat about the fisc and its potential effect on many of our institutions, and, moreover, that we rethink some approaches to making these determinations.

References

Metcalf, Charles E. 1972. *An Econometric Model of the Income Distribution.* Chicago: Markham Publishing Company.

Mirer, Thad W. 1973. "The Effects of Macroeconomic Fluctuations on the Distribution of Income." *Review of Income and Wealth,* Series 4, no. 19, pp. 385-405.

Sawers, Larry, and Wachtel, Howard M. 1975. "Theory of the State, Government Tax and Purchasing Policy, and Income Distribution." *Review of Income and Wealth,* Series 21, March, pp. 111-124.

5 The Burden of Taxation

Edgar K. Browning

One of the accepted maxims in economics is that the burden, or incidence, of the entire tax system (federal, state, and local) is roughly proportional to income. A slightly progressive federal tax system is believed to be offset by a slightly regressive state and local tax system. In one form or another, this conclusion is stated in virtually every principles of economics and public finance textbook.[1] This generalization is almost certainly incorrect.

The empirical basis for statements concerning tax incidence by income class rests on several studies that allocate tax burdens by income class (Colm and Tarasov 1940, Musgrave et al. 1951, 1974; Gillespie 1965; Herriot and Miller 1971; Pechman and Ockner 1974). The two most recent studies, those by Musgrave et al. (1974) and Pechman and Okner (1974), are the most thorough. They estimate the incidence of the tax system using alternative assumptions about the incidence of various taxes. Under competitive incidence assumptions, the tax system is found to be modestly progressive at the very top and bottom of the income distribution but proportional over the broad middle-income classes. When different assumptions are used for the property tax, corporate income tax, and social security payroll tax, even this modest degree of progressivity vanishes. Under certain combinations of assumptions, the tax burden on the poor is a higher percentage of income than for higher income taxpayers.

There is a common error in all studies of tax incidence: these studies use rules of thumb for the allocation of tax burdens that are correct, in general, only if all income is in the form of capital and labor income. Government transfers, however, have become an important source of income, especially for the lower income classes. Once the existence of transfer income is incorporated into the general equilibrium analysis of tax incidence, a very different pattern of burdens by income class emerges for some taxes. For example, in all existing studies, excise and sales taxes are a major regressive element in the tax system. When low-income families have a large proportion of their income in the form of transfers, however, these taxes can be shown to be quite progressive. This single change makes the overall tax system substantially more progressive than

I would like to thank William Breit, Edwin Burmeister, William R. Johnson, Ronald N. McKean, and Charles E. McLure, Jr., for comments on earlier drafts. The paper was revised while I was a visiting scholar at the University of California at Los Angeles. Reprinted from Edgar K. Browning, "The Burden of Taxation," *Journal of Political Economy* 86, no. 4 (1978):649-671 by permission of the University of Chicago Press.

previously realized. Of perhaps even greater interest, this sharp progressivity is largely independent of whatever assumptions are made concerning the incidence of the property tax, corporate income tax, or social security payroll tax.

Tax Incidence and the Price Level

How a tax may affect the absolute level of prices is widely believed to be largely irrelevant in determining the distribution of real tax burdens. Tax incidence is held to be a function of changes in relative prices, as Musgrave (1959, p. 370) has noted: "Resulting changes in the distribution of real income will be independent of the particular pattern of change in absolute prices. *Incidence is not a function of changes in absolute prices but of changes in relative prices.*" McLure (1970) has recently demonstrated this point rigorously in the context of a simple general equilibrium model.

In other words, the distribution of real tax burdens is the same whether the price level rises or remains unchanged when a tax is introduced. The rationale for this position can be seen most easily by considering a general sales tax that applies to all goods and services at equal rates. Two distinctly different outcomes are conceivable. First, product prices could rise by the amount of the tax while factor prices remain unchanged. Second, product prices could remain unchanged while factor prices fall in proportion to the size of the tax. Both outcomes, however, are the same in real terms: factor prices have fallen relative to product prices in both cases.

One qualification to the view that absolute prices do not matter for tax incidence has been recognized: it must be assumed that there are no assets fixed in money terms. However, a more important problem has not been considered. Government transfers are an important source of income, and if these transfers are fixed in money terms tax incidence depends on what happens to the absolute price level. Consider a person whose entire income is in the form of a government transfer. If a general sales tax raises the price level, and the size of the transfer in money terms is fixed, a burden is placed on this transfer recipient by the tax since the higher price level reduces the real value of the transfer. Conversely, if the price level is unchanged by the tax, the transfer recipient would bear no burden from the tax, since the purchasing power of his transfer would be unaffected.

The conventional view that tax incidence does not depend on what happens to the price level is based on a simple theoretical model in which all income is derived from factor earnings. In the context of that model the proposition is correct. The proposition may not be correct when government transfers are an important source of income. In this case the incidence of a tax can depend on what happens to the price level and the money value of transfers; either or both may be affected by changes in the tax system. This raises an important methodological issue concerning the appropriate assumptions in a study of tax incidence.

Existing incidence studies allocate the burden of an excise tax in proportion to outlays on the taxed product, and the burden of a sales tax in proportion to total consumption outlays. Insofar as transfer income is concerned, this procedure is valid only under highly restrictive assumptions. For example, this procedure would be correct if the overall price level rises in proportion to the size of the tax (total tax revenue as a percentage of national income), and if transfers in money terms are unaffected. In the case of an excise tax on a particular product, the price of the taxed product would rise by the amount of the tax per unit, with no change in any other product or factor price. Under these circumstances, a person whose only income is a fixed money transfer would be burdened to the extent that he consumes the taxed product. In effect, existing incidence studies depend for their validity on the assumption that sales and excise taxes reduce the real value of all government transfers exactly in proportion to the size of the tax.

There are at least two problems with this position as a justification for the procedures used to allocate tax burdens in tax incidence studies. First, it must be assumed that the price level rises exactly in proportion to the size of the tax. As a matter of macroeconomic theory, it is far from clear why the introduction of a tax (in a balanced-budget framework where the revenues are spent by the government) or the substitution of one tax for another (in a differential incidence approach) would increase prices by precisely that amount. Any different impact on the price level would make this method of allocating tax burdens incorrect.

The second problem is even more severe. It must also be assumed that the money value of transfers remains unchanged when the price level rises. Given the legislation governing existing transfer policies, this assumption is simply untenable. The single most important transfer program, social security, now has benefit levels linked to the consumer price index. When prices rise benefits rise, keeping real benefits approximately unchanged. A number of other programs also have monetary benefit levels that automatically increase when absolute prices rise. This is true of all in-kind programs (Medicare, Medicaid, food stamps, housing assistance, and others), since an increase in the absolute prices of the subsidized goods increases the monetary value of the subsidy (Food stamp subsidies are also related to the consumer price index).

Even for transfer programs that do not automatically increase money benefits when the price level rises, it is clear that legislatures make ad hoc adjustments in response to price level increases. The official poverty lines are increased when prices rise, and legislators are quite aware that money benefits must be increased to keep the real positions of recipients unchanged.

In view of these considerations, what assumptions should be used in tax incidence analysis about the impact of taxation on the price level and on the size of government transfers? My preference is to assume that the monetary authorities act to keep the price level unchanged and that the money value of transfers also remains unchanged. This has the effect of keeping the real value of transfers constant. (Alternatively, and equivalently, it could be assumed that the money value of transfers is varied in proportion to any change in the price level.) Assuming that the real value of transfers is unaffected by tax policy not only appears realistic but also has the advantage that tax incidence is once again independent of what happens to the absolute price level. The distribution of tax burdens under this assumption turns out, however, to be quite different from that estimated in previous incidence studies.

In assuming that the real value of transfers is kept fixed (by keeping the price level and the money value of transfers unchanged), I do not mean to suggest that the effect of changes in the price level on income distribution should be ignored. As a practical matter, however, there seems no way to determine exactly how much of a given rise in prices is due to taxation or how much money transfers will rise in response. Since many factors in addition to taxation influence the absolute price level and the determination of transfer levels, it seems preferable to regard the impact of absolute price level changes as a separate issue. Thus I share McLure's (1970, p. 266) position on this issue: "Redistributions of income can result from inflationary or deflationary policies, including those of taxation. But these are best considered as separate phenomena resulting from the chosen macroeconomic policy, rather than from the particular tax in question."

The Incidence of Sales and Excise Taxes

It will be convenient to begin with a brief description of the general equilibrium analysis of the incidence of sales and excise taxes. Although the initial portion of the analysis is familiar to many economists, it is important to identify carefully the theoretical basis for the procedure that has been used to allocate the burden of these taxes by income class in incidence studies. Once this basis is understood, a major error in all existing incidence studies will be apparent. In addition, the excise tax case is of considerable importance in evaluating the incidence of other taxes, such as the corporate income tax, since certain incidence assumptions are equivalent to assuming that the economy responds to these taxes as if they were, at least in part, excise taxes themselves.

The basic model used throughout the analysis is the familiar Harberger general equilibrium model. Since the structure of this model has been explained in detail many times, only its most important features are outlined here.[2] The economy is assumed to be perfectly competitive, both in factor and product markets. Two products, x and y, are produced. Two factors of production, labor L and capital K, are employed in the production of each product. Total factor supplies are assumed fixed, but factors are fully mobile between sectors, at least in the long-run framework employed. All disposable income is consumed: there is zero net saving.

Since the equations that describe this model are one fewer than the number of unknowns, it is necessary to choose one product or factor to serve as numéraire or to add an equation that specifies how the general price level is determined.[3] The latter method for closing the system is followed here: it is assumed that the monetary authorities act to keep the general level of prices unchanged, thereby keeping national income, measured in dollars, unchanged.

There are two major approaches to the analysis of tax incidence. Balanced-budget incidence identifies the combined effects of a tax plus an assumed expenditure policy on the distribution of private disposable incomes. Differential incidence identifies the effects of substituting one tax for another on the distribution of income when government expenditures are held constant. Neither approach is without problems, but the choice between them generally does not involve substantive issues. As Mieszkowski (1969, p. 1105) notes: "In practice, however, the differences between the two approaches are minor as most results on differential incidence can easily be translated into absolute burdens by using the proportional income tax as a 'reference point'."[4] The balanced-budget approach is used here, primarily for ease of exposition. This approach necessitates incorporating the effects of the expenditures financed by the tax into the analysis. To accomplish this, following Harberger (1962) and McLure and Thirsk (1975), we assume that the government uses the tax revenue to finance purchases of products in a manner that is distributionally neutral. Roughly speaking, this means that the government purchases goods in amounts that offset the reduction in private purchases due to the income effects of the tax, but not its substitution effects.[5]

Using this framework, let us now examine the imposition of a general sales tax that is levied at equal rates on the sales of both goods, x and y. Since the tax is levied at the same rate on both goods, it does not affect relative product prices. Moreover, under our assumption that the price level is fixed, the absolute prices of both goods remain unchanged. Under these conditions the tax produces a proportionate reduction in the prices paid to factors of production. Total outlays on goods x and y now exceed total payments to factors of production by the amount of tax revenue collected.[6]

The incidence of the general sales tax—its effect on the distribution of disposable real incomes—depends on its effects on household budgets operating through changes in the uses of income and through changes in the sources of income.[9] On the uses side, real incomes are unaffected by a truly general sales tax, since there is no change in the prices of products purchased. On the sources side, factor earnings have fallen in proportion to the size of the tax. Thus if the sales tax raises revenue equal to 10 percent of national income, each household's factor earnings will have fallen by 10 percent.

When there are no government transfers, the tax burden of the sales tax could be allocated in proportion to either factor earnings or consumption outlays since these two sums are equal for each household in the zero saving model. This provides a justification for allocation in proportion to consumption outlays (the procedure actually used in incidence studies), but this justification is no longer valid when factor earnings are not the only source of income for households. A household whose entire income is in the form of a government transfer, for example, would bear no burden under the sales tax since product prices are unchanged. (We are assuming that the money value of transfers is unchanged.) Allocation of the tax burden in proportion to consumption outlays is thus incorrect when these outlays are financed from transfer payments rather than from factor earnings.

Actually, what is important in determining the incidence by income class of a general sales tax is the proportion of income received as transfers. For example, if the tax produces a 10 percent reduction in factor prices, a household whose entire income is factor earnings would bear a burden equal to 10 percent of its income. If, on the other hand, half of a household's income is factor earnings and half is a transfer payment, the tax burden of a 10 percent reduction in factor prices would be equal to only 5 percent of its total income. The larger the proportion of income received as transfers, the smaller the tax burden as a percentage of total income. If all households received the same percentage of their total income as transfer payments, it would still be possible to allocate the tax burden in proportion to either consumption outlays or factor earnings. When households receive different percentages of their total incomes as transfers, however, allocation of the tax burden in proportion to consumption outlays overstates the burden for those who receive above-average proportions of their incomes as transfers and understates the burden for those who receive below-average proportions of their incomes as transfers. The correct procedure in this case is to allocate the tax burden in proportion to factor earnings, not in proportion to consumption outlays.

Table 5-1 shows that the proportions of income received as transfers differ greatly among population quintiles, as would be expected. Transfer income is 65 percent of total income in the lowest quintile but falls steadily as one moves up the income distribution until it is only 8 percent for the highest quintile.[8] Although estimates reported in table 5-1 should be considered rough, other studies confirm the disproportionate importance of transfer income in lower-income classes.[9] Thus the lowest quintile tends to be insulated to a large degree from the effects of a general sales tax. A general sales tax reduces factor prices, but the lowest quintile receives only 35 percent of its income as factor income.

This analysis suggests that the burden of a general sales tax should be allocated according to factor earnings rather than consumption. There are two complications to be considered, however. First, when we drop the assumption of zero savings, the tax has further effects, since it tends to favor those who save a

Table 5-1
Sources of Income, 1972
(in billions of dollars)

Quintile	*Total Income*	*Labor Income*	*Capital Income*	*Transfer Income*
Lowest	77.0 (100)	18.4 (24)	8.3 (11)	50.3 (65)
Second	111.0 (100)	66.4 (60)	12.9 (12)	31.7 (28)
Third	150.1 (100)	111.3 (74)	13.2 (9)	25.6 (17)
Fourth	197.3 (100)	156.0 (79)	16.5 (8)	24.8 (13)
Highest	350.4 (100)	266.4 (76)	55.1 (16)	28.9 (8)
Total, all quintiles	885.8 (100)	618.5 (70)	106.0 (12)	161.3 (18)

Source: Calculated from data summarized in Browning, 1976.
Note: Numbers in parentheses are percentages.

large proportion of their incomes. Second, actual sales taxes in the United States are not truly general taxes that strike all goods and services but instead exempt many goods and therefore alter relative product prices. The significance of these factors can be better evaluated after the incidence of an excise tax is examined, since the analysis of such a tax emphasizes the importance of changes in relative prices.

Consider the imposition of a per unit excise tax on the sale of product x. The tax leads to a higher price for x (relatively and absolutely[10]), and consumers purchase a smaller quantity. Output of x falls as labor and capital are released from employment in production of x. Full employment can be achieved only with a reduction in absolute factor prices, so industry y will be led to increase its employment. If we assume that factor intensities are the same in both industries (an assumption used throughout this chapter), there is a proportionate reduction in the prices of both factors.[11] With lower factor prices, costs are reduced for industry y, so output increases, and its larger output is sold at a lower price.

Figure 5-1 is a diagram of the final equilibrium using partial equilibrium constructs.[12] With units of output defined so that initial prices are equal, x_1 and y_1 are produced in the absence of the tax. A tax of T_x per unit (equal to $P'_x - P''_x$) is imposed on industry x. In the final general equilibrium, costs of production exclusive of the tax (net payments to factors per unit of output) are lower for both industries because of the reduction in factor prices, as shown by the downward shift in both supply curves (exclusive of the tax on x). The final

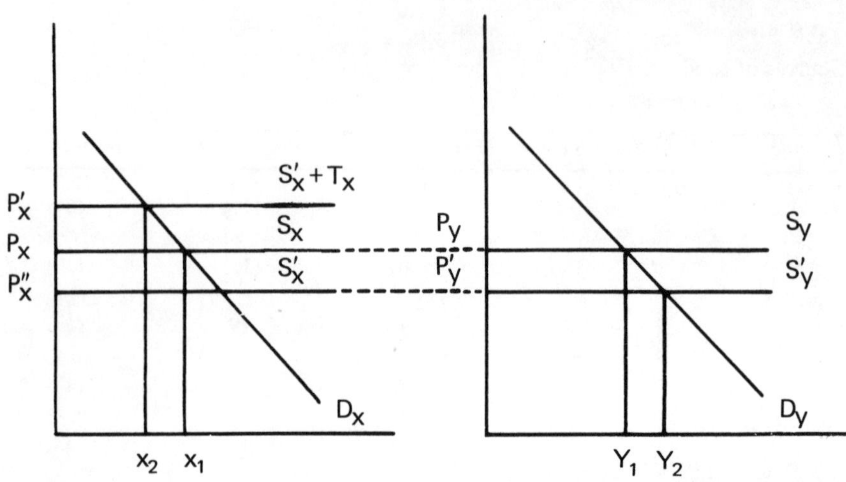

Figure 5-1. Changes in Prices and Outputs with an Excise Tax

price of x inclusive of the tax is higher, and the final price of y is lower, with opposite movements in output levels. We are assuming that the level of national income in money terms remains unchanged. Thus national income with the tax in place, $P'_x x_2 + P'_y y_2$, is equal to national income in the absence of the tax, $P_x x_1 + P_y y_1$.[13]

An excise tax affects households, operating through changes in both the sources and the uses of income. For any person or income class the total tax burden is the sum of these two effects. On the sources side there is, just as with a general sales tax, a reduction in factor earnings proportionate to the amount of tax revenue as a percentage of national income. An additional effect flows from the change in product prices. Since one price is higher and the other lower, whether a person is harmed further or benefited by this change depends on the proportion of income spent on each item. Persons who spend a higher-than-average proportion on x are harmed while those who spend a lower-than-average proportion (higher than average on the lower-priced good) are benefited. There is a zero net effect for those who spend the same percentage on x as society as a whole.[14]

In existing tax incidence studies excise taxes are generally allocated in proportion to consumption of the taxed good rather than in the manner just described. Just as with the general sales tax, if each household's income is solely in the form of factor earnings, then allocation in proportion to consumption of the taxed good generates the same estimated tax burden as estimating the effects on sources and uses of income separately and then summing,[15] for in this case the tax is neutral on the sources side (the same percentage for all), and any deviations from proportionality that exist occur to the extent that persons spend on x a percentage of their income that differs from the national average. Thus those who spend a higher than average proportion on x bear a total tax burden as a percentage of income that is greater than the average (and conversely), and this is exactly the result produced when the tax burden is allocated in proportion to consumption of good x.

When income derives from transfers in addition to factor earnings, however, this justification for allocating the burden of an excise tax in proportion to consumption of the taxed good is not valid. As a simple example, consider once again a person whose entire income is in the form of a government transfer. An excise tax has no effect on his income on the sources side since he has no factor earnings. If he spends a proportion of his income on x equal to the national average, there is no net burden on the uses side, since the loss from consuming the higher-priced good is exactly offset by the gain from consuming the lower-priced good. Thus he has a zero tax burden, but use of the conventional method of allocating the tax burden would imply, incorrectly, a substantial burden on this person. When transfer income is an important source of income, allocation in proportion to consumption of the taxed good is generally wrong, just as in the case of a general sales tax. To get the right answer it is necessary to use the theoretically correct, but more cumbersome, approach of estimating the effects on the sources and uses sides of the budget and then summing.

Estimating Tax Burdens by Income Class

To develop a general method for allocating the tax burden of excise and sales taxes by income class, we begin by defining the total income of the ith income class Ii in the absence of these taxes as

$$I_i = L_i P_L + K_i P_K + T_i = x_i P_x + Y_i P_y, \tag{5.1}$$

where L_i and K_i are the quantities of labor and capital, P_L and P_K their prices, and T_i the amount of government transfers. Income on the sources side is thus the sum of labor, capital, and transfer income. Income on the uses side is equal to the sum of the prices times quantities of the two products.

Defining units so that all factor and product prices are initially unity, the percentage change in the disposable real income (the average tax rate) of the ith class following the imposition of the tax is

$$dI_i/I_i = f_i dP_L + g_i dP_K + h_i dT_i - [a_i dP_x + (1 - a_i) dP_y], \tag{5.2}$$

where f_i, g_i, and h_i are the fractions of total income received as labor, capital, and transfer income, and a_i is the fraction of total outlays made on good x.[16] Since we are assuming that the tax has no effect on the size of the transfer, dT_i equals zero, and equation 5.2 may be rewritten as

$$dI_i/I_i = f_i dP_L + g_i dP_K - [a_i dP_x + (1 - a_i) dP_y]. \tag{5.3}$$

The first two terms on the right side of equation 5.3 measure that part of the percentage burden of the tax due to changes in factor earnings (the sources side), while the term in brackets is that part of the percentage change due to changes in product prices (the uses side).

For society as a whole, the percentage change in real income is given by

$$dI/I = F dp_L + G dp_k - [A dP_x + (1 - A) dP_y], \tag{5.4}$$

where F and G are the average fraction of total income received as labor and capital income, and A is the average fraction of total outlays made on good x. Since the weights that define an unchanged price level are A and $(1 - A)$, the term $[AdP_x + (1 - A)dP_y]$ is always zero: what some persons in their roles as consumers gain, others lose. In the aggregate the entire burden can be assigned on the sources of income side; net factor payments fall short of the total outlays on products by the amount of tax revenue.

Net effects on real income resulting from changes in relative product prices occur only to the extent that consumption patterns deviate from the national average. For any income class that spends the same fraction of income on good x as the national average (when $a_i = A$) there is no effect on real income from the uses side. Then the tax burden can be allocated entirely on the sources side for this income class. In the following application, this is assumed to be so for every income class. How much this assumption may bias the results is considered later.

Table 5-2 shows some of the results of the tax incidence study by Pechman

Table 5-2
Effective Tax Rates, 1966: Competitive Incidence Assumptions

Decile	*Individual Income Tax*	*Corporate Income Tax*	*Property Tax*	*Sales and Excise Taxes*	*Payroll Taxes*	*Other*	*Total Taxes*
First	1.1	1.7	2.1	8.9	2.6	0.4	16.8
Second	2.3	2.1	2.6	7.8	3.8	0.4	18.9
Third	4.0	2.2	2.6	7.1	5.4	0.4	21.7
Fourth	5.4	1.9	2.1	6.7	6.1	0.4	22.6
Fifth	6.3	1.7	1.8	6.4	6.3	0.3	22.8
Sixth	7.0	1.5	1.6	6.1	6.2	0.3	22.7
Seventh	7.5	1.6	1.7	5.7	5.8	0.3	22.7
Eighth	8.3	1.8	1.8	5.5	5.4	0.3	23.1
Ninth	8.8	2.2	2.2	5.0	4.8	0.3	23.3
Tenth	11.4	8.1	5.1	3.2	2.2	0.2	30.1
All deciles	8.5	3.9	3.0	5.1	4.4	0.3	25.2

Source: Pechman and Okner, 1974, table 4-9.

and Okner (1974). These estimates are of the average tax rates by population deciles for each major tax taken separately and then for all taxes together under competitive incidence assumptions.[17] These assumptions produce the most progressive pattern of incidence from among the eight different combinations of incidence assumptions employed. Even so, progressivity is only moderate except for the lowest two deciles and the highest decile. Note the contribution to the tax system by sales and excise taxes. These taxes are estimated to be quite regressive, falling from an average rate of 8.9 percent for the lowest decile to a rate of 3.2 percent for the highest. Sales and excise taxes were, of course, allocated in proportion to total consumption, or consumption of taxed items in generating these estimates. This method of allocating these taxes is incorrect.

Using the data reported in table 5-1, I have estimated the average tax rates by quintile due to sales and excise taxes on the assumption that the uses side can be ignored. Assuming that these taxes represent 5.1 percent of total income, as Pechman and Okner did, one can see that they are equivalent to a proportional tax of 6.2 percent on factor earnings. Thus $dP_L = dP_K = -0.062$. The average tax rate (more precisely, minus the average tax rate) can then be calculated using equation 5.3 and the labor and capital shares of total income from table 5-1. For example, the average tax rate for the lowest quintile is 0.24 (0.062) + 0.11 (0.062), or 2.2 percent. Although these taxes depress factor prices by 6.2 percent, this results in a loss of only 2.2 percent of the total income of the lowest quintile, since it receives only 35 percent of its income as factor earnings. Table 5-3 gives the results of these calculations for all income classes on the assumption that the average tax rate for both deciles contained in each quintile is equal to the average rate for the quintile.

Instead of being regressive elements in the tax system, the incidence of sales and excise taxes is progressive, as is shown in table 5-3. Average tax rates rise

Table 5-3
Effective Tax Rates Based on Factor Earnings

Decile	*Sales and Excise Taxes*	*Total Taxes*
First	2.2	10.1
Second	2.2	13.3
Third	4.5	19.1
Fourth	4.5	20.4
Fifth	5.1	21.5
Sixth	5.1	21.7
Seventh	5.4	22.4
Eighth	5.4	23.0
Ninth	5.7	24.0
Tenth	5.7	32.6
All deciles	5.1	25.2

from 2.2 percent for the lowest quintile to 5.7 percent for the highest. This progressivity results because excise and sales taxes are equivalent to proportional taxes on factor earnings under the stated conditions, and factor earnings are a smaller percentage of total income in the lower-income classes. Moreover, this change also makes the total tax system progressive throughout the income scale, with rates varying from 10.1 percent for the lowest decile to 32.6 percent for the highest decile. This one change in the method of allocating tax burdens has a striking effect on the estimated progressivity of the entire tax system. Pechman and Okner found that under competitive assumptions the tax rate for the top decile was less than twice the tax rate for the lowest decile. According to table 5-3, the tax rate for the top decile is actually more than three times the tax rate for the lowest decile.

The assumption that each of the two lowest deciles receives 65 percent of its income as transfer income (the average for the lowest quintile) probably tends to overstate the tax burden for the lowest decile and to understate it for the second decile. It is likely that the lowest decile receives more than 65 percent of its income as transfer income while the second decile receives less. If we assume that the lowest decile receives 80 percent of its income as transfers and the second decile 50 percent, then the average tax rates due to sales and excise taxes would be 1.1 percent 3.1 percent, respectively. This would make the overall average tax rate for the lowest decile only 9 percent. I believe it highly likely that at the present time the average tax rate for the lowest decile is substantially lower than 10 percent. (Similarly, it is likely that the tax rate for the highest decile is now well above 32.6 percent.) Not only have transfers become mre important for low-income classes in recent years, but the tax burden due to other taxes has become smaller than in 1966, the base year for the Pechman and Okner study.[18]

Now let us return to the question of the possible bias introduced by ignoring changes on the uses side. If all income classes spend the same percentage of their consumption outlays on taxed goods, then there is no net burden or benefit on the uses side for any income class due to changes in relative product prices. The relevant questions are whether consumption patterns are similar in this sense and, if not, how great a difference this implies for the actual tax burdens that are borne. Taking the latter question first, consider a hypothetical example to see that moderate differences in consumption patterns lead to only small burdens and benefits on the uses side.

Suppose that in the context of our simple model an excise tax of 0.17 is applied to good x. (Recall that initial prices are unity.) On average, assume that 30 percent of national income is spent on good x (thus $A = 0.3$). This tax results in $dP_x = 0.119$ and $dP_y = 0.051$, and produces revenue equal to 5.1 percent of national income.[19] Any income class that devotes 30 percent of its disposable income to good x would then bear a zero burden on the uses side of the budget (since $0.3(0.119) + 0.7(-0.051) = 0$), and the tax burden could be accurately estimated on the sources side alone, as we have done. Now suppose that the lowest quintile devotes about one-sixth more of its income, or 35 percent, to purchases of good x. There is then an additional tax burden on the uses side; expressed as a percentage rate of tax, it would be 0.009 (equal to 0.35 (0.119) + 0.65(–0.051)), which must be added to the 0.022 rate calculated for the sources side. The overall rate would be 3.1 percent, still well below the national average of 5.1 percent. As this example makes clear, moderate differences in consumption patterns among income classes have relatively small effects on the sizes of tax burdens. Ignoring tax effects on the uses side introduces only a small bias into the estimates unless there are pronounced differences in consumption patterns.

In fact, a variety of evidence suggests that consumption patterns by income class do not differ significantly from the national average. When Pechman and Okner computed sales and excise taxes as a percentage of consumption outlays for income classes, they found that the percentages were nearly the same for all deciles (1974, p. 81). This implies that consumption patterns are quite similar in the relevant sense. In a survey of family expenditures by the Bureau of Labor Statistics (1971, pp. 104-105), it was found that low-income families actually devote a smaller-than-average proportion of their expenditures to alcohol and tobacco (goods subject to high excise taxes), although the difference was minor. Similarly, price indexes weighted appropriately for the poor show little difference from the consumer price index, once more suggesting a general similarity in consumption patterns (Hollister and Palmer 1972). While these facts are merely suggestive, I believe that they show it is reasonable to assume that changes in the relative prices of consumer goods have effects of distinctly secondary importance, and their neglect will not unduly bias the results.

In evaluating this judgment, one must recognize that taxes other than excises may affect relative product prices. This is true, for example, of the corporate income tax. Whatever is assumed about the incidence of the corporate income tax, it tends to raise corporate sector prices and lower noncorporate sector prices. Low-income classes devote a larger-than-average share of their expenditures to food and housing, mainly noncorporate products, and therefore probably gain on the uses side for this tax. Similarly, some states exempt "necessities" in their sales taxes, and this too may turn relative prices in favor of the poor. If the combined effect of all taxes on relative product prices is considered, it seems quite likely that low-income classes might gain from changes on the uses side. But the magnitude of any effect on the uses side due to changes in relative prices of consumer goods is not likely to be great.

There is one systematic difference among income classes on the uses side of household budgets: low-income households consume a larger fraction of their incomes. In 1960-1961, consumption expenditures by families with incomes under $3,000 averaged 116 percent of their aftertax incomes, while the national average was 91 percent (BLS 1971, table B-17). Insofar as general sales taxes tend to raise the prices of all consumer goods relative to capital goods, this suggests net burdens on the uses side at low incomes and net benefits to heavy savers at high incomes.

Although this issue deserves further investigation, there are several reasons for believing that differences in the percentage of income consumed have little quantitative significance for the study of tax incidence. First, sales taxes are not truly general taxes, for they always exempt certain classes of consumer goods, and the relative prices of these goods will be reduced. Second, while sales taxes may tend to favor savings on the uses side of household budgets, other taxes, such as the corporate income tax and the property tax, penalize saving relative to consumption. Overall it is far from clear that those who consume a large proportion of their income are harmed relative to others. Third, differences in consumption relative to income derive in part from the annual accounting period used in measuring income. According to the permanent income hypothesis, if income were measured over longer time periods, there would be little if any difference in the percentage of income consumed at different income levels. Finally, even if we ignore these three factors, moderate differences in the percentage of income consumed introduce only small burdens and benefits on the uses side, as suggested by the preceding numerical example, because it is only the deviation from the average that is relevant.

While it would be wrong to conclude from this discussion that changes on the uses side are always negligible, in the context of examining the tax burden of the entire tax system by broad income classes it appears reasonable to ignore the uses side. When that is done, as we have seen, competitive incidence assumptions yield a pattern of effective rates that is distinctly progressive. The system is still progressive even when incidence assumptions generally thought to be regressive are used.

Corporate, Property, and Payroll Taxes

Incidence studies have emphasized that the distribution of the tax burden by income classes depends importantly on what assumptions are made about the incidence of major taxes. The most controversial taxes are the corporate income tax, property taxes, and the employer portion of the social security payroll tax. Under competitive conditions the long-run incidences of these taxes are straightforward. The corporate income tax is borne in proportion to the amount of capital owned, whether the capital is employed in the corporate or the noncorporate sector. Property taxes also impose a tax burden in proportion to the amount of capital owned, regardless of the locality in which it is employed. The employer portion of the social security payroll tax is borne in proportion to the covered earnings of workers, just as is the employee portion (Harberger 1962; Mieszkowski 1972; Brittain 1972; and Aaron 1975).

Many economists have been uneasy with estimates of tax incidence based on these assumptions. Because of noncompetitive elements in the economy, it is felt that the changes in factor and product prices, employment and output, required for the competitive conclusions to hold may not occur. Thus a more or less arbitrary part of each tax is assumed to be "shifted to consumers" and then allocated in proportion to consumption outlays. When substituted for the competitive incidence allocations, this invariably produces a more regressive pattern of tax rates.

Table 5-4 illustrates this point for the three taxes under consideration. The figures are from the Pechman and Okner study (1974). Under competitive incidence assumptions, the three taxes taken together are progressive up through the third decile and then approximately proportional until the tenth decile. The regressive incidence assumptions are that half the corporate tax and half the employer portion of payroll taxes are allocated according to consumption and that the portion of the property tax on improvements is allocated according to outlays on shelter and consumption. When the taxes are allocated according to these rules, the overall pattern of incidence changes dramatically. As shown in the last column of table 5-4, incidence becomes regressive throughout the income scale. In particular, the estimated average tax rate for the lowest decile more than doubles.

Allocating these taxes in proportion to consumption, however, is incorrect for the same reason that the allocation of excise and sales taxes in this way is wrong. To develop this point more fully, consider the corporate income tax. In the competitive model the corporate income tax is treated as a levy on capital

Table 5-4
Effective Tax Rates, by Income Decile

	Competitive Assumptions				*Regressive Assumptions*			
Decile	*Corporate Income Tax*	*Property Tax*	*Payroll Taxes*	*Total*	*Corporate Income Tax*	*Property Tax*	*Payroll Taxes*	*Total*
Lowest	1.7	2.1	2.6	6.4	6.1	6.4	4.5	17.0
Second	2.1	2.6	3.8	8.5	5.4	5.1	4.5	15.0
Third	2.2	2.6	5.4	10.2	5.0	4.6	5.4	15.0
Fourth	1.9	2.1	6.1	10.1	4.4	3.8	5.7	13.9
Fifth	1.7	1.8	6.3	9.8	4.1	3.3	5.8	13.2
Sixth	1.5	1.6	6.2	9.3	3.9	3.2	5.6	12.7
Seventh	1.6	1.7	5.8	9.3	3.7	3.2	5.4	12.3
Eighth	1.8	1.8	5.4	9.0	3.7	3.2	5.0	11.9
Ninth	2.2	2.2	4.8	9.2	3.9	3.2	4.5	11.6
Tenth	8.1	5.1	2.2	15.4	5.2	2.9	2.5	10.6
Total	3.9	3.0	4.4	11.3	4.4	3.4	4.4	12.2

Source: Pechman and Okner, 1974, table 4-9.

earnings in the corporate sector. By depressing net earnings in the corporate sector, capital migrates to the noncorporate sector until the net returns in the two sectors are equalized. Under plausible conditions the net return to capital falls by the amount of the tax; so on the sources-of-income side the burden is in proportion to the ownership or capital (Harberger 1962). There are also changes on the uses-of-income side, since corporate prices rise and noncorporate prices fall. These changes are always ignored in incidence studies, presumably for much the same reasons explained in the last section.

Since the competitive model implies a rise in corporate prices, what exactly does it mean to substitute an alternative incidence assumption in which the tax is "shifted to consumers"? Most analysts are unclear on this point: they simply allocate the burden in proportion to consumption. It is obviously important, however, to be clear about exactly how the system responds to the tax compared with the response of a competitive system. To say that corporate prices rise does not distinguish this case from the competitive case. I suspect that what most writers have in mind is the assumption that corporations act as if the tax were an excise tax. In some cases this meaning is explicit, as when Musgrave and Musgrave (1976, p. 423) state, "The general equilibrium adjustment to the tax will be similar to that of an excise tax imposed on the output of this sector."

I will proceed on the assumption that this is what is meant when it is said that the tax is shifted to consumers rather than being borne by capital. Comparing tax incidence under these alternative assumptions then means comparing the incidence of a proportional tax on capital income to the incidence of an excise tax. Under conventional rules of thumb, the part of the corporate tax treated as an excise tax has a regressive incidence. But, as demonstrated in the last section, an excise tax is not regressive; it is progressive. So it is not clear that the assumption that part of the corporate income tax affects the system as an excise tax will produce a more regressive pattern of tax rates.

To examine quantitatively the effect of altering incidence assumptions on the incidence of the corporate income tax, ignore the changes on the uses side for competitive and regressive assumptions. Then the tax burden can be allocated fully on the sources side:

$$dI_i/I_i = f_i dP_L + g_i dP_K. \tag{5.5}$$

For any income class competitive assumptions imply that the tax is a proportionate tax on capital income, so

$$dP_K = R/Y_K^T, \tag{5.6}$$

where R is total revenue and Y_K^T is total capital income for the nation. The effective tax rate for any income class is then simply $g_i R/Y_K^T$. Alternatively, when regressive assumptions are used and the tax is treated as an excise tax, there is a proportionate change in P_K and P_L equal to

$$dP_K = dP_L = R/(Y_K^T + Y_L^T), \tag{5.7}$$

with initial prices of unity. Here Y_L^T is total labor income, so the term on the right is simply the tax expressed as a percentage of factor earnings.

Now it is a simple matter to compare the average tax rate by income class for the corporate tax under these two incidence assumptions. The average rate under competitive assumptions is $g_i R/Y_K^T$, while when treated as an excise tax, the average rate is $(f_i + g_i) R/(Y_K^T + Y_L^T)$. ($R$ is either the total revenue of the tax or whatever part of it is being treated as an excise tax.) Thus for any income class where $g_i/(f_i + g_i)$ is greater (less) than $Y_K^T/(Y_K^T + Y_L^T)$, the tax burden of the corporate income is less (greater) when the tax affects the system as does an excise tax than when it is borne in proportion to capital income. The data necessary for this comparison for quintiles are contained in table 5-1. Performing the required calculations shows that treating part of the corporate income tax as an excise tax reduces the average tax rates for the lowest, second, and highest quintiles while increasing it for the third and fourth quintiles. Thus to the extent that the corporate income tax is "shifted to consumers," the tax system becomes more progressive at the bottom of the income scale. This finding is, of course, in sharp contrast to existing estimates, which suggest that the corporate income tax becomes less progressive under these conditions.

Exactly the same conclusion is true for the property tax, since we would once again be comparing a proportionate tax on capital to an excise (or general sales) tax. The employer portion of the payroll tax is more complicated because it is not a proportional tax on labor income but instead proportional only up to the ceiling on covered earnings. Since the data in table 5-1 do not permit identifying how much of labor income in each quintile represents covered earnings, no general expressions for this tax can be evaluated.

Table 5-5 indicates the quantitative significance of altering incidence assumptions. Incidence under competitive assumptions was calculated from table 5-1 by using the percentages of total income generated as tax revenue for each tax as reported by Pechman and Okner (as given in the last row).[20] Since the data base differs from the Pechman and Okner study, and I am using quintiles rather than deciles, the average tax rates do not correspond exactly with those shown in table 5-4. Nevertheless, agreement is fairly close, especially the general pattern of incidence for all three taxes considered together.

The four columns to the right give the average tax rates under the following incidence assumptions: half of the corporate tax, half of the property tax, and half of the payroll tax are treated as if they were excise taxes and are thus allocated in proportion to factor earnings. The results are interesting. For all three taxes the average tax rates fall for the two lowest quintiles. Taking the

Table 5-5
Effective Tax Rates, by Income Quintile

	Competitive Assumptions				*Regressive Assumptions*			
Quintile	*Corporate Income Tax*	*Property Tax*	*Pay-roll Tax*	*Total*	*Corporate Income Tax*	*Property Tax*	*Pay-roll Tax*	*Total*
Lowest	3.6	2.2	3.2	9.0	2.6	2.0	2.5	7.1
Second	3.9	3.2	5.8	12.9	3.7	2.8	4.8	11.3
Third	2.9	2.4	6.3	11.6	3.4	2.7	5.4	11.5
Fourth	2.6	2.1	5.6	10.3	3.4	2.6	5.1	11.1
Highest	5.2	4.3	3.5	13.0	4.8	3.7	4.3	12.8
Total	3.9	3.0	4.4	11.3	3.9	3.0	4.4	11.3

three taxes together, the combined rate for the lowest quintile falls from 9.0 percent to 7.1 percent when the regressive assumptions are used. The rate also falls significantly for the second quintile, but there is very little change for the top three quintiles.[21]

Not much significance should be attached to the exact changes reported in table 5-5. Perhaps to a greater extent than in most studies, the data for the distribution of income, as given in table 5-1, are imperfect. In particular, estimates of capital income and transfer income are only rough estimates. I would therefore refrain from arguing that substituting regressive assumptions for competitive assumptions necessarily results in a significantly lower tax burden for low-income classes. What can be concluded, I think, is that using regressive assumptions is not likely to imply a significantly different pattern of incidence than using competitive assumptions. That conclusion depends primarily on the fact that lower-income classes receive a higher proportion of their income as transfers, with the proportion falling sharply in higher-income classes.

Restating our conclusions to this point: Under competitive assumptions when excise and sales taxes are treated correctly, the entire tax system is more progressive than generally recognized. It is now apparent that replacing the competitive assumptions with regressive assumptions for the controversial taxes does not greatly modify that conclusion. Thus the overall tax system is quite progressive, independent of assumptions concerning the incidence of the more controversial taxes.

Conclusion

This chapter has investigated the incidence of several major taxes in a setting where low-income groups receive a large part of their total income in the form of transfers. Its major conclusions are that the tax system is substantially more progressive than is suggested by existing incidence studies and that this remains true even under regressive assumptions concerning the incidence of taxes. In fact, it is possible that the more "regressive" the appropriate assumptions, the smaller the tax burden on the poor. These conclusions should, of course, be checked in a full-scale incidence study that takes proper account of transfer income in allocating tax burdens (I am currently engaged in such a project).

These findings are of importance in their own right, but the general approach also has significant implications for many controversial issues in tax reform. To take but one example, a major obstacle to the substitution of a value-added tax (VAT) for the corporate income tax has been the belief that the change would make the tax system more regressive. The analysis developed here shows this belief to be unfounded. If the corporate income tax is shifted entirely to consumers (acts as an excise tax), then it has the same incidence as a VAT since tax burdens in both cases should be allocated in proportion to factor earnings. On the other hand, if the corporate tax is borne partly or wholly in proportion to capital ownership, substitution of the VAT might actually lighten the tax burden on the poor.

The significance of transfer income concentrated in low-income classes also has relevance that extends beyond tax analysis. That the poor receive a large share of their income as transfers effectively insulates them from the distributional effects of innumerable policies in addition to taxation. It is a common experience for economists to qualify their recommendation for some efficient policy on the grounds that its distributional effects harm the poor. Yet in many cases such a qualification may be unwarranted because policies generally thought to significantly burden the poor may do so to only a modest degree, if at all. Whether our concern is with monopoly, price ceilings, unions, pollution taxes, or public utility pricing, the general equilibrium approach to the distribution of burdens and benefits developed here is appropriate. Once the issues in these diverse areas are analyzed within an appropriate general equilibrium framework, it can be seen that the poor will seldom bear any significant burden from policy changes, and they may well benefit from changes commonly thought to harm them. In any event, the quantitative effects are likely to be small. Recognition of this should make the tasks of policy analysts and decision makers far easier, since they can concentrate more on the efficiency aspects of policy choices.

Notes

1. For a sampling, see Samuelson, 1973, pp. 175-177; McConnell, 1972, pp. 147-149; Dolan, 1977, pp. 65-66; Musgrave and Musgrave, 1976, pp. 389-402; Herber, 1975, pp. 165-166; Due and Friedlaender, 1973, pp. 142-143; and Singer, 1976, pp. 39-41.

2. For a complete development of this model, see Harberger, 1962,

Mieszkowski, 1967, 1969, and McLure, 1970, 1975. A very helpful, simplified exposition is given by McLure and Thirsk (1975).

3. See McLure, 1975, pp. 136-137, for a discussion of the possible choices. I follow McLure and Thirsk (1975) in assuming the money level of national income constant.

4. Thurow (1975) discusses several criticisms of both approaches to the analysis of tax incidence.

5. For a more complete discussion, see McLure, 1970, 1975. The assumption that expenditures are distributionally neutral facilitates converting the balanced-budget results into differential incidence terms. Any difference in tax burdens under two taxes of equal yield using balanced-budget incidence is automatically the difference that would be produced by substituting one tax for another.

6. Since we are using a balanced-budget framework, the reduction in the total purchases of x and y by households is exactly offset by an increase in purchases by the government. Total output remains unchanged.

7. Musgrave (1959, pp. 217-223) was one of the first economists to emphasize that the net effect of a tax on a person's real income occurred through these two conceptually different types of effects.

8. See Browning, 1976, for a discussion of this data. Labor income is from the *Consumer Population Survey* and includes wage and salary income, nonfarm self-employment income, and farm self-employment income, adjusted for underreporting. Capital income includes dividends, net rental income, private pensions (adjusted for underreporting), plus accrued capital gains. Transfer income includes cash transfers (adjusted for underreporting) and in-kind transfers. (Public schools are included as in-kind transfers, but if they are deleted, the results would not be significantly affected.) Ideally, we would like still more inclusive measures. For example, the employer portion of the payroll tax should be included in labor income since we wish it to measure before-tax labor income. Similarly, capital income should include imputed income from owner-occupied housing. These omissions are not large enough or distributed unevenly enough, however, to significantly affect the results.

9. A study by the Congressional Budget Office (1977, table A-4) estimates that transfer income was 95 percent of total income of the lowest quintile in 1976. Although I believe this estimate to be biased upward, there is no doubt that lower-income groups receive a far greater proportion of their total income as transfer income than do higher-income groups.

10. With the price level fixed, a relative increase in one price implies an absolute increase, and vice versa.

11. If the taxed industry is more capital intensive than other industries, the price of capital will, of course, fall by more than the price of labor. The assumption of equal factor intensities is implicitly made in all incidence studies: only with this assumption would the procedures used to allocate the burdens of excise taxes be correct.

12. Partial equilibrium diagrams cannot, of course, be used to rigorously analyze the reaction to the tax, but they can be used to give a "picture" of what happens under the stated assumptions. Used in this way, they help to clarify the analysis. For other uses of the partial equilibrium constructs in this way, see McLure and Thirsk, 1975, and Harberger 1966.

13. The manner in which the government spends the tax revenue is already incorporated in the demand curves. Thus although total output of y increases, this does not necessarily imply that individuals are consuming more y than in the absence of the tax.

14. This also means, of course, that there is a zero net effect on the uses side for society as a whole. In common with most incidence analysis, this ignores the excess burden resulting from the allocative effects of the tax.

15. More precisely, if nonfactor income is the same percentage (including zero) for each person, this procedure generates the correct results. See the discussion of the importance of the share of income received as transfers.

16. Equation 5.2 is a variation of equation 9 in McLure, 1970. Although McLure does not explicitly derive this equation, it can be derived from his equation 10a.

17. Although I shall refer to the assumptions underlying the figures in the table as competitive, they differ in one minor respect: half of the corporate income tax is allocated in proportion to dividends rather than in proportion to capital income in general. This does not produce a significantly different pattern of incidence than fully competitive assumptions. See Pechman and Okner, 1974, chap. 4).

18. The Congressional Budget Office (1977) estimates that income and payroll taxes are only 1 percent of income for the lowest quintile, while my estimate (1976) is 1.7 percent. As can be seen in table 5-2, Pechman and Okner estimated a combined rate for these taxes for the bottom decile of 3.7 percent. Although there are differences in procedures and income definitions in these studies, it is likely the burden from income and payroll taxes on low-income groups has been reduced over the past decade. One reason for this is the rapid growth of cash and in-kind transfers over the past decade. These forms of income are not taxable under the income or payroll tax.

19. Assume that the *cum* tax quantities are 30 for x and 70 for y and that national income is 100. Then we have (1) $(1 + dP_x)30 + (1 - dP_y)70 = 100$; (2) $dP_x + dP_y = T_x = 0.17$; and (3) $30T_x/100 = 0.051$. The figures in the text can be calculated from these relationships.

20. This procedure was not used for the payroll tax, since it does not fall in proportion to the factor earnings base, as do the other two taxes. For the payroll tax each quintile's tax rate was computed by averaging the tax rates for the two deciles it contains, using the rates estimated by Pechman and Okner. This procedure overstates the rate for each quintile slightly.

21. Since a tax on capital income leads to a lower rate for the lowest quintile when allocated according to capital plus labor income, it might be

thought that the rate would rise when a tax on labor income is allocated according to capital plus labor income. This is true if the tax on labor income is proportional, but the payroll tax is regressive at higher levels of labor incomes. Thus when this regressive labor income tax is allocated in proportion to capital plus labor income, the rate also falls for the lowest quintile.

References

Aaron, Henry J. 1975. *Who Pays the Property Tax?* Washington, D.C.: Brookings Institution.

Brittain, John A. 1972. *The Payroll Tax for Social Security.* Washington, D.C.: Brookings Institution.

Browning, Edgar K. 1976. "The Trend toward Equality in the Distribution of Net Income." *Southern Economic Journal* 43 (July):912-923.

Bureau of Labor Statistics. 1971. *Consumer Expenditures and Income: Survey Guidelines.* Bulletin 1684.

Colm, Gerhard, and Tarasov, Helen. 1940. *Who Pays the Taxes?* A Study Made for the Taxpayer National Economic Committee, Monograph 3, Investigation of Concentration of Economic Power, Seventy-Sixth Congress, 3rd sess.

Dolan, Edwin, G. 1977. *Basic Economics.* Hinsdale: Dryden Press.

Due, John F., and Friedlaender, Ann F. 1973. *Government Finance: Economics of the Public Sector,* 5th ed. Homewood, Ill.: Richard D. Irwin.

Gillespie, W. Irwin. 1965. "Effect of Public Expenditures on the Distribution of Income." In R.A. Musgrave, ed., *Essays in Fiscal Federalism.* Washington, D.C.: Brookings Institution.

Harberger, Arnold C. 1962. "The Incidence of the Corporation Income Tax." *Journal of Political Economy* 70 (June):215-240.

_______. 1966. "Efficiency Effects of Taxes on Income from Capital." In M. Krzyzaniak, ed., *Effects of the Corporation Income Tax.* Detroit, Mich.: Wayne State University Press.

Herber, Bernard P. 1975. *Modern Public Finance,* 3d ed. Homewood, Ill.: Richard D. Irwin.

Herriot, Roger A., and Miller, Herman P. 1971. "The Taxes We Pay." *Conference Board Record* 8. (May).

Hollister, Robinson G., and Palmer, John J. 1972. "The Impact of Inflation on the Poor." In K. Boulding and M. Pfaff, eds., *Redistribution to the Rich and Poor.* Belmont, Calif.: Wadsworth Publishing.

McLure, Charles E., Jr. 1970. "Tax Incidence, Macroeconomic Policy, and Absolute Prices." *Quarterly Journal of Economics* 82 (May):254-267.

McLure, Charles E., Jr. 1975. "General Equilibrium Incidence Analysis: The Harberger Model after Ten Years." *Journal of Public Economics* 4 (February):125-161.

McLure, Charles E., Jr., and Thirsk, Wayne R. 1975. "A Simplified Exposition of the Harberger Model. I: Tax Incidence." *National Tax Journal* 28 (March):1-28.

McConnell, Campbell R. 1972. *Economics,* 5th ed. New York: McGraw-Hill.

Mieszkowski, Peter M. 1969. "Tax Incidence Theory: The Effects of Taxes on the Distribution of Income." *Journal of Economic Literature* 7 (December):1103-1124.

_______. 1967. "On the Theory of Tax Incidence." *Journal of Political Economy* 75 (June):250-262.

_______. 1972. "The Property Tax: An Excise or a Profits Tax?" *Journal of Public Economics* 1 (April):73-96.

Musgrave, Richard A. 1959. *The Theory of Public Finance.* New York: McGraw-Hill.

Musgrave, R.A. Carroll, J.J., Cook, L.D., and Frane, L. 1951. "Distribution of Tax Payments by Income Groups: A Case Study for 1948." *National Tax Journal* 4 (March):1-53.

Musgrave, Richard A., Case, Karl E., and Leonard, Herman. 1974. "The Distribution of Fiscal Burdens and Benefits." *Public Finance Quarterly* 2 (July):259-311.

Musgrave, Richard A., and Musgrave, Peggy B. 1976. *Public Finance in Theory and Practice,* 2d ed. New York: McGraw-Hill.

Pechman, Joseph A., and Okner, Benjamin A. 1974. *Who Bears the Tax Burden?* Washington, D.C.: Brookings Institution.

Samuelson, Paul A. 1973. *Economics,* 9th ed. New York: McGraw-Hill.

Singer, Neil M. 1976. *Public Microeconomics,* 2d ed. Boston: Little Brown.

Thurow, Lester C. 1975. "The Economics of Public Finance." *National Tax Journal* 28 (June):185-194.

U.S. Congressional Budget Office. 1977. *Poverty Status of Families under Alternative Definitions of Income.* Washington, D.C.: U.S. Government Printing Office.

Commentary

Charles E. McLure, Jr.

In his classic *Theory of Public Finance* Musgrave (1959, chap. 10) emphasizes that tax incidence is most usefully analyzed in terms of changes in relative prices rather than absolute prices. Moreover, he notes that incidence on the side of sources of income is a matter of changes in relative factor rewards and incidence on the side of uses is a matter of changes in relative product prices. Where differential analysis is under examination, there is, by assumption, no net burden of taxation. Thus it is simplest (but not essential) to think of zero-sum redistributions on the sides of both uses and sources of income. Where balanced budget analysis is concerned, the tax burden equals revenue collected (in a world of fixed factor supplies, with excess burdens ignored). In such a case it may be attractive to think of the tax as imposing a burden equal to revenues on either the uses or the sources side of income and involving redistribution on the other side. Of course, where (sources or uses side) the burden *appears* to lie depends on what happens to absolute prices, but being determined by changes in relative prices the real result is independent of changes in absolute price levels (see also McLure 1970, 1971).

Musgrave (chap. 15) also described the following equivalences between taxes in a world of two goods, two factors, and no saving:

$$
\begin{array}{llll}
T_{kx} & \text{and} & T_{ky} & = T_k \\
T_{Lx} & \text{and} & T_{Ly} & = T_L \\
T_x & \text{and} & T_y & = T_c/T_I
\end{array}
$$

where T_x is the tax levied on the production or consumtpion of product X, T_k is the tax on the factor services of capital, and T_{kx} is the tax on capital services employed in producing good X. Analogous notation pertains to taxes on good Y and to taxes on labor services, T_L. Any line or column on the preceding table can be read to mean that a tax levied at the same percentage rate on the first two entries is equivalent to the third entry. In the bottom right-hand corner we indicate that a general tax on consumption, T_c, and a general tax on all income, T_I, are themselves equivalent in a world without saving.

Edgar Browning has implicitly suggested that this description of tax equivalences is incomplete because it ignores the existence of transfer payments. He argues that estimates of tax incidence at various income levels, because they neglect the role of transfers, are generally inaccurate. In particular, they are valid only for a set of assumptions that he believes to be generally invalid.

Browning would note that an additional source of household income, transfers, should be added to what is taxed in the third column. Once this is done it is necessary to distinguish between total income of households, which includes transfers, and factor income, which does not. Unless transfer income is taxed, the equivalence remains between a tax on consumption (or production) and a tax on factor income, not a tax on total income. This has a crucial implication, which is the heart of Browning's paper: consumption taxes and excise taxes, as well as income taxes, should be allocated on the basis of factor income rather than on the basis of consumption of the taxed item. The question, then, is whether transfer income is taxed.

Where income taxes are concerned there seems to be little controversy. Despite strong equity and efficiency arguments for their inclusion in the tax base, both money transfers and in-kind transfers are generally excluded from the tax base. The real question arises when we come to taxes on consumption. In order to know the real incidence of such taxes we should know whether taxes raise the price level and, if they do, whether transfers are adjusted to reflect the taxes and keep real income of the recipients of transfers constant. These alternatives are as follows:

Case I Product prices constant; factor earnings fall. Browning result: primary incidence on sources side

Case II Factor earnings constant; product prices rise

A. Normal transfers rise to reflect price rise. Browning result: primary incidence on sources sides

B. Nominal transfers constant. Conventional result: primary incidence on uses side

Only in case IIB do we have the traditional result that consumption taxes are borne in proportion to consumption and therefore burden recipients of transfers, as well as other consumers. Under the assumptions of either case I or case IIA the taxes are borne in proportion to factor incomes, so that recipients of transfers escape their burden.

Stripped of the incidence analyst's sometimes confusing methodology, Browning's point is fairly simple. In the conventional scenario of case IIB, the tax induces an increase in absolute product prices which burdens the transfer recipient because his nominal income does not adjust. In a real sense the transfer recipient owns an asset that is fixed in nominal terms. In the Browning result of case IIA nominal transfers rise to reflect the tax-induced increase in product prices and keep real transfers constant, but incomes of factor owners do not similarly adjust. Thus the tax is borne by recipients of factor income on the sources side. In case I, which Browning takes to be even more likely, nominal factor earnings fall when a tax is imposed; the result is identical to that in case IIA but is obtained more directly.

The logic of Browning's argument is impeccable, but its general applicability is less certain. To some extent it may be unfair to take case I as most descriptive of reality and to argue that any effects on absolute prices should be attributed to marcoeconomic policies. (Since I have taken this line in previous writings, I cannot argue too hard against it.) If, however, Browning is forced to retreat to case II, the burden of proof on him is substantially greater, for now he must demonstrate that transfers do indeed move in lockstep with prices, including in particular tax-induced increases in prices. While we cannot expect Browning to provide that demonstration in this paper, one must hope that in future research he will go beyond the largely unsupported assertions made here. In the meantime perhaps we should consider his estimates to be reasonable alternatives to the conventional estimates rather than unique replacements.

I would also suggest, as an aside, that the proper analytical framework may not be immutable. In earlier times when transfers were small and perhaps viewed as a form of public philanthropy, case IIB might have been the appropriate analytical context. But the growth of transfers, the indexation of social security, the genesis of the concept of welfare rights, and so on may have made case IIA a more tenable assumption.

Second, in his concluding section Browning has gone well beyond incidence analysis to make statements about the likely distributional implications of an array of policies that are questionable, at best. Under the conventional analysis the poor may bear significant burdens as a result of policies adopted for allocative reasons such as effluent charges or peak-load pricing. Browning assures us that we have nothing to fear on this score, because his analysis tells us that the poor will be burdened little by such policies and may even benefit from them. Presumably this conclusion comes from his assumption that case I is the relevant one. But if we are in the world of case II, which I prefer to believe, we must worry about whether transfers will rise to reflect tax-induced price increases rather than advance policy proposals based on belief in an automatic adjustment mechanism. It is one thing to analyze incidence on the belief that case I or IIA is relevant and another thing to base policy on that belief without worrying that case IIB describes the real world. It simply does not ring true when one suggests that sales taxes need not exempt food and that value-added taxes should not be considered regressive because transfers will automatically adjust.

Third, like so many analyses of incidence based on aggregates for income classes, Browning's analysis ignores horizontal equity. But the neglect is unusually bothersome in the present case, especially when one considers how sanguine Browning is that case IIB is not relevant. Consider the position of a low-income household that is dependent on transfers and does not consume an item that based on consumer surveys had a low-income elasticity of demand. Such a household might well favor a tax on such items, because it knows (or at least Browning does) that transfer payments will be adjusted to leave the real income of the average transfer recipient unchanged. While this level of sophistication might have existed in recent discussions of combining energy taxes with per capita rebates, the general tenor seems a bit farfetched.

Finally, it seems that one must be fairly careful in following Browning's line of reasoning, even if one accepts it in certain circumstances. We have not distinguished between incidence studies for the nation as a whole and studies for a given state or locality. But it seems that Browning's approach is likely to be increasingly inappropriate as one moves to smaller and smaller jurisdictions.

To see this, consider social security, the largest single transfer program. Browning is correct in saying that because of indexing, recipients of social security are isolated from increases in prices induced by nationwide increases in consumption taxes. On the average, they are isolated from price increases induced by state and local sales and excise taxes. But recipients of social security residing in a given (small) state are not isolated from the effects of an increase in the sales and excise taxes of that state; the indexing is determined by the effect that the state's tax increase has on the nation's cost of living, whereas the burden to the consumer is determined by the effect on the cost of living in the state. Of course, Browning does not suggest that his analysis would be relevant for the analysis of state or local taxes. But experience, especially in the property tax field, must make one wary that analysis acceptable in the national context will be applied in the state or local context where it is appropriate. (The analogy to the now-conventional "new view" of the incidence of the property tax should be apparent. For a simplified exposition that should help to clarify the present discussion, see McLure, 1977.)

References

McLure, Charles E., Jr. 1970. "Tax Incidence, Absolute Prices, and Macroeconomic Policy." *Quarterly Journal of Economics* 84 (May):254-267.

_______. 1971. "Tax Incidence with Imperfect Factor Mobility." *Finanzarchiv* 30:27-48.

_______. 1977. "The 'New View' of the Property Tax: A Caveat." *National Tax Journal* 30 (March):69-75.

Musgrave, Richard A. 1959. *The Theory of Public Finance.* New York: McGraw-Hill.

6 Simultaneous Equations Models of Sex Discrimination

Solomon W. Polachek

There is little disagreement that sex differences exist within our economy. It has been shown that women earn less than men and that their occupational structure differs such that women predominate in jobs with more menial task assignments. Yet in the literature on discrimination controversy exists as to where within the economy the underlying causes of inequality lie.

On the one hand, some studies claim this disparity to be demand determined. Such hypotheses imply that firms discriminate by not hiring women for "good" jobs. Women are therefore relegated to secondary jobs, thereby causing occupational segregation. Because those in "bad" jobs receive lower wages, a large market wage gap develops.

Studies concentrating on supply aspects of the market propose a different scenario to explain the same market observations. These studies claim that differing life-cycle labor force expectations cause differences in human capital investment between men and women, thereby causing women to supply themselves to less skilled jobs and to obtain lower wages.

While both theories are plausible and consistent with numerous sets of data, each provides a different explanation of sex inequality as well as a different policy recommendation for remedying the situation. Demand-oriented theories imply a policy forcing firms to hire females in all occupations and in some cases in numbers equal to their representation in the population. Supply-oriented theories imply policies that encourage continuous life-cycle labor force participation of women. Examples are day care centers and legislation requiring employers to offer more flexible hours of work.

Since in reality both theories appear to be applicable, both supply and demand policies may be helpful. However, the appropriate policy mix is important. Inefficiencies throughout the economy will result if predominantly demand-oriented policies are used when the problem is predominantly supply oriented, and vice versa. In part to alleviate the losses associated with the inefficiencies of choosing an inappropriate policy, I develop models to help ascertain whether sex differences are predominantly supply or demand oriented.

I wish to thank Thomas Kniesner, Jacob Mincer, and members of the Labor and Applied Economics Workshop at the University of North Carolina, Chapel Hill, for valuable comments. Francis Horvath, David Raber, and Douglas Waldo provided valuable computational assistance. This work was financed in part by the Department of Labor. A version of this chapter appeared as U.S. Department of Commerce Technical Information Service Paper PB-256-805.

To answer questions regarding the identifiability of sex differences, both the labor market (governing wages and occupations) as well as the human capital market (governing educational choices and on-the-job training) are analyzed separately, within simultaneous equations settings. I conclude strongly that sex differences in the acquisition of human capital cannot be ignored in understanding sex differences in wages and occupational structure. While I find that sex differences in wages and occupation are related to differences in levels of labor market experience and education, human capital differences may themselves stem from discrimination either in the human capital market or in expectations of sex discrimination in the labor market. Nevertheless, if the goal is to equalize male-female labor market status, efficient government policy must encourage the equal acquisition of human capital both in school and in labor force behavior.

Sex Differences in the Labor Market

Numerous studies outline sex differences in the labor market. Most concentrate on wage discrimination; some deal with occupational segregation. It is well known that females are found in jobs with the most menial task assignments (Bergmann 1971, Edgeworth 1922, Lucas 1974, and Zellner 1972). Table 6-1 presents data on sex differences in occupational distribution for 1960 and 1970. Men have a higher probability of being in (nonteaching) professional, managerial, craft, and operative occupations. Women have a higher probability of being in clerical, household, and service jobs. Some researchers (Bergmann 1971) claim

Table 6-1
Occupational Distribution by Sex
(in percents)

	1960		*1970*	
Occupation	*Male*	*Female*	*Male*	*Female*
Professional	12	15	16	15.5
Teachers	1	6	2	9
Residual	11	9	14	6.5
Managers	13	4	12	4
Clerical	9	29.5	8.5	35
Sales	8	7.5	8	7.5
Craft	25	1.5	24	2
Operative	25	19.5	22.5	15
Household	–	7	–	4
Service	8	16	9	17
Total	100	100	100	100

Source: 1960 Census of Population, 1970 Census of Population.

that wage discrimination stems chiefly from employment discrimination by firms. Because firms refuse to hire women in "nonfemale" high-wage jobs, females tend to have an obviously different occupational structure that is a cause of observed wage differentials. Such a hypothesis is referred to as occupational segregation.

The importance of this hypothesis can be analyzed by creating indexes that compute the portion of wage differentials that can be attributed to differences in occupational distribution. Such indexes measure what females would earn if they had a male occupational distribution (Y_{FM}), and similarly what the wage rates of males would be if they had a female occupational structure (Y_{MF}).[1] The percentage of the original wage gap closed by these measures $[(Y_{FM} - Y_F)] + (Y_M - Y_{MF}) / 2(Y_M - Y_F)]$ represents the explanatory power of occupational segregation as a source of wage differentials (table 6-2). (For a further description of the measures see Chiswick et al., 1974.) These measures indicate that occupational segregation explains at most 20 percent of the wage differential; for the strata of single males and females, occupational segregation somehow decreases the wage gap. That is, the wage for single men and women would widen were it not for sex differences in occupational structure.

We find then sex differences in both wages and occupational structure, but occupational differences account for a small fraction of the observed wage differentials. Perhaps there exists a common cause for occupational as well as wage differences.

Sex Differences in Human Capital

Figure 6-1 shows that life-cycle earnings differ dramatically, not only by sex, but by marital status as well. Earnings differentials remain relatively small for single, never-married males and females, yet are extremely large between married men and women. As I have shown (1975), these differences are related to aspects of family structure such as length of marriage and number and spacing of children. To test the hypothesis that human capital acquisition varies by sex, marital status, and number of children, we now explore sex differences in labor market behavior and schooling choices.

The National Longitudinal Survey shows that married women have the lowest participation in the labor force, single men and women an intermediate level, and married men the most continuous participation over the life cycle. Table 6-3 provides a more detailed profile of labor force participation by women.

Labor force behavior is only one form of human capital. In part it represents experience and opportunities for on-the-job training. Other forms of human capital also differ by sex. Analysis of nationwide data on individual educational choices indicate that sex differences abound.[2] Table 6-4 focuses on

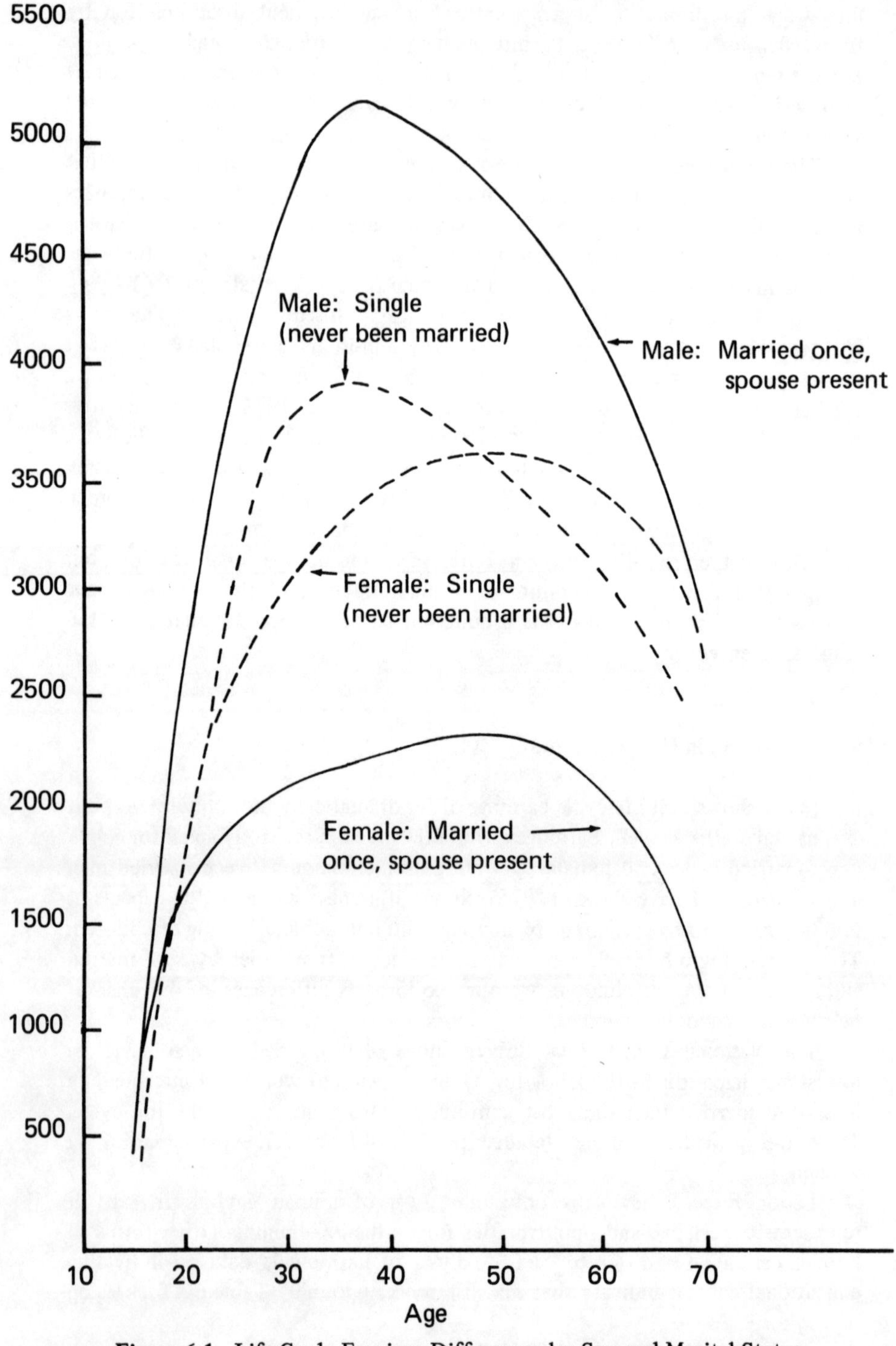

Figure 6-1. Life-Cycle Earnings Differences by Sex and Marital Status

Table 6-2
Effect of Occupational Classification on Wages

Female and Male Wages	Hourly (in dollars)			Annual (in dollars)		
	1960	1970[a]	1970	1960	1970[a]	1970
A.						
Y_F	1.81	3.01	3.00	2,391.04	3,975.27	3,957.16
Y_M	2.63	4.54	4.54	4,941.04	8,580.30	8,567.32
Y_{FM}	1.87	3.23	3.29	2,706.92	4,796.51	4,949.53
Y_{MF}	2.49	4.46	4.37	4,372.93	7,600.86	7,328.14
$(Y_{FM}-Y_F/Y_MY_F)$	0.07	0.14	0.19	0.12	0.18	0.21
$(Y_M-Y_{MF})/Y_M-Y_F)$	0.17	0.05	0.11	0.22	0.21	0.27
$(Y_{FM}-YF)+(Y_M-Y_{MF})/2(Y_M-Y_F)$	0.12	0.10	0.15	0.17	0.20	0.24
N_M	38,916	397,452	400,628	38,916	397,452	400,628
N_F	18,925	223,254	227,151	18,925	223,254	227,151
B. *Married males and females*[b]						
Y_F	1.82	3.00	2.98	2,331.70	3,909.37	3,892.96
Y_M	2.78	4.79	4.79	5,599.56	9,663.43	9,657.66
Y_{FM}	1.72	3.13	3.18	2,341.28	4,563.82	4,662.57
Y_{MF}	2.71	4.79	4.70	5,159.99	9,131.39	8,853.12
$(Y_{FM}-Y_F)/(Y_M-Y_F)$	−0.10	0.07	0.11	0.003	0.11	0.13
$(Y_M-Y_{MF})/(Y_M-Y_F)$	−0.07	0.00	0.05	0.13	0.09	0.14
$(Y_{FM}-Y_F)+(Y_M-Y_{MF})/2(Y_M-Y_F)$	−0.09	0.04	0.08	0.07	0.10	0.14
N_M	24,158	305,997	307,467	24,158	305,997	307,467
N_F	8,796	131,717	133,907	8,796	131,717	133,907
C. *Never-been-married males and females*						
Y_F	1.90	3.07	3.07	2,483.48	3,614.58	3,593.85
Y_M	2.06	3.52	3.53	2,518.85	3,875.14	3,863.84
Y_{FM}	1.84	2.96	2.98	2,225.89	3,362.18	3,432.72
Y_{MF}	2.27	3.75	3.71	2,799.85	4,204.87	4,179.09
$(Y_{FM}-Y_F)/(Y_M-Y_F)$	−0.38	−0.24	−0.20	−7.28	−0.97	−0.60
$(Y_M-Y_{MF})/(Y_M-Y_F)$	−1.31	−0.51	−0.39	−7.94	−1.27	−1.17
$(Y_{FM}-Y_F)+(Y_M-Y_{MF})/2(Y_M-Y_F)$	−0.84	−0.38	−0.29	−7.61	−1.12	−0.88
N_M	5,883	66,371	67,027	5,883	66,371	67,027
N_F	4,348	51,730	52,586	4,348	51,730	52,586

[a]1970 data in terms of 1960 occupational classification.

[b]1960 data represent married once, spouse present? 1970 data are for married, spouse present.

Y_F ñ mean female earnings.

Y_M = mean male earnings.

Y_{FM} = what females would earn with male occupational distribution.

$(Y_{MF}$ = what males would earn with female occupational distribution.

$(Y_{FM}-Y_F)/(Y_M-Y_F)$ = measure 1 of explanatory power of occupational distribution.

$(Y_M-Y_{MF})/(Y_M-Y_F)$ = measure 2 of explanatory power of occupational distribution.

$(Y_{FM}-Y_F)+(Y_M-Y_{MF})/2(Y_M-Y_F)$ = mean explanatory power of occupational segregation.

N_M = number of males.

N_F = number of females.

Table 6-3
Percentage of Female Lifetime Labor Force Participation, by Marital Status and Education

	Education			
Marital Status	*Elementary*	*High School*	*College*	*Graduate School*
Married, spouse present	27.4	33.8	36.4	50.0
Married, spouse absent	28.3	33.4	54.1	NC
Widowed	31.7	32.4	44.9	56.5
Divorced	38.1	51.8	62.4	50.0
Separated	46.1	47.5	49.6	68.2
Never married	28.2	66.9	88.9	97.2
Total	30.1	36.9	41.4	59.1

Source: 1967 National Longitudinal Survey (NLS) of Work Experience of Females 30-44 Years of Age, in Herbert S. Parnes et al., *Dual Careers* (Washington, D.C.: U.S. Department of Labor, 1970).

Note: Lifetime labor force participation = total years worked divided by total exposure (age minus education minus 6) to the labor force.

NC = not calculated (too few observations)

a subsample of 718 students who had attended at least four years of college and had declared a major field of study. The results presented here show significant differences in the choice of college majors by sex. Classifying college majors into forty-two groups indicates male specialization in physical sciences (with the exception of mathematics), engineering, and business. Females, on the other hand, tend to specialize in education, nursing, and to some extent liberal arts fields such as English, speech and drama, fine arts, and music. Contrary to popular belief few women, compared with men, enter the biological sciences. Statistical testing that both males and females have the same distribution of majors rejects the hypothesis of a significant similarity.[3]

Analysis of these educational differences seems to indicate strong motivational differences between men and women (table 6-5). For example, in the matrix of simple correlations, females take significantly fewer high school science and mathematics courses but are faster readers (simple correlations are –0.273, –0.250, and 0.150 respectively). They take more summer school courses (0.116), do more volunteer work during the summer (0.119), and take more art and music courses (0.121). Females indicate that they go to college less "to earn more" (–0.312) than to "develop socially" (0.137) and "marry well" (0.168), but their high school and college grades exceed those of males (0.233 and 0.225 respectively) as does their class standing (0.304). Although a rather small (0.020) correlation between aptitude and sex indicates few enrollment

Table 6-4
Distribution of College Major Stratified by Sex, 1959

Major	*Description*	*Number of Males*	*Percentage of Males*	*Number of Females*	*Percentage of Females*
1	Architecture	8	2.0	0	0.0
2	English	7	1.7	31	10.1
3	Fine arts	4	1.0	5	1.6
4	History	24	5.9	10	3.2
5	Journalism	4	1.0	2	0.6
6	Language	0	0.0	5	1.6
7	Music	3	0.7	8	2.6
8	Philosophy	2	0.5	0	0.0
9	Speech or drama	4	1.0	11	3.6
10	Theology	7	1.7	1	0.3
11	Other	8	2.0	4	1.3
12	Anatomy	2	0.5	1	0.3
13	Biochemistry	1	0.2	0	0.0
15	Zoology	10	2.4	0	0.0
16	Other biology	10	2.4	7	2.3
17	Chemistry	14	3.4	5	1.6
18	Earth science	7	1.7	0	0.0
19	Mathematics	16	3.9	13	4.2
20	Physics	5	1.2	1	0.3
21	Other physical science	2	0.5	1	0.3
22	Economics	11	2.7	2	0.6
23	Political science	7	1.7	2	0.6
24	Psychology	12	2.9	5	1.6
25	Sociology	8	2.0	8	2.6
26	Other social science	5	1.2	3	1.0
27	Chemical engineering	3	0.7	0	0.0
28	Civil engineering	11	2.7	0	0.0
29	Electrical engineering	11	2.7	0	0.0
30	Mechanical engineering	16	3.9	0	0.0
31	Other engineering	15	3.7	0	0.0
32	Agriculture	15	3.7	2	0.6
33	Business	95	23.2	21	6.8
34	Education	20	4.9	91	29.5
35	Home economics	0	0.0	17	5.5
36	Law	1	0.2	1	0.3
37	Medicine	6	1.5	2	0.6
38	Nursing	0	0.0	27	8.8
39	Physical education	14	3.4	11	3.6
40	Other (technical)	18	4.4	4	1.3
41	Other (nontechnical)	4	1.0	7	2.3
	Total	410		308	

$\chi^2 = 292.97$

Source: Eckland, 1972. Reprinted with permission from the *Industrial and Labor Relations Review* 31, no. 4 (July 1978).

differences on the basis of ability, a greater bias exists according to parents' wealth. If one takes parents' levels of education as a measure of permanent income, a greater family income increases the probability of a daughter's attending college. Presumably, consistent with market expectations, parents prefer to finance their son's college education to a greater extent than their daughter's education.

Ordinary least-squares regressions on being in any particular major (table 6-6) indicate that after adjusting for ability, labor force, and marital expectations, sex differences exist in choice of college majors. Females tend to major in education and the humanities, and males in science, engineering, and mathematics.

In summary, we find that acquisition of human capital differs by sex. Women on the average tend to participate less in the labor force. For those that are married and have children, intermittent labor force participation accounts for females' being out of the labor force at least ten years to bear and raise children. For women with lesser amounts of education and more children, labor force intermittency becomes more exaggerated. Differences in the acquisition of human capital occur long before the age of labor force entry. Schooling choices differ dramatically, by sex, starting at least as early as high school. Females tend toward education and humanities, while males major in science, engineering, and mathematics.

The differences in human capital and especially in human capital acquired in school before job market entry may explain sex differences in labor market achievement. If no sex differences in human capital existed, then sex differences in wages and occupation would have to be caused by discrimination. But given the observed sex differences in human capital, further testing is needed to discern whether sex discrimination causes sex differences in the demand for human capital or whether sex differences in human capital are caused by other factors.

Simultaneous Equations Approaches

Sex differences in the labor market and sex differences in human capital acquisition have been examined. With respect to labor market variables, wages and occupational status differ. With respect to human capital, life-cycle labor market experience and schooling choices differ. It is plausible that differences in human capital may explain the observed differences in wages and occupations, but it is also possible that anticipated labor market discrimination affects human capital choices so that a simultaneous relation exists. This section applies simultaneous equations techniques to analyze wages and labor market experience, occupation and labor market experience, and occupational prestige and levels of schooling. These models attempt to discern the causality between labor market performance and human capital.

Table 6-5
The Relationship between Sex and College-Related Variables (N = 718)

Variable Description	*Simple Correlation with Sex*[a]
Semesters of high school mathematics	−0.273
Semesters of high school science	−0.250
Reading speed	0.150
Diligence in doing homework (1 = very diligent; 4 = not diligent)	−0.260
Attended summer school	0.116
Attended remedial classes	−0.051
Worked during summer	−0.419
Summer art or music classes	0.121
Summer volunteer work	0.119
High school grade point average (0 = D or less; 9 = A)	0.233
Parents highly influential on college attendance	−0.011
Attended college because college graduate earns more	−0.312
Attended college because liked idea of college	−0.067
Attended college because friends went to college	0.012
Attended college to develop socially	0.137
Attended college to marry well	0.168
Attended college because of its academic reputation	0.113
Attended college because of its excellence in field of interest	0.052
Attended college because of admission standards	−0.063
Believes women can have career and children simultaneously	0.121
Anxious to marry during college	0.678
Freshman grade average (0 = D or less, 9 = A)	0.174
Scholastic standing in high school	0.304
Labor force commitment (percentage of time did not work since leaving school)	0.535
Aptitude score (overall)	0.020
Usefulness of college in job preparation (1 = useful; 4 = not useful)	−0.101
Necessity of college for current or last job	0.029
Father's education (0 = None; 9 = Ph.D. or professional degree)	0.107
Mother's education	0.107
Number of brothers and sisters	−0.043
Marital status (0 = married, divorced, or widowed; 1 = never married)	−0.001
Years married	0.031
Major	
Humanities	0.099
Social science	−0.076
Engineering, math, or physical science	−0.273
Fine arts	−0.030
Education	0.371
Business	−0.201
Medical fields	0.202
Home economics	0.180

Source: Eckland, 1972. Reprinted with permission from the *Industrial and Labor Relations Review* 31, no. 4 (July 1978).
Note: Any correlation coefficient r such that $|r| > 0.073$ is significant at $\alpha = 0.05$ and $|r| > 0.086$ at $\alpha = 0.01$.
[a]Male = 0; female = 1.

Wage Differentials: An Instrumental Variables Approach

The earnings function relates wages to investment in schooling and on-the-job training as well as to a number of additional standardizing exogenous variables. The function is usually fitted in the following form:[4]

$$\ln W =$$

$$\underset{(30.7)}{4.36} + \underset{(7.4)}{0.055S} + \underset{(2.2)}{0.007e_1} \underset{(-1.8)}{-0.005h} + \underset{(4.9)}{0.017e_2} + \underset{(3.6)}{0.064 \ln(\text{wks})} - \underset{(-0.5)}{0.011 \ln(\text{hrs})}$$

$$R^2 = 0.26 \text{ (}t\text{-values in parentheses)} \qquad (6.1)$$

where

$\ln(W)$ = logarithm of observed hourly wage rate

S = years of schooling

e_1 = first work experience segment of the life cycle

h = years out of the labor force

e_2 = second segment of work experience

$\ln(\text{wks})$ = logarithm of weeks worked

$\ln(\text{hrs})$ = logarithm of hours worked per week

Potential labor market experience is broken into work (e_1 and e_2) and nonwork (h) segments of the life cycle. The negative coefficient of h indicates that large nonwork segments reduce wages. In addition, the coefficient obtained by adding a series of interaction terms between job experience (e_1) and labor force intermittency (i) is negative (table 6-7) thereby implying that the expectation of labor force intermittency causes a decline in on-the-job training even while at work.

This interpretation of the negative impact of labor force intermittency on wages may be called into question. Presumably women with greater earnings power have stronger job aspirations and work commitments than other women throughout their lifetimes. Hence the earnings function in equation 6.1 may well have causality running in the opposite direction. Since lifetime work experience may depend on prior wage levels and expectations, the experience variables are in part determined as well as determining. If so, the residual of the wage equation is correlated with the experience variable, and the estimates of the coefficients may be biased.

One econometric approach to estimating equation 6.1 in the presence of endogeneity of explanatory variables is to use instrumental variables. Estimated

Table 6-6

Ordinary Least-Squares Estimates of the Determinants of Choice of College Major, 1959 ($N = 569$)

Regression Coefficients	*Humanities*	*Social Science*	*Engineering Physical Science*	*Fine Arts*	*Education*	*Business*	*Medical Related*	*Home Economics*	*Other*
a	0.0110	0.0039	0.0088	0.0010	−0.0080	−0.0070	−0.0016	−0.0016	−0.0065
	(2.74)	(1.24)	(1.98)	(0.49)	(2.11)	(1.73)	(0.63)	(1.01)	(1.91)
a_q	−0.0121	−0.0023	0.0219	−0.0016	0.0025	−0.0109	0.0036	−0.0001	−0.0011
	(2.59)	(0.63)	(4.25)	(0.67)	(0.57)	(2.29)	(1.22)	(0.00)	(0.26)
a_v	9.9534	−0.0014	−0.0080	−0.0147	0.0211	0.0304	0.0130	−0.0028	−0.0120
	(2.81)	(0.10)	(0.39)	(1.48)	(1.18)	(1.58)	(1.10)	(0.36)	(0.74)
e_m	−0.0009	0.0165	−0.0084	0.0034	−0.0237	0.0068	0.0005	−0.0039	0.0096
	(0.10)	(1.92)	(0.69)	(0.60)	(2.30)	(0.62)	(0.10)	(0.88)	(1.02)
m	0.0785	0.0763	−0.1207	−0.0049	−0.0251	0.0193	−0.0192	0.0298	−0.0340
	(1.55)	(1.92)	(2.16)	(0.17)	(0.53)	(0.37)	(0.61)	(1.47)	(0.79)
h	0.0304	−0.0192	−0.0185	−0.0312	0.0321	−0.0687	0.0312	−0.0239	0.0678
	(0.52)	(0.41)	(0.28)	(1.01)	(0.58)	(1.15)	(0.85)	(1.01)	(1.35)
b_1	−0.0299	−0.0470	0.0749	−0.0108	−0.0326	0.0858	−0.0001	0.0064	−0.0468
	(0.90)	(1.80)	(2.04)	(0.62)	(1.04)	(2.54)	(0.00)	(0.48)	(1.65)
b_2	−0.0952	0.0547	−0.0233	−0.0100	0.0158	0.0009	0.0217	0.0106	−0.0249
	(2.92)	(2.14)	(0.65)	(0.59)	(0.52)	(0.00)	(1.07)	(0.81)	(0.89)
S	0.0190	−0.0530	−0.1573	0.0005	0.2582	−0.1326	0.0708	0.0626	−0.0761
	(0.50)	(1.78)	(3.76)	(0.00)	(7.25)	(3.45)	(3.38)	(4.14)	(2.36)
C	0.3202	0.0275	−0.009	0.0079	0.1588	0.2438	0.0212	0.0150	0.2065
R^2	0.07	0.04	0.14	0.01	0.15	0.09	0.05	0.05	0.02

Source: Eckland, 1972. Reprinted with permission from the *Industrial and Labor Relations Review* 31, no. 4 (July 1978).

Note: t-values in parentheses.

Table 6-6 continued

a = aptitude (see table 6-3)
a_q = proxy for quantitative ability (number of semesters of high school math and science)
a_v = proxy for verbal ability (index of reading speed; see table 6-3)
e_m = proxy for quality of preschool investment (education of mother)
m = family expectation variable (current marital status; 1 = never married; 0 = married, divorced, widowed)
h = labor force expectation variable (percentage of time worked since school)
b_1 = behavioral variable (whether respondent believes college graduates earn more)
b_2 = behavioral variable (whether respondent believes college develops one socially)
S = sex (1 = female, 0 = male)
C = constant

Table 6-7
Ordinary Least-Squares Regressions Measuring the Effect of Labor Force Intermittency on Wages and the Rate of Change of Wages over the Life Cycle (N = 933)

Explanatory Variables	*(1)*	*(2)*	*(3)*	*(4)*	*(5)*	*(6)*
c	4.46	4.53	4.50	4.43	4.27	4.44
	(41.6)	(42.0)	(41.9)	(30.84)	(29.9)	(30.35)
S	0.057	0.055	0.056	0.056	0.064	0.055
	(9.68)	(9.48)	(9.52)	(9.45)	(9.18)	(9.45)
e_1	0.009	0.006	0.008	0.006	0.009	0.006
	(2.99)	(1.91)	(2.38)	(1.94)	(1.33)	(0.87)
e_1^2					−0.0001	−0.0000
					(−0.22)	(−0.03)
h	−0.005	−0.005	−0.003	−0.005	−0.008	−0.009
	(−1.66)	(−1.76)	(−1.21)	(−1.67)	(−1.57)	(−1.66)
h^2					0.0002	0.0002
					(1.00)	(0.92)
e_2	0.020	0.019	0.020	0.017	0.020	0.019
	(6.56)	(5.63)	(6.08)	(5.03)	(2.57)	(2.43)
e_2^2					−0.0001	−0.0001
					(−0.22)	(−0.28)
i		−0.129		−0.074		−0.077
		(−4.06)		(−1.88)		(−1.87)
i^*h			−0.007			
			(−3.43)			
i^*e				−0.013		−0.013
				(−1.49)		(−1.36)
ln (wks)				0.045	0.063	0.045
				(2.43)	(3.41)	(2.37)
ln (hrs/wk)				−0.015	−0.011	−0.016
				(−0.64)	(−0.47)	(−0.72)
Health					0.070	
					(2.00)	
R^2	0.25	0.26	0.26	0.27	0.26	0.27

Source: Observations of white married once, spouse present females who worked in 1966 from the National Longitudinal Survey (NLS) survey of females 30-44 years of age, in Herbert S. Parnes et al., Dual Careers (Washington, D.C.: U.S. Department of Labor, 1970).
Note: Dependent variable is ln of hourly wages; t values in parentheses.

c = constant
S = years of schooling
e_1 = first set of experience
h = home time (time not at work between periods j_1 and j_2)
e_2 = duration of last job
i = dummy variable equaling 1 if not at work after j_2 (measure of job intermittency)
$i * h$ = interaction of i and h (measures whether depreciation is higher during home time if labor force intermittency exists)

Table 6–7 continued

i^*e	=	interaction of intermittency and investment in period e_1
ln(wks)		standardization for weeks worked per year
ln(hrs)	=	standardization for hours worked per week
health	=	dummy variable equaling 1 for good health

values of *e* and *h* are used to reestimate the earnings function, as shown in table 6-8 where a comparison ordinary least-squares regression is also reported. Note that the use of instrumental variables strengthens the dependence of female wages on job experience. The experience coefficient increases, and the magnitudes of the home time variables more than double. Statistical significance of both the experience and home time variables increases. These results imply that even when experience is determined as a function of exogenous variables, years of experience or nonexperience in the labor force affect earnings. Thus although the dependence of earnings on experience was expected to be overestimated because of a simultaneous equations bias, this is not the case. Little if any spurious correlation seems to exist. The large amount of time out of the labor force occurs not because of low wages in labor market but apparently because of home responsibilities. This is apparent when noting the impact of children on labor supply in the instrumental variable equation.

Despite these strong results, certain biases could mar the findings. The instrumental variables approach used here neglects the fact that other factors such as children or spouse's education may also be endogenous.

Occupational and Educational Choices

We now specify a model relating occupational status to educational attainment. Those with larger amounts of schooling are hypothesized to attain jobs of higher prestige levels. Conversely, entry barriers affecting the demand for women in certain occupations may affect schooling choices. While such expectations of future discrimination may affect schooling, different labor market aspirations may be the cause of sex differences in educational choices. In this section a model is proposed to test the impact of education and success in the labor market as well as the impact of future occupational expectations on schooling choice.

Such a model can be represented as the simultaneous system:

$$o = f(k, X_1), \tag{6.2}$$

$$k = g(o, X_2), \tag{6.3}$$

Table 6-8

National Longitudinal Survey Wage Regressions: Ordinary Least-Squares and Two-Stage Least-Squares Estimation ($N = 923$)

	Instrumental Equations[a]					*Wage Equations*			
Dependent Variable	*e*		*h*		*Dependent Variable*	*OLS*		*2SLS*	
	b	*t*	*b*	*t*		*b*	*t*	*b*	*t*
constant	−4.38	−2.3	4.38	2.3	constant	4.493	43.0	4.492	41.4
health	−0.003	−1.0	0.003	−1.0	*e*	0.009	3.0	0.018	5.1
reside	−0.028	−2.4	0.028	2.4	*h*	−0.006	−2.0	−0.014	−4.1
loc	0.759	2.2	−0.759	−2.2	school	0.062	11.4	0.058	10.2
ln hrs	0.59	1.9	−0.590	−1.9	kids	−0.011	−1.5	0.004	0.4
ln wks	1.331	5.8	−1.331	−5.8	R^2	0.21			
kids	−0.568	−5.8	0.568	5.8					
school	0.093	1.1	−0.093	−0.09					
expos	0.333	8.8	0.667	17.7					
educh	−0.024	−0.3	0.024	0.3					
tenure	0.576	14.1	−0.576	−14.1					
R^2	0.39		0.46						

[a]With the exception of the expos coefficients (which sum to 1), the sum of the coefficients across the *e* and *h* equations sum to 0 illustrating the restriction that $e+h$=expos=age minus education minus six.

[b]Endogenous variables:

health = duration of health limitations in months
reside = number of years in current residence
loc = size of place of residence
ln hrs = logarithm of hours worked per week
ln wks = logarithm of weeks worked per year
kids = number of children
school = years of schooling
expos = age minus education minus six
educh = years education of husband
e = work experience
h = years of home time
tenure = number of years spent on current or last job

where

o = labor market status (measured by NORC) occupational prestige scores.[5]

k = purchased human capital (level P schooling obtained)

X_1, X_2 = exogeneous variables such as ability (verbal versus quantitative), marital status, number of children, and percentage of time not worked since leaving school (to measure labor force commitment)

Equation 6.2 represents the market governing occupational choice, and equation 6.3 the human capital acquisition market. The markets are interrelated in the sense that acquisition of human capital (k) is in part functionally related to intended occupation (o), while at the same time occupation is related to one's acquired human capital. Using a simultaneous equations model implies that k and o, when taken as endogenous variables, can be interpreted as expectations. Thus $f'_k = \partial o/\partial k$ can be defined as the effect of differences in human capital (measured by level of schooling) on occupation, and $g'_o = \partial k/\partial o$ can be thought of as representing the effect of expected occupational status on accumulation of schooling.

In the context of this model the sources of discrimination can be identified depending on the relationship between k and o in equation 6.2 and between o and k in equation 6.3. If the acquisition of human capital is not rewarded by better jobs ($f'_k \cong 0$) when those with high occupational aspirations purchase human capital ($g'_o > 0$), then demand discrimination exists. On the other hand, if aspirations of high occupational attainment do not motivate the obtaining of human capital ($g'_o \cong 0$) even though the acquisition of human capital is rewarded by better jobs ($f'_k > 0$), then sex differences result from supply-side considerations.

Both f' and g' should exceed zero. Some rewards should be obtained from schooling, and expectations of occupational attainment should affect schooling decisions. Thus it is not so much the magnitudes of each of these partial derivatives that are important as their relative sizes in comparison to each other and in comparison to those of males. Table 6-9 contains the results of estimation of this model for working males and females (1960 U.S. Census 1/1000 sample). Higher occupational expectations increase levels of schooling more for males than females (0.907 versus 0.118). Thus it appears that if males and females have equal occupational expectations (measured in terms of expected occupational prestige), males obtain more schooling than females. Equally surprising is that the return from such investment in schooling pays off more for females (in terms of occupational prestige units) than for males. The "prestige rate of return" to schooling for women is 0.366; for men it is only 0.205. Thus this model indicates that in the analysis of market returns in prestige units rather than in

Table 6-9
Joint Determination of Schooling and Occupational Prestige: Three-Stage Least-Squares Estimation

	Female (N = 8,963)		*Male (N = 27,021)*	
Explanatory Variables	*Occupational Prestige*	*Schooling*	*Occupational Prestige*	*Schooling*
Constant	4.896 (72.93)	1.308 (1.11)	4.735 (130.6)	−3.265 (5.08)
Size of place	0.002 (0.80)		0.017 (14.80)	
Age	−0.026 (−1.96)	−0.083 (−3.10)	0.133 (16.76)	−0.251 (15.14)
Schooling	0.366 (23.22)	0.	0.205 (35.30)	
Hours worked	0.006 (4.67)		0.009 (10.62)	
Weeks worked	−0.012 (−5.89)	0.002 (0.71)	0.004 (1.37)	−0.006 (1.11)
Total income	0.018 (13.09)	−0.001 (−0.18)	0.017 (11.09)	−0.001 (−0.15)
Family size	−0.007 (−6.54)	0.002 (1.14)	−0.0001 (−0.20)	0.001 (0.90)
Hours/week-spouse		0.319 (48.59)		0.522 (85.00)
Occupational prestige[a]		0.118 (0.62)		0.907 (7.83)

Source: U.S. Census of Popultation, 1960.

Note: Log-log specification so that each coefficient can be interpreted as an elasticity. *t*-values in parentheses.

[a]Occupational prestige is measured by the National Opinion Research Center (NORC) survey and, unlike Duncan indexes, is independent of income and education.

dollars, women fare better than men. They obtain more prestigious jobs per year of "expected" schooling and similarly obtain less schooling for a given "expected" level of job prestige.

Conclusions

My intention in this paper is not to present a comprehensive analysis of all aspects of sex discrimination but to illustrate supply and demand sources of sexual inequality and to provide simultaneous equations techniques to help distinguish between the alternative causes. Sex differences abound. Females have smaller wages and achieve lower occupational status.

While many have attributed sex differences to demand discrimination, I find that numerous human capital variables difer not only by sex but by marital status and family size within sex groups. Such is the case for labor market experience and educational choices. Because of these findings I hypothesized that males and females supply different sets of skills to the labor market and hence obtain varying remuneration and job status. Wages and job status do indeed differ by experience and educational choices. Yet relating differences in occupation and wages to such human capital variables does not prove them to be the cause of sex differences in labor market attainment; instead the relationship may be the reverse.

Discrimination could cause sex differences in demand for human capital. In order to test for such causality, simultaneous equations models were applied. In the wage equation, instrumental variables strengthened the dependence of earnings on labor force experience. Schooling and the continuity of labor force experience, even when measured as instrumental variables, make a difference.

These results indicate a strong relationship between labor market status and human capital, and a lesser dependence of schooling on occupational expectations. Sex differences in human capital are important and cannot be ignored in understanding sex differences in labor market attainment. Even when adjusted for the possibility of reverse causality, human capital variables maintained their importance.

In the last section I attempted to disentangle cause and effect when using occupational prestige as a measure of labor status. For a given expectation of occupational prestige, females obtain less schooling than males.

Despite these results, further work is necessary to better measure the impact of supply versus demand effects of discrimination. I suggest concentration on three aspects of discrimination. First, further work is necessary on simultaneous equation systems of wages, occupational and educational choices, and labor market experience. Such models could incorporate fertility decisions as well. Second, I propose more concentration on narrower aspects of human capital. Whereas in this paper I analyze educational choices and labor force continuity, additional research on kinds of job experience, intensity of investment, and kinds of schooling would be helpful. Third, more emphasis should be placed on refining measures of job remuneration. Task assignment, occupational prestige, skill depreciation rates, and job characteristics compatible with child rearing should be included.

Notes

1. These measures are computed as follows:

$$Y_{FM} = \frac{\sum_{\text{OCCUP}} W_{\text{OCCUP}_F} \cdot M_{\text{OCCUP}}}{\sum_{\text{OCCUP}} M_{\text{OCCUP}}} = \text{female earnings if they had a male occupational distribution}$$

$$Y_{MF} = \frac{\underset{\text{OCCUP}}{} W_{\text{OCCUP}_M} \cdot F_{\text{OCCUP}}}{\underset{\text{OCCUP}}{\Sigma} F_{\text{OCCUP}}} = \text{male earnings if they had a female occupational distribution}$$

where M_{OCCUP} and F_{OCCUP} represent the number of males and females in the occupation OCCUP, and W_M and W_F represent their wage rates.

2. The Eckland (1972) data is used in this analysis. These data represent a detailed follow-up study (performed in 1970) of a group of predominantly white men and women who were high school seniors in 1955. Other recent data sources for individual information on college major as well as associated demographic characteristics are the NORC June 1961 College Graduate Study (National Opinion Research Center, University of Chicago), the National Longitudinal Survey (Center for Human Resources, Ohio State University), and the Research Triangle Institute-National Longitudinal Survey (RTI-NLS). The group surveyed by NORC consisted of a sample of students graduating from 135 randomly chosen colleges. For more information on the sample see Davis, 1964. The survey consisted of five waves: (1) April 1961 with a sample of 33,782, (2) spring 1962 with a sample of 31,075, (3) February 1963 with a sample of 29,738, (4) March 1964 with a sample of 24,385, and (5) April 1968 with a sample of 4,868. This last wave represents an 81 percent response rate to a 30 percent sample of those who responded to all previous waves. The groups surveyed in the NLS data consist of a national sample of males and females fourteen to twenty-five years of age, women thirty to forty, and men forty to fifty-five. For a further description see Parnes et al., 1970. However, neither source contains information beyond 1964. The RTI-NLS data are from a national survey containing information on students who were high school seniors in 1972. While this data set is the most recent available, it contains serious drawbacks in that it only contains choices through the freshman year of college.

3. The computed χ^2 value in 292.27 with thirty-nine degrees of freedom is significant at $a < 0.01$.

4. The data used are the National Longitudinal Survey (NLS) described in Parnes et al. (1970).

5. Unlike Duncan measures of occupational prestige NORC occupational prestige scores are computed independent of education and wage rate. Thus in this model we are not regressing a variable on part of itself.

References

Bergmann, Barbara R. 1971. "The Effect on White Incomes of Discrimination in Employment," *Journal of Political Economy* 79:294-313.

Chiswick, Barry, O'Neill, June, Fackler, James, and Polacheck, Solomon, 1974.

"The Effect of Occupation on Race and Sex Differences in Hourly Earnings." *Proceedings of the American Statistical Association* 219-228.

Davis, James Allan. 1964. *Great Aspirations: The Graduate School Plans of America's College Seniors.* Chicago: Aldine.

Eckland, Bruce K. 1972. "Subject Index for Use with the 1970 Survey Questionnaire." Working Paper No. 2, Institute for Research in Social Science, University of North Carolina, Chapel Hill.

Edgeworth, F.Y. 1922. "Equal Pay to Men and Women for Equal Work." *Economic Journal* 32:431-457.

Lucas, Robert E.B. 1974. "The Distribution of Job Characteristics." *Review of Economics and Statistics* 56:530-540.

Parnes, Herbert S., Shea, John R.; Spitz, Ruth S.; and Zeller, Frederick A. 1970. *Dual Careers.* Washington, D.C.: U.S. Department of Labor.

Polacheck, Solomon. 1975. "Potential Biases in Measuring Male-Female Discrimination." *Journal of Human Resources* 10:205-229.

Zellner, Harriet. 1972. "Discrimination against Women, Occupational Segregation, and the Relative Wage." *American Economic Review* 62, no. 2:157-60.

Commentary

Jane Alison Weiss

Solomon Polachek has addressed three interesting questions and their interrelations: Why are women's wages consistently less than two-thirds that of white men? Why are women differentially allocated to the job market than white men? Why are women's acquisitions of human capital both different from and less than those of white males? Previous research by Polachek and others has shown the explanatory power of human capital variables in accounting for male-female wage differentials. In chapter 6 Polachek has attempted to consider the degree to which occupational segregation and barriers to entry to educational institutions influence both the acquisition of human capital and the later earnings of women. Taking on the argument that occupational segregation resulting from discrimination in hiring practices and the concomitant lower wages may discourage women from investing in human capital, Polachek presents a diverse array of data and employs simultaneous equations models to disentangle the reciprocal effects of these variables and to assess the impact of human capital variables.

Polachek concludes that while "sex differences in wages and occupation are related to differences in levels of labor market experience and education, human capital differences may themselves stem from discrimination either in the human capital market or in expectations of sex discrimination in the labor market." His findings, (table 6-9) however, indicate greater support for the argument that women's occupational prestige is determined by their educational attainment than for the argument that their educational attainment is determined by occupational prestige. Polachek concludes that social policy should include as an important component programs to encourage women to acquire human capital. No serious student of occupations and wage attainment would argue with this conclusion; education and on-the-job training play an important part in the attainment of both individuals and of groups within the population. However, some major difficulties should prevent the serious reader from taking the findings of this substantial work at face value.

The first problem Polachek encounters lies in the data employed. The use of data from the National Longitudinal Survey on women aged thirty to forty-four in 1966 to assess the form government policy should take for women in their teens in the 1980s (or later) presents a number of acute problems. These women (had they chosen to do so) would have entered college between 1940 and 1954. This group reflects both period and cohort characteristics that distinguish them dramatically from younger, contemporary groups of women. As Wilson and Portes observe (1975, p. 391), "The drastic alteration of the positions of women and blacks . . . may be such that the assumption of aggregate equilibrium on which the tenability of causal inferences rests (Blalock 1968) may not be warranted for the affected groups."

The dramatic increase in both women's educational attainment (women were 39 percent of the college population in 1965, while the 1979 freshman class is 51 percent female) and their employment (in 1965, 39 percent of all women worked, today 51 percent are employed) implies a set of circumstances underlying the attainment processes very different from those of fifteen to forty years ago (the lag depends on whether we are considering the education or occupation data). A major change affecting the educational attainment of women is the passage of legislation that made illegal the use of quotas to restrict the proportion of women in college (usually to a ratio of two men to one woman). It seems strange to discuss education as a good that women choose when, in fact, women's "choices" not only have been limited by their socialization but have been concretely delimited by admissions quotas.

The process of occupation and earnings attainment is, in fact, quite different for older and younger women. Ward (1978), using the combined National Opinion Research Center (NORC) General Social Survey for the years 1974-1977, compares the processes involved in the occupation and earnings attainment of younger (eighteen to forty-four) and older (forty-five to sixty-four) women workers and reports sharply different findings for the two groups. Among the older women, occupational prestige and marital status were the primary determinants of earnings; among younger women education and experience were the major determinants. Thus the argument that women make educational and occupational choices that give precedence to their roles as wives and mothers is supported among older women, but there is no significant relationship between marital status and earnings in the sample of younger women. The findings in the sample of younger women more closely resemble the typical white male model, with education and experience acting as the major determinants of earnings. (The unstandardized coefficients for these variables in the sample of younger women were at least twice the magnitude of those in the sample of older women.) Major structural changes that have occurred in the last twenty years have sharply affected women's employment rates and their employment histories. Hence it is impossible to generalize from a study at one period to a later period of time for a group undergoing such changes as women have.

Examination of a sample of middle-aged women in the 1960s will seriously underestimate the impact of human capital variables on women entering the labor force in the future. The reasons underlying a shift in the effects of human capital acquisition among women relate to changes in the structure of the labor market and to the increased human capital acquisition that has followed from the vastly expanded enrollments of women in colleges and universities (with, among other things, the removal of quotas); changes in aspects of the social structure will have important effects on women's occupation and earnings attainments beyond the simple effects of human capital acquisition. Further, women's occupational expectations and their acquisition of human capital will be directly determined by these structural changes.

I have not, of course, invalidated Polachek's findings with these observations; I simply wish to limit their area of application to an explanation of attainment for middle-aged women in the 1960s. Nor have I called into question the use of a model whose estimates change significantly over time.

A serious concern with this line of research is the epistemic correlation between the acquisition of human capital and the indicators employed to measure it. When male-female comparisons in these areas are drawn, serious qualitative differences are not captured by the quantitative measures generally employed. I shall discuss problems with the measures used for job experience, schooling, and occupational prestige.

Polachek (1975) himself has observed that there are different kinds of job experience, and the failure to capture these distinctions biases the findings. Griffin (1978) demonstrates, indeed, that firm-specific work experience has greater effects on wages than overall experience, and the deletion of firm-specific experience from the model biases the estimates of experience. Polachek has included two measures of experience, one measuring the first set of experience and one the duration of the last job. If duration of last job means length of time on current job, then Polachek has addressed this problem; if not, then the likelihood of bias from this source remains. The problem, however, is larger than simply dividing job experience into general and firm-specific categories. When male job experience and female job experience are compared, it is important to consider the differences in the jobs themselves. This does not consist of dividing them into "good" jobs and "bad" jobs, as Polachek maintains. Rather, it consists of dividing them into jobs that have career ladders and those that do not; the differences between the two will clearly affect the way in which job experience affects wage attainment (Blau and Jusenius 1976). Because women are overwhelmingly located in jobs that do not have career ladders, the effects of job experience are likely to be simply incremental, resulting from simple increases in salary over time. Those whose job experiences are derived from jobs with career ladders will reflect both the incremental increase and increases resulting from job advancement.

As Polachek observes, the content of schooling is vastly different for men and women and thus should have differential effects on their occupation and wage attainment. One must seriously question, then, what a simple linear measure of educational acquisition will tell us about the comparative effects of education attainment on occupation and wage attainment for males and females.

Polachek argues that women receive higher occupational prestige for each year of "expected" schooling than men do. On average, women's occupational prestige scores are as high as those of men. This means, of course, not that there is sexual equality in occupational attainment but that men are distributed at both ends of a prestige scale while women are located in the middle (Ward 1979). In addition, women are more likely than men to be employed in white-collar jobs. Thus a comparison based on male and female occupational prestige may give us little if any information about the way in which human capital acquisition relates to any absolute measure of occupational "prestige." White-collar jobs obtain higher prestige scores than blue collar jobs; hence women generally receive higher prestige scores than men with comparable stocks of human capital. It seems clear that the blue collar-white collar distinction muddles the comparison of male-female occupational prestige.

It seems important to consider which factors cause the effects of human capital variables to change over time (specifically with reference to women). This issue points to a major weakness in the human capital approach to occupational and earnings inequality: the assumption of an open and perfectly competitive market. This assumption implies that individuals operate independently of the social structure, in that each is free to make the same choices as all others. The pernicious effects of the existing hierarchically organized social structure on the perceptions and ambitions of individuals is ignored.

The work of Boudon (1973), White (1970), and others has shown that the movements of individuals cannot be analyzed independently of the structure through which they move. This is particularly true when the researcher is analyzing groups of individuals who have held distinctly different positions within social institutions. Sørenson (1977, p. 969) has argued that the task at hand is the formulation of a model of "how opportunities for change in attainment are created in this structure." Burawoy (1977, p. 1035) observes that "the interpretation of status attainment can be undertaken only with reference to the historically specific social structure in which it occurs—in particular the patterns of empty places which define the educational and occupational structures."

The necessity for considering changes in social structure has been emphasized as well by Thurow and Lucas (1972). They observe that if income were determined primarily by educational attainments, then the significant shifts in the distribution of education since World War II should have precipitated similar shifts in the distribution of income. There have, of course, been no such shifts.

Likewise, the considerable increase in the educational attainments of women have not led to an increase in their relative earnings, and the increasing shift to continuous work history patterns has had no effect on their relative earnings as human capital theory would predict. This relates directly to the fact that productivity is inherent in jobs, not in individuals (Thurow 1975).

Polachek observes that if females possessed the same occupational distribution as males, the wage gap would be closed by only 20 percent. It seems likely that this rough representation of occupational segregation would account for more of the differences today, as the gap in educational attainments is narrowing. More precise measures of occupational segregation and the structure of labor markets must be obtained and included in models of earnings and occupational attainment. Without the inclusion of these structural variables these micromodels remain underspecified (Hannan 1971), and the greatest methodological precision will not increase our understanding of the processes being analyzed.

References

Blau, Francine, and Jusenius, Carol L. 1976. "Economists' Approaches to Sex Segregation in the Labor Market: An Appraisal." *Signs: Journal of Women in Culture and Society* 1, no. 3, part 2:181-199.

Boudon, Raymond. 1973. *Mathematical Structures of Social Mobility.* New York: Elsevier.

Burawoy, Michael. 1977. "Social Structure, Homogenization, and 'the Process of Status Attainment in the United States and Great Britain.'" *American Journal of Sociology* 82, no. 5:1031-1042.

Griffin, Larry J. 1978. "On Estimating the Economic Value of Schooling and Experience: Some Issues in Conceptualization and Measurement." *Sociological Methods and Research* 6, no. 3.

Hannan, Michael T. 1971. *Aggregation and Disaggregation in Sociology.* Lexington, Mass.: Lexington Books, D.C. Heath.

Polachek, Solomon W. 1975. "Potential Biases in Measuring Male-Female Discrimination." *Journal of Human Resources* 10:205-229.

Sørenson, Aage, B. 1977. "The Structure of Inequality and the Process of Attainment." *American Sociological Review* 42, no. 6:965-978.

Thurow, Lester C. 1975. *Generating Inequality.* New York: Basic Books.

Thurow, Lester C., and Lucas, Robert E.B. 1972. *The American Distribution of Income.* Washington, D.C.: U.S. Government Printing Office.

Ward, Kathryn B. 1978. "The Earnings Attainment of Middle-Aged and Older Women." Master's thesis, University of Iowa.

_______. 1979. "Alternative Approaches to the Measurement of Occupations." University of Iowa.

White, Harrison. 1970. *Chains of Opportunity: System Models of Mobility and Organizations.* Cambridge, Mass.: Harvard University Press.

Wilson, Kenneth L., and Portes, Alejandro. 1975. "The Educational Attainment Process: Results from a National Sample." *American Journal of Sociology* 81, no. 2:343-363.

7 Do Women Earn Less under Capitalism?

John R. Moroney

The Lord said to Moses, "Say to the people of Israel, when a man makes a special vow of persons to the Lord at your valuation, then your valuation of a male from twenty years old up to sixty years old shall be fifty shekels of silver, according to the shekel of the sanctuary. If the person is a female, your valuation shall be thirty shekels."

Leviticus 27:1-4.

It is widely known, and almost universally deplored, that in the United States the average earnings of women are low relative to those of men. The earnings ratios vary according to the definitions of wages and employment and according to the year of observation. But practically all computations pertaining to the past three or four decades yield ratios in the range 0.50 to 0.65.[1] Furthermore, women do not fare any better in at least one highly visible branch of U.S. government employment. During the year 1974 the median earnings of female and male employees in the U.S. Senate were $10,260 and $17,670, respectively, yielding a ratio of 0.58 (Capitol Hill Women's Political Caucus, 1975). Such comparatively low earnings have recently been attributed to pervasive sex discrimination, which has in turn been described by some critics (Goldberg 1970, Edwards, Reich, and Weisskopf 1972, Harris and Silverman 1973, and Harris 1975) as an inherent institution of capitalism–especially American capitalism.

What is not so widely known, but should be, is that the average earnings of women are low in comparison with those of men in virtually every country whose government publishes wages classified by sex. Yet the relative earnings of women display considerable variation internationally. During the past two decades they have approximated 65 percent to 70 percent of men's earnings in Finland, Norway, Israel, and France. Among the socialist nations of Czechoslovakia, Hungary, and Poland, they have clustered tightly in the neighborhood of 67 percent of male earnings. But women have earned, on the average, less than

I am pleased to acknowledge the helpful comments and suggestions of Murray Feshbach and Janet G. Chapman, Evsey Domar, Helen Kearney, Gertrude E. Schroeder, and Jane Weiss. It is not implied that these scholars necessarily agree with the views expressed in this chapter. This article is reprinted, with amendments, with permission of the *Economic Journal* where it originally appeared in September, 1979, volume 89, © by the Royal Economic Society, Cambridge University Press.

60 percent than men in the predominantly English-speaking countries (Australia, Canada, United Kingdom, and the United States).

Accordingly, this chapter has three purposes. The first is to tabulate ratios of average, economywide earnings of men and women workers, as well as earnings ratios in the manual trades, in several countries for which comparable data are available. The second is to conduct some exploratory tests concerning differences in relative earnings in different types of economic systems. Such tests should, at a minimum, be useful in evaluating the assertion that capitalism per se engenders particularly depressed relative earnings of women. Finally, we consider certain patterns of female occupational assignment in the Soviet Union, China, and Cuba, communist countries whose governments, regrettably, have not published earnings classified according to sex.

The Radical Indictment

Modern radical political economists have ascribed the subordinate status of women in the marketplace to several allegedly capitalistic institutions.[2] They contend that the nuclear family and a relentless drive for male supremacy within the family unit have forced women into specialized roles of child rearing and family maintenance. Since these activities are not compensated by wages, they do not offer women an opportunity for wealth accumulation, the principal source of status and power in capitalism. According to the radical view, these suppressive forces have been assisted under capitalism by a transfer of production from the home to the factory and the creation of a wage-labor market primarily for the participation and benefit of men. The segregation of women into nonmarket work creates a reserve army of labor, however, that can be tapped at low wages especially when shortages of male labor develop.

Although the preceding summary is necessarily a simplification omitting much richness of detail, I believe it represents a fair consensus of the modern radical viewpoint. Some modern critics, however, do not associate a subordinate status of women exclusively with capitalism. Mitchell (1966), for example, notes that patriarchal family structures existed in precapitalist feudal societies and are present in contemporary noncapitalist societies of tropical Africa, as well as in the postcapitalist bureaucracies of the Soviet Union and Eastern Europe. Similarly, Glazer and Waehrer (1977) emphasize that women have retained subordinate status not only in the mixed-capitalist economies of the United States and Great Britain but also in the Soviet Union and East Germany. They state that women have superior job opportunities in socialist countries but continue to bear the double burden of housewife and worker. Indeed, they conclude (1977, p. 48), "socialism has not automatically brought sexual equality, although socialism may be a necessary condition for the liberation of women."

Other critics stress certain contradictions between capitalist economic development and women's subordinate role in the nuclear family. Yet they attempt to forge a causal link between capitalism and a menial economic status of women. Davies and Reich (1972, pp. 348-356) suggest that as capitalist countries mature economically, the comparative growth of service and white-collar occupations, in which women are traditionally concentrated, induces greater female labor force participation. Other forces stimulating labor force participation, especially of married women, are the increased production of preprocessed commodities and labor-saving appliances.

According to this view, such trends should have diminished the importance of the nuclear family as a social unit and should have mitigated the degree of female bondage within the family. Thus Davies and Reich declare as contradictory the fact that the nuclear family has, if anything, become more entrenched in the United States during the period 1900-1969. They attribute this fact, and the persistence of women's subordinate economic status, to "the collective interests, ideologies and actions of males as a caste and capitalists as a class" (1972, p. 354). The patriarchal nuclear family as linked to collective male chauvinism as follows (1972, p. 354): "Males as a caste enjoy privileges within the family as it is now constituted and they have supported its perpetuation. . . . The unequal power relationship between husband and wife is at root based on the general unavailability for most women of adequate alternative sources of income and on the social conditioning of children in the family to a patriarchal society." It is evident, however, that patriarchal value systems preceded by several millennia the development of capitalist ideology: the roles of husband as household leader and of wife as helpmate may be dated from Genesis.

There are three arguments used by modern radicals to tie the nuclear family and women's inferior status to the interests of capitalists. First, a sexually segmented labor market, fostered by capitalists, allegedly obscures common class interests and solidarity among female and male workers. However, no empirical evidence has been offered to support this contention. Indeed, the radicals' point seems inconsistent with the observation that heightened group consciousness *requires* considerable social segmentation, as manifested in recent ethnic and women's rights movements.

Second, the family and school system are identified as the institutions that reproduce and maintain the labor force. They are decried as the agents through which children are indoctrinated to the essential hierarchical values of capitalism. This logic is not persuasive. The family and school system are the basic units of reproduction and education in all modern societies. Hierarchical social systems pervade the military, governmental, and economic systems of all countries. It remains to be established whether capitalistic hierarchies differ substantively from others or whether there are special features of capitalism particularly well served by the nuclear family and extrafamilial schooling.

Third, the nuclear family allegedly nourishes the ethos of possessive individualism, an ethic singularly suited to capitalism. This viewpoint, too, must be questioned on logical grounds. For it is within the nuclear family, particularly with children, that material resources and human energies are distributed according to individual need rather than competitive performance.

To summarize, it is by no means clear to me why capitalists, as a class, should attempt to perpetuate the nuclear family. Some empirical evidence should perhaps be brought to bear on this point. If one accepts the radical syllogism linking capitalist development to the perpetuation of the nuclear family, it follows that the nuclear family should atrophy with the demise of capitalism. Yet the onset of socialism in Eastern Europe following World War II did not, in itself, affect marriage rates: during the capitalist and postcapitalist period in Eastern Europe, 1932-1975, marriage rates in Czechoslovakia, Hungary, and Rumania mirrored the trends in the United States, except for a comparatively (and understandably) larger increase in U.S. rates during the years 1946-1948. Similarly, marriage rates in the German Democratic Republic have been quite similar to those in the Federal Republic of Germany. Indeed, since 1970 the rates in East Germany have consistently been larger, and the gap has widened. Although these facts are by no means offered as a conclusive refutation of the radical thesis, they seem to cast doubt on it.

Modern radical doctrine holds that the subordination of women in the labor market is a central characteristic of capitalism. The underlying causes are identified to be the symbiotic forces of patriarchal nuclear family structure and the class interests of capitalists. Socialism, by eliminating capitalists as a class, is posited as a necessary condition for advancing the relative earnings of women. The New Left theses, as a system, may certainly be questioned on logical grounds. But problems of logic aside, the issue of relative earnings remains to be evaluated empirically.

Scope of the Study

The macroeconomic scope of this chapter is perhaps best clarified by stating that the average aggregate earnings of both sexes are taken as data. No attempt is made to analyze their underlying causes, except to classify them into two broad categories. Imagine first an economy consisting of several occupations, each including men and women. If, within each occupation, the frequency distribution of skills and earnings were identical for both sexes, one could say this economy is free of intraoccupational wage discrimination. But if women were either excluded or underrepresented among the higher-paying groups, this occupational differentiation would cause their average economywide earnings to be comparatively low.[3] An international study of occupational discrimination would require, at a first level, a detailed study of the occupational distribution of skills, by sex. Explaining the sex-related distribution of skills would require, at a deeper level, country-specific facts concerning the patterns of schooling and vocational training by which different skills are acquired. Adequate information, classified by sex, is apparently not available at either level for many countries other than the United States.[4]

At the other extreme, imagine that relative to the labor force women are proportionately represented in all categories of skills. If within each (or even one) category women are paid less than men of equal skills, and in no occupation are they paid more, one could say there is pure intraoccupational wage discrimination. This circumstance, as well, would cause the average aggregate earnings of women to be comparatively low. International comparisons of purely intraoccupational wage discrimination could in principle be based on (female-male) earnings ratios within tightly defined occupations or industries characterized by homogeneous skills. Only a few countries, notably Canada, Sweden, and the United States, publish earnings classified according to sex at the level of detail required.[5]

Both types of differentiation are present in all real economic systems. In decentralized market economies characterized by full employment (or a fortiori by involuntary unemployment), the presence of one probably depends on the existence of the other. Even in centrally planned economies, in which a bureaucratic (and nondiscriminatory) allocation of labor by sex might in principle be feasible, the two types of differentiation coexist.

I do not deal explicitly with either type of sex-related differentiation. Instead, I describe the consequences of both, as they are manifested in average aggregate earnings ratios. For the purpose of comparing market differentiation in different types of economic systems, such economywide earnings ratios are the proper focal point. Unfortunately, median earnings of men and women are published by only a few socialist countries, Czechoslovakia, Hungary, and Poland.[6] Accordingly, I discuss the patterns of occupational segregation and the relative earnings they imply in Cuba, China, and the Soviet Union.

Basic Facts on Relative Earnings

All earnings discussed here are pretax labor incomes. The relative earnings in table 7-1 are economywide ratios, and those in table 7-2 are ratios in the manual trades. The latter are singled out because the blue-collar trades include workers from comparatively homogeneous social classes.

Three points should be borne in mind when one is reading the tables and interpreting the statistical tests. First, in all countries the earnings ratios refer to full-time, year-round workers. Although the definitions differ slightly from country to country and over time, a full-time, year-round worker is ordinarily employed for at least thirty hours per week and fifty weeks per year (Lydall, 1968, pp. 51 ff).

Table 7-1
Economywide Ratios of Female to Male Earnings, Annual

Capitalist	*Year*	*Earnings Ratio*		*Year*	*Earnings Ratio*
Australia	1962	0.607	United Kingdom	1953-54	0.536
	1964	0.591		1968	0.530
	1966	0.578		1970	0.537
	1967	0.582		1972	0.557
	1969	0.584		1974	0.564
	1971	0.607		1975	0.615
Austria	1957	0.613	United States	1939	0.583
Belgium	1964	0.632		1949	0.641
Canada	1950-1951	0.607		1959	0.589
	1960-1951	0.602		1963	0.586
Finland	1960	0.642		1966	0.579
France	1951	0.717		1969	0.585
	1952	0.704		1971	0.595
	1954	0.732		1973	0.566
	1956	0.696		1974	0.572
	1957	0.684	*Socialist*		
	1959	0.688	Czechoslovakia	1949	0.662
	1961	0.699		1959	0.662
	1963	0.700		1962	0.659
	1970	0.667		1968	0.666
Israel	1962-1963	0.700		1970	0.671
Japan	1955	0.459	Hungary	1962	0.697
	1975	0.562		1972	0.725
			Poland	1972	0.665

Sources:

1. Ratios for the United Kingdom, 1968-1972, are computed from earnings published in *Annual Abstract of Statistics, 1973*, table 162, p. 156. Ratios for 1974 and 1975 are computed from earnings reported in *Annual Abstract of Statistics, 1976*, table 169, p. 172.
2. Ratio for France, 1970, is computed from earnings published in *Annuaire Statistique de la France, 1974* (1974, table 8, p. 521).
3. Ratios for United States, 1963, 1966, 1969, 1971, 1973, 1974, are computed from U.S. Bureau of Census, *Current Population Reports*, various issues.
4. Ratios for Czechoslovakia are computed from earnings published in Michal, 1973, p. 415.
5. Ratios for Poland and Hungary, 1972 are computed from earnings published in Michal, 1975, p. 267.
6. Ratios for Australia, 1962 and 1964, are computed from earnings published in the *Year Book of Australia, 1967*, p. 328; for 1966 and 1967 from ibid., *1969*, p. 279; for 1969 from ibid., 1971, p. 263; and for 1971 from ibid., *1972*, p. 263.
7. Ratio for Japan, 1975, is computed from earnings published in *Monthly Labor Statistics and Research Bulletin*, 1976, pp. 42-43.
8. All other ratios are computed from earnings published in Lydall, 1968.

Second, all ratios in table 7-1 refer to the median earnings of females divided by those of males. The ratios in table 7-2 are computed from arithmetic mean earnings in Norway and from median earnings in the other countries. The

Table 7-2
Ratios of Female to Male Earnings in Manual Trades

Capitalist	*Year*	*Earnings Ratio*		*Year*	*Earnings Ratio*
Australia	1964	0.576	Norway	1966	0.650
	1967	0.563		1968	0.658
	1969	0.562		1970	0.657
	1971	0.596		1972	0.662
	1973	0.634		1974	0.660
Austria	1926	0.546		1975	0.655
	1947	0.653	United Kingdom	1960	0.534
	1953	0.704		1963	0.502
Belgium	1964	0.612		1965	0.490
Canada	1940-1941	0.541		1967	0.494
	1950-1951	0.593		1969	0.488
	1960-1961	0.542		1971	0.510
Chile	1964	0.651		1973	0.517
France	1951	0.700		1975	0.574
	1952	0.693	United States	1939	0.571
	1954	0.707		1949	0.644
	1956	0.674		1959	0.527
	1957	0.652		1969	0.558
	1959	0.650		1971	0.574
	1961	0.649		1973	0.528
	1963	0.654		1974	0.546
Germany (F.R.)	1957	0.602	*Socialist*		
	1962	0.638	Hungary	1962	0.685
Netherlands	1963	0.562	Poland	1957	0.674
	1968	0.628		1958	0.643
	1973	0.639		1961	0.645
				1962	0.639

Sources:

1. Ratios for Australia are computed from earnings published in *Year Book of Australia, 1969*, p. 276; ibid., *1971* , p. 255; ibid., *1972*, p. 264; ibid., *1974*, p. 272.
2. Ratios for the Netherlands are computed from earnings published in *Statistical Yearbook of the Netherlands, 1974*, table 2, p. 304, and average hours per week published in *Social Statistics: Labour Force Sample Survey*, 1973, p. 118.
3. Ratios for Norway are computed from hourly earnings and average hours per week published in *Yearbook of Nordic Statistics, 1976*, table 159, p. 228, and table 44, p. 70.
4. Ratios for the United Kingdom, 1963-1967, are computed from earnings published in *Annual Abstract of Statistics, 1973*, table 158, p. 153; and for 1969-1975 from earnings published in ibid., *1976*, table 167, p. 171.
5. Ratios for the United States, 1969-1974 are computed from earnings published in *U.S. Census of Population, 1970*, tables 240 (p. 1=818) and 241 (p. 1-824); *Current Population Reports*, no. 85, p. 139; ibid., no. 97, p. 149; and ibid., no. 101, p. 143.
6. All other ratios are computed from median earnings published in Lydall, 1968.

critical point ensuring international comparability of earnings ratios is similarity in shape of the female and male wage distributions within each country. Dissimilarity in their shapes across countries does not invalidate an international comparison. Since Lydall (1968) found the distributions of manual earnings of females and males to be practically identical in all non-Scandinavian countries listed in table 7-2, one may expect the alternative earnings ratios to be quite comparable.

Third, within each country the distribution of earnings for both sexes is lognormal leptokurtic (Lydall 1968). This fact can be explained by several theoretical hypotheses, including those of Gibrat (1931), Roy (1950a, b), and Mincer (1958, 1974). Within a country, and for a given time period, the estimated ratio of median (or mean) female earnings to median (or mean) male earnings is a random variable whose probability distribution is not known. It seems reasonble to suppose that the earnings ratios in different countries are independent. To assume independence among the sequential observations within a country is more questionable. Accordingly, several tests of independence are conducted.

Consider first the data in table 7-1. Both the chi-square and the one-sample Swed-Eisenhart tests indicate that the observations in France, as well as those in the United States, may be accepted as independent at $P \leqslant 0.05$. However, the chi-square test for independence is not recommended when expected frequencies are as small as they are in the present applications (Cochran 1954). Since the Swed-Eisenhart test requires a minimum of nine observations, Kendall's nonparametric test for trend was applied to the observations in Australia and the United Kingdom. There is no trend in the Australian data, but there is a mild trend in the U.K. earnings ratios. If we consider the observations in table 7-2, Kendall's nonparametric test shows that during the respective sample periods relative earnings do not display significant trends in any of the English-speaking countries.

Let us focus more closely on the earnings ratios in table 7-1. It is clear that, on the average, women in all countries earn substantially less than men. The earnings ratios are remarkably similar in Australia, Canada, the United Kingdom, and the United States. The mean and median ratios in these countries are, respectively, 0.582 and 0.584. The non-English-speaking capitalist countries are characterized by relatively higher earnings of women. The mean ratio in these countries is 0.660, the median 0.688. These values are strikingly close to the mean (0.676) and median (0.666) of the socialist economies. It is unfortunate that more observations could not be obtained from socialist countries. But most East European governments, including that of the Soviet Union, have never published earnings classified by sex.[7] Regrettably, neither has China or Cuba.[8]

Several hypotheses can nonetheless be tested. Since we are dealing with small samples of random variables whose population distributions are not known, it seems preferable to employ nonparametric tests that involve no assumptions concerning theoretical population distributions. Specifically, we conduct pairwise tests for equality of median earnings ratios. A chi-square test (with correction for continuity) is used when the combined number of observations in both subsamples is greater than twenty and when each cell in the contingency table has an expected frequency at least as large as five (Cochran 1954). Otherwise, the Fisher-Yates test is used (Finney 1948, Cochran 1952). The level of significance in the following tests is $P \leqslant 0.05$.

Relative earnings of women differ between the group of English-speaking countries and the group of non-English-speaking capitalist economies. The test for equality of median earnings ratios yields a computed X^2 of 12.4. Since the critical value of X^2 at the 5 percent significance level is 3.84, the hypothesis of equality is decisively rejected.

The median earnings ratio for the non-English-speaking capitalist countries (0.688) closely approximates that of the socialist countries (0.666). The Fisher-Yates test indicates that these medians are not significantly different from one another. This result does not hinge on the relatively large number of observations for France. If one selects arbitrarily either any one or any two observations from France, discards the others, and reapplies the Fisher-Yates test, one still cannot reject the hypothesis of equality of medians for these two groups of countries.

The distinction between relative earnings in the English-speaking countries and the socialist economies is more substantive. According to the Fisher-Yates test, the socialist median is significantly larger than that in the English-speaking economies.

The ratios of manual earnings in table 7-2 may also be classified in three groups. Australia, Canada, the United Kingdom, and the United States from a reasonably homogeneous group with a mean of 0.551 and a median of 0.546. The non-English-speaking capitalist countries display a higher mean (0.648) and median (0.652).[9] Finally, Hungary and Poland have a mean (0.657) and median (0.645) nearly identical to those of the second group of capitalist countries.

A test of the difference between medians of the English-speaking and non-English-speaking capitalist countries yields a calculated X^2 of 26.3, which is highly significant. The Fisher-Yates tests indicate that the median of the socialist countries is significantly greater than that of the English-speaking countries, but it is not significantly different from the median of the other capitalist economies.

These tests cast serious doubt on the proposition that relative earnings of women have differed systematically according to the broadly defined systems, capitalism and socialism. For the purpose at hand, such a simple and broad distinction is not very fruitful. The earnings ratios in tables 7-1 and 7-2 nontheless permit two clear conclusions: women have been paid considerably less than men, on the average, in all countries reviewed, and their relative earnings have been at the bottom of the scale in the English-speaking economies. Why women have earned comparatively less in these countries than in the other capitalist economies remains to be established. One cannot resist speculating that different legal institutions may have played some role. Australia, Canada, the United Kingdom, and the United States have shared a tradition of common law, whereas the other capitalist countries in our sample have been governed under civil codes.[10] Kanowitz (1969) and others have suggested that the common law doctrine of coverture and its associated system of property rights have particularly discouraged the acquisition of human and nonhuman capital by women. This is a provocative assertion that would seem to merit systematic study.

In fairness to the New Left position, one must record that many modern radicals deny that the bureaucratic systems of Eastern Europe are truly socialistic. They champion instead the participatory socialist economies of China and Cuba as models for expunging sex differentiation in the marketplace. It is lamentable that earnings, systematically classified by sex, have not been published in either of these countries or in the Soviet Union. Nevertheless, some suggestive evidence concerning female labor force participation and average sectoral wage rates is available for these economies.

Sex-Based Differentiation in China, Cuba, and the Soviet Union

Howe (1973) presents what appears to be the most comprehensive study of wage structures in Communist China. He documents some narrowing of average wage scales across occupations, as well as within particular enterprises, since 1949. In the 1950s intraenterprise wage spans (across occupations) were in the range fourfold to sevenfold, and some further compression may have occurred since (1973, pp. 38ff).[11] Yet he reports no information whatsoever concerning sex-specific wage structures. There is some evidence (Chen 1967) that the salaried, nonagricultural labor force in the 1950s consisted chiefly of men and that men were concentrated in branches paying comparatively high wages. The composition of the work force in 1955, by selected branch, appears in table 7-3. There were considerable differences in female labor force participation among

Table 7-3
Distribution of Salaried Labor Force in Selected Branches, China 1955

Branch	*Percentage Male*	*Percentage Female*	*Average Wage (Yuan per Year)*
Industry	81.6	18.4	664
Construction	96.7	3.3	701
Banking, insurance	83.3	16.7	586
Culture, education, and health	78.5	21.5	548
Total	86.9	13.1	610

Source: Chen, 1967, tables 11.7, p. 482, and 11.17, pp. 492-93.

branches. The average annual wage in the construction branch, in which women represented only 3.3 percent of the work force, was approximately 25 percent higher than that in culture, health, and education, in which women constituted 21.5 percent of employment. To my knowledge, these are the only published statistics concerning labor force participation of women in China. The economic position of women in that vast land awaits careful documentation.

A similar pattern of occupational differentiation appears in Cuba. Blutstein et al. (1971), pp. 355 ff) report that Cuba has not published official figures concerning female employment, but demographers estimate that before the revolution men constituted approximately 83 percent of the paid labor force. Estimates for the year 1970 indicate that females represented between 20 percent and 23 percent of the work force (Blutstein et al. 1971, p. 356).[12] An estimate of female participation and average wage rates, by sector, appears in table 7-4. With an aggregate female participation rate of 20 percent to 25 percent as a benchmark, women are proportionately represented in the higher-paying industrial and financial sectors but are overly concentrated in the lower-wage service and commercial sectors. Women are also highly concentrated in the low-wage agricultural sector (in which the average wage was 1,059 pesos per year in 1966).

The Cuban government has never published official statistics concerning male and female wage rates and employment by sector or by occupation. A more conclusive investigation is therefore not currently possible. There seems to be little doubt that the economic position of Cuban women has improved somewhat since the revolution; but the New Left claims of rapid gains toward sexual equality in the marketplace or of a comparatively higher status of women vis-á-vis their position under capitalism, stand as articles of faith unsupported by scientific evidence.

Considerably more information is available in the Soviet Union. It must be

Table 7-4
Labor Force Participation by Sector in Cuba, 1970, and Average Sectoral Earnings, 1966

Sector	*Percentage Male*	*Percentage Female*	*Average Wage (Pesos per Year)*
Industry	78	22	2063
Administration and finance	75	25	1928
Education, culture	32	68	1733
Services	48	52	940
Commerce	66	34	1502
Business	66	34	n.a.

Source: Labor force participation obtained from Randall, 1974b, p. 6. Average wages, by sector, obtained from Roberts, 1970, pp. 194-195.

Note: These are wages in the state sector, and earnings in the private sector are excluded.

recalled that the Soviet Union has never published earnings statistics, classified by sex, either for occupational categories, for individual sectors, or in the aggregate.[13] However, average wage rates and the sex composition of the work force have been estimated for various sectors of the Soviet economy. A thirteen-sector classification was recently published by Dodge (1976, p. 183), and data taken from his study for the year 1973 appear in table 7-5. A very clear inverse relation between average sectoral earnings and female labor force participation is present: the correlation coefficient between these variables is –0.656, significant at $P \leqslant 0.01$. This pattern is consistent with Moskoff's (1974) more detailed, fifty-six branch study of average wage rates and female labor force participation for the year 1966. Moskoff found that the average monthly wage ranged from a maximum of 281.4 rubles for engineers and technical personnel in the fish-processing industry (34 percent of whom were women) to a minimum of 70 rubles for pharmacists (95 percent were women). Using Moskoff's data (fifty-six observations), I computed a correlation coefficient between average monthly earnings and female labor force participation, by branch, of –0.550 (significant at $P \leqslant 0.001$).[14]

The occupational assignments of men and women in the Soviet Union are highly differentiated, leading to considerable differentials in male and female incomes. Indeed, scattered evidence on the overall relative earnings of women suggests that they are quite comparable to those in the non-English-speaking capitalist economies. A study by Soviet sociologists Gordon and Klopov (1973), presumably covering the years 1967-1968, reports that in a typical Soviet industrial center the average earnings of women and men were, respectively, 84

Table 7-5
Labor Force Participation and Average Earnings, by Sector, in the Soviet Union 1973

Sector	*Percentage Male*	*Percentage Female*	*Average Salary (Rubles per Month)*
Transport	76	24	156.7
Construction	71	29	163.6
Agriculture	56	44	117.3
Arts	55	45	99.0
Science and Science Service	51	49	147.3
Industry (production workers)	51	49	147.2
Housing	47	53	102.0
Government and economic administration	37	63	126.0
Communications	32	68	107.5
Education, culture	27	73	120.5
Trade, catering	24	76	101.8
Credit, insurance	20	80	123.1
Public health, welfare	15	85	99.0

Source: Dodge, 1976, p. 183.

and 131 rubles per month (an earnings ratio of 0.64!). Similarly, Chapman (1975) cites a study conducted in Leningrad in the mid 1960s showing that women's earnings were, on the average, 69.3 percent of those of men. She suggests that the greater part of such observed differentials is attributable to sex differentiation in occupational assignment rather than to unequal pay for equivalent work.

The general principle of inequality of earnings is well established and vigorously defended by certain leading Soviet sociologists. For example, Mokronosov (1973, p. 24) writes:

> The specific nature of socialism, its difference from developed communism, consists in the fact that at this state of the development of production the normal functioning of the latter is possible only on the basis of the *constant attachment* [his italics] of particular groups of society to qualitatively dissimilar types of labor. This does not occur by law; it is caused by the objective conditions of societal production. . . . Marx, characterizing precisely this feature of socialism, wrote that along with equal rights to the means of production, there are unequal rights for unequal labor.

Similar argumentation is given by Shkaratan (1973a, p. 13), who writes: "The social division of labor inherent in socialism thereby emerges as the foundation of actual inequality of groups of workers who, owing to the operation of the law of distribution according to work, end up with unequal shares in the national income of society." In another essay, Shkaratan (1973b, p. 76) reviews certain facts concerning sex differentiation in early training patterns. For example, among tenth-grade graduates in Leningrad, 1963-1967, 4.7 percent of the boys and 33.7 percent of the girls took jobs as nonmanual, office workers. By contrast, 62.6 percent of the boys but only 24.7 percent of the girls became skilled (and comparatively well-paid) manual workers. Shkaratan (1973b, p. 76) justifies such patterns by stating that "the division into personnel in skilled manual labor and personnel in nonmanual labor not requiring a specialized education is *increasingly* [my italics] based on natural factors rather than having a social character." Hardly ammunition for the women's movement!

Summary and Conclusions

Any criticism of an economic system must necessarily be comparative. To be substantive, however, it should demonstrate the superiority of some workable alternative. Comparatively low earnings of women, and differences in occupational distributions of men and women, are oft-cited evils of capitalism, and socialism (either in a parliamentary or a totalitarian form) has been chronicled by certain radical economists as a mitigating alternative. Yet those who have claimed an improved economic position of women under socialism have not documented their views. Accordingly, this chapter has sketched a picture of women's comparative earnings in different countries.

Several findings stand out. First, on the average, women have persistently earned less than men in those societies for which data are at present available. This fact is of course consistent with a range of theoretical hypotheses, some of which are grounded in discrimination toward women and some of which are not.[15]

Second, there is substantial evidence that the relative earnings of women are significantly lower in the United States than in certain socialist countries. But more than that, women's relative earnings are uniformly lower in the English-speaking countries.

Third, our findings do not support the claim that capitalism as a system engenders disproportionately low earnings of women. On the contrary, the capitalist economies studied here may be classified in two groups, distinguished obviously only by differences in language and legal traditions. There are almost certainly more fundamental social distinctions between the English-speaking countries as a group and the others. These differences and their influence on women's relative earnings seem to be fertile grounds for study.

Fourth, there is no substantive distinction between the relative earnings of women in Austria, Belgium, Chile, Finland, France, the Federal Republic of Germany, Israel, the Netherlands, and Norway, on thy one hand, and Czechoslovakia, Hungary, Poland, and (based on the limited information available) the Soviet Union. The institutions of socialism, at least as practiced in these East European economies, have not raised the relative earnings of women by comparisons with those in a range of capitalist countries.

The capitalist system, of course, is not a monolithic social structure. It was never adopted in any country as a social contract but has evolved in somewhat different forms in various countries. Private ownership of reproducible and human capital, a wage-labor market, and the nuclear family are cornerstones of all modern capitalist societies. Except for predominantly private ownership of capital, these institutions prevail in the European communist countries as well. The similarities between women's relative earnings in the non-English-speaking capitalist countries and the East European economies suggest that private versus state ownership of capital is not a crucial variable affecting the position of women in the marketplace.

In some respects this chapter raises more questions than it answers. Two areas in particular seem to merit further study. First, more detailed investigations of the relative earnings of women in different economic systems would be of great interest. Such studies should ideally include more data for socialist countries, as they become available, and should concentrate some attention on the changing responsibilities of men and women in nonmarket activities.[16] Second, a study of the economic roles of men and women in capitalist countries governed by common law and those ruled by civil law seems to be a path worth following.

Notes

1. Kahne (1975) provides a comprehensive survey and guide to the literature dealing with economic participation of women in the United States. For a discussion of relative earnings, see especially pp. 1258 ff. and the references cited. See also Tsuchigane and Dodge (1974).

2. Some sociologists recognize that these institutions are found in non-capitalistic societies. See Mitchell, 1966, Rowbotham, 1974, Rubin, 1978, and Zaretsky, 1976.

3. The presence of occupational differentiation is well established both in capitalist and socialist countries. Using the assumption that female and male earnings within sectors are equal (because earnings classified by sex are not available), Moskoff (1974) estimated that pure occupational differentiation would have caused women's earnings in the Soviet Union in 1966 to be 88 percent of men's earnings. The overall earnings gap appears to be in the range 30 percent to 35 percent, rather than 12 percent.

4. The statistical yearbooks of Hungary and Yugoslavia, for example, report enrollment and graduation, by sex, in broad vocationalcategories. But the distribution of employment, by skill category and sex, is not reported at a level of detail required for a comprehensive study.

5. For example, Gunderson (1975) recently examined female-male earnings differentials within the narrowly defined six-digit *Dictionary of Occupational Titles* in Ontario, Canada. He found that the average wage differential between the sexes for jobs with identical descriptions was 22 percent. Within occupations having incentive wage systems, the average differential diminished to 14 percent. Ayers and Moroney (1978) investigated hourly wages of men and women in three-digit manufacturing industries for several European countries, using data published by the Organization for Economic Cooperation and Development, Statistical Office of the European Communities and the International Labour Organization *Yearbook of Labour Statistics*. The hourly wage differentials, in percentage terms, are considerably smaller than the monthly or annual earnings differentials.

6. Some New Left economists, for example Edwards, Reich, and Weisskopf (1972), would disavow this classification, arguing instead that the economies of East Europe are state socialist and those of England, France, Norway, and Sweden are state capitalist. Such an alternative classification would seem capricious, if not impossibly arbitrary, for empirical purposes.

7. Lydall (1968) also discovered this in his research extending through 1967. I have consulted the national yearbooks and other sources for Bulgaria,

the Democratic Republic of Germany, Rumania, Yugoslavia, and the Soviet Union and have not found any earnings published by sex. Toussaint Hocevar of the University of New Orleans, a specialist in the economies of Eastern Europe, indicates in private correspondence that he not been able to discover sex-specific earnings in other publications of these East European countries. Schroeder (1972) and Moskoff (1974) report that the Soviet Union has never published earnings classified by sex, and I have recently confirmed this point in correspondence with the Soviet specialist Murray Feshbach.

8. I have consulted the statistical yearbooks and several other statistical reference works concerning Cuba. I have also reviewed thoroughly a number of sources for China, including Chen, 1967, Howe, 1973, Bureau of Economic Analysis, 1973, and other references cited in these publications, all of which indicate that earnings classified by sex have never been published in China. Some reasons for the scanty wage statistics for China are discussed in Howe, 1973, and Bureau of Economic Analysis, 1973.

9. An earlier version of this paper included earnings ratios in the manual trades during the period 1963-1973 for Denmark, Finland, and Sweden, as well as for Norway. These ratios were comparatively high, with a mean of 0.736, and showed a distinct upward trend. These were ratios of hourly earnings, however, and are therefore not comparable to the ratios appearing in table 7-2. In particular, the increase in the ratio of women's to men's hourly earnings in Norway, from 0.720 to 0.780 between 1965 and 1975, has been exactly offset by a more rapid decrease in the average weekly hours worked by women (from 33.9 to 28.1 hours per week), thus leaving the ratio of women's to men's weekly earnings absolutely stable. It was possible to make this adjustment to full-time weekly earnings for Norway, using data published in the *Yearbook of Nordic Statistics* (1977, tables 44 and 159), but not for the other Scandinavian countries, because the average number of hours worked per week by men and women is not published for those countries.

10. Norway does not have such a distinctive civil law heritage as the other non-English-speaking countries but is plainly much closer to the civil law than to the common law group.

11. During a visit to China in December 1972–January 1973, Eckstein (1977, pp. 298 ff) found that current wage spans within enterprises were typically in the range three to fivefold. These differentials are quite comparable to those in U.S. or European firms. Eckstein (1977) reported earnings differentials between apprentices, on the one hand, and senior professional or political figures, on the other, in China to be approximately twentyfold, which he nonetheless believes to be lower than those present in the United States.

12. These estimates are consistent with those reported by Randall (1974a, p. 23), a feminist who is quite sympathetic to changes occurring in the status of women in the Cuban labor force.

13. See Chapman, 1975, and the Russian expert Schroeder, who writes in

her survey of Soviet wage statistics (1972, p. 313): "Soviet socialism has promised to achieve greater equality of incomes than results from capitalist exploitation of man by man. Quite possibly greater equality has been achieved, especially in the past fifteen years.... [Yet] nothing at all can be said as to whether equal pay for equal work prevails with respect to the earnings of males and females."

14. The relevant data are published in Moskoff's article (1974). On written request, I will be pleased to mail the data on which the computations are based.

15. Battalio, Kagel, and Reynolds (1978) provide an example of earnings differences based strictly on differential productivity. They find in an experimental economy in which men and women work on the same task (weaving woolen belts on hand looms) under identical conditions that the average hourly output of females is 78 percent that of men.

16. Legislation designed to modify the nonmarket activities of men and women in Scandinavian countries is described by Leijon (1975). See also the national reports recently summarized by Darling (1975).

References

Annuaire Statistique de la France. 1974. Paris: Institut National de la Statistique et des 'Etudes 'Economiques.

Annual Abstract of Statistics. London: Her Majesty's Stationery Office, various issues.

Ayers, R.M., and Moroney, J.R., 1978 "Male-Female Earnings Differentials: Cross-Section and Time Series Evidence for Western Europe." Tulane University.

Battalio, Raymond C., Kagel, John H., and Reynolds, Morgan O. 1978. "A Note on the Distribution of Earnings and Output per Hour in an Experimental Economy." *Economic Journal* 88 (December):822-829.

Blutstein, Howard I.; Anderson, Lynne C.; Betters, Elinor C.; Lane, Deborah; Leonard, Jonathan A.; and Townsend, Charles. 1971. *Area Handbook for Cuba*. Washington, D.C.: U.S. Government Printing Office.

Capitol Hill Women's political Caucus. 1975. "Sexists in the Senate? A Study of Differences in Salary by Sex Among Employees of the U.S. Senate." May.

Chapman, Janet G. 1975. "Equal Pay for Equal Work?" Paper prepared for a conference on Women in Russia, Stanford University. May 29-June 1.

Chen, Nai-Ruenn. 1967. *Chinese Economic Statistics.* Chicago: Aldine Press.

Cochran, William G. 1954. "Some Methods for Strengthening the Common X^2 Tests." *Biometrics* 0 (December):417-451.

_______. 1952. "The X^2 Test of Goodness of Fit." *Annals of Mathematical Statistics* 23:315-345.

Darling, Martha, ed. 1975. *The Role of Women in the Economy.* Paris: Organization for Economic Cooperation and Development.

Davies, Margery, and Reich, Michael. 1972. "On the Relationship between Sexism and Capitalism." In Richard C. Edwards et al., *The Capitalist System: A Radical Analysis of American Society.* Englewood Cliffs, N.J.: Prentice-Hall.

Dodge, Norton. 1976. "The Role of Women in the Soviet Economy." In *Economic Aspects of Life in the USSR.* Brussels: NATO Directorate of Economic Affairs.

Eckstein, Alexander. 1977. *China's Economic Revolution.* Cambridge: Cambridge University Press.

Edwards, Richard C., Reich, and Michael, and Weisskopf, Thomas. 1972. *The Capitalist System: A Radical Analysis of American Society.* Englewood Cliffs, N.J.: Prentice-Hall.

Emerson, John P. 1973. *Administrative and Technical Manpower in the People's Republic of China.* Bureau of Economic Analysis. International Population Reports Series p-95, no. 72. Washington, D.C.: U.S. Government Printing Office.

Finney, D.J. 1948. "The Fisher-Yates Test of Significance in 2 χ 2 Contingency Tables." *Biometrika* 35:145-156.

Gibrat, R. 1931. *Les Inégalites* Économiques. Paris: Librairie du Recueil Sirey.

Glazer, Nona, and Waehrer, Helen, eds. 1971. *Women in a Man-Made World.* Chicago: Rand McNally College Publishing Co.

Goldberg, M.P. 1970. "The Economic Exploitation of Women." *Review of Radical Political Economics* 2 (Spring):35-47.

Gordon, L.A., and Klopov, E.V. 1973. "Some Problems of the Social Structure of the Soviet Working Class." In Murray Yanowitch and Wesley A. Fisher eds., *Social Stratification and Mobility in the USSR.* White Plains, N.Y.: International Arts and Sciences Press.

Gunderson, Morley. 1975. "Male-Female Wage Differentials and the Impact of Equal Pay Legislation." *Review of Economics and Statistics* 57 (November):462-469.

Harris, Alice K. 1975. "Stratifying by Sex: Understanding the History of Working Women." In Richard C. Edwards, Michael Reich, and David M. Gordon, eds., *Labor Market Segmentation.* Lexington, Mass.: D.C. Heath.

Harris, Alice K., and Silverman, Bernard. 1973. "Women in Advanced Capitalism." *Social Policy* 4 (July/August):16-22.

Howe, Christopher. 1973. *Wage Patterns and Wage Policy in Modern China, 1919-1972.* Cambridge: Cambridge University Press.

Kahne, Hilda. 1975. "Economic Perspectives on the Roles of Women in the American Economy." *Journal of Economic Literature* 8 (December):1249-1292.

Kanowitz, Leo. 1969. *Women and the Law.* Albuquerque, N.M.: University of New Mexico Press.

Leijon, Anna-Greta. 1975. "Sexual Equality in the Labor Market: Some

Experiences and Views of the Nordic Countries." *International Labor Review* 112 (August-September):109-123.

Lydall, Harold F. 1968. *The Structure of Earnings.* London: Oxford University Press.

Michal, Jan. 1973. "Size Distribution of Earnings and Household Incomes in Small Socialist Countries." *Review of Income and Wealth,* Series 19, pp. 407-427.

_______. 1975. "An Alternative Approach to Measuring Income Inequality in Eastern Europe." In Z. Fallenbuchl, ed., *Economic Development in the Soviet Union and Eastern Europe,* vol. 1: *Reforms, Technology, and Income Distribution.* New York: Praeger.

Mincer, Jacob. 1958. "Investment in Human Capital and Personal Income Distribution." *Journal of Political Economy* 66:281-302.

_______.1974. *Schooling, Experience, and Earnings.* New York: National Bureau of Economic Research.

Mitchell, Juliet. 1966. "Women: The Longest Revolution." *New Left Review.* reprinted in Nona Glazer and Helen Waehrer, eds., *Women in a Man-Made World.* Chicago: Rand McNally College Publishing Co., 1977.

Mokronosov, G.V. 1973. "On the Criteria of Interclass Differences in Socialist Society." In Murray Yanowitch and Wesley A. Fisher, eds. *Social Stratification and Mobility in the USSR.* White Plains, N.Y.: International Arts and Sciences Press.

Monthly Labour Statistics and Research Bulletin. 1976. Vol. 28, no. 3. Japan: Statistics and Information Department, Minister's Secretariat, Ministry of Labour.

Moskoff, William. 1974. "An Estimate of the Soviet Male-Female Income Gap." *Association for Comparative Economic Studies Bulletin.* 16 (Fall):21-31.

Randall, Margaret. 1974a. *Cuban Women Now.* Toronto: The Women's Press.

_______. 1974b. *Cuban Women Now: Afterword 1974.* Toronto: Women's Press.

Roberts, C. Paul, ed. 1970. *Cuba, 1968, Supplement to the Statistical Abstract of Latin America.* Los Angeles: Latin American Center of the University of California.

Rowbotham, Sheila. 1974. *Woman's Consciousness, Man's World.* Baltimore, Md.: Penguin Books.

Roy, A.D., 1950a. "The Distribution of Earnings and of Individual Output." *Economic Journal* 60:489-505.

_______. 1950b. "A Further Statistical Note on the Distribution of Individual Output." *Economic Journal* 60:831-836.

Rubin, Gayle. 1978. "The Social Nature of Sexism." In Richard C. Edwards, Michael Reich, and Thomas E. Weisskopf, eds. *The Capitalist System: A Radical Analysis of American Society*, 2d ed. Englewood Cliffs, N.J.: Prentice-Hall.

Schroeder, Gertrude E. 1972. "An Appraisal of Soviet Wage and Income Statistics." In Vladimir Treml and John P. Hardt eds., *Soviet Economic Statistics.* Durham, N.C.: Duke University Press.

Shkaratan, O.I. 1973a. "Sources of Social Differentiation of the Working Class in Soviet Society." In Murray Yanowitch and Wesley A. Fisher, eds., *Social Stratification and Mobility in the USSR.* White Plains, N.Y.: International Arts and Sciences Press.

_______. 1973b. "Social Groups in the Working Class of a Development Socialist Society." In Murray Yanowitch and Wesley A. Fisher, eds., *Social Stratification and Mobility in the USSR.* White Plains, N.Y.: International Arts and Sciences Press.

Social Statistics: Labour Force Sample Survey. 1973. Luxembourg: Organization for Economic Cooperation and Development.

Statistical Yearbook of the Netherlands, 1974. 1975. The Hague: Central Bureau of Statistics.

Tsuchigane, Robert, and Dodge, Norton. 1974. *Discrimination against Women in the United States.* Lexington, Mass.: D.C. Heath.

U.S. Bureau of the Census. 1973. *Census of Population: 1970,* vol. 1: *Characteristics of the Population,* part 1. United States Summary, section 2. Washington, D.C.: U.S. Government Printing Office.

U.S. Bureau of the Census. *Current Population Reports.* Washington, D.C.: U.S. Government Printing Office, various issues.

Year Book of Australia. Canberra: Australian Bureau of Statistics, various issues.

Yearbook of Nordic Statistics, 1976. 1977. Stockholm: Nordic Council.

Zaretsky, Eli. 1976. *Capitalism, The Family, and Personal Life.* New York: Harper and Row.

Commentary

Cynthia B. Lloyd

John Moroney has raised an extremely interesting and provocative question in his Chapter, "Do Women Earn Less under Capitalism?" The current concern in the United States over the deterioration of the female-male earnings ratio naturally raises the question how women are faring relative to men in other countries. Is the prevailing wage gap between the sexes in the United States a universal phenomenon, or does its existence and severity depend on the nature of the surrounding economic system? The debate within the economics profession between radical and neoclassical economists centers on the determinants of income inequality, including inequality between the sexes. The radical economists point to certain characteristics of the capitalistic system as prime determinants of the earnings gap between men and women. However, little attention has been given in this debate to comparative analysis as a way of testing whether the sources of the problem are specific to capitalism. There is much talk at the popular level about the unusually active participation of women in certain socialist economies like Russia and China. However, there is little awareness of the division of labor between the sexes within these labor markets or of the relative economic status of the sexes in these societies. Therefore, this paper is a welcome beginning to what I hope will be a developing cross-national investigation of wage determination and inequality.

Moroney begins his discussion with a review of the radical literature relating capitalism to women's economic position. In this literature the nuclear family has been seen as the key factor within capitalistic society that has reinforced male supremacy, particularly as production has shifted from the home to the factory in the process of industrialization. However, as Moroney correctly points out, the institutions within capitalism (nuclear family, wage labor) that have been viewed as enhancing male supremacy exist within socialist societies as well. Still the question remains: Is there something unique within these institutions in a capitalistic society such as the United States that maintains and reinforces women's inferior economic status to an unusual degree? Although the radical literature cited is unclear on this point, it is still useful to look at the actual female-male earnings ratios.

The main contribution of this paper is the collection and presentation of male-female earnings ratios for an international cross section of countries. These data yield two findings that are clear and indisputable: (1) Women on average earn less than men in all the countries sampled, and (2) noticeable differences

The preparation of this discussion was supported by a Ford Foundation grant through the Center for Social Science Research for research in sex roles and social change.

exist between countries in male-female ratios. Moroney does not attempt to analyze the sources of these differentials but instead asks the central question, Do women earn less under capitalism? In order to answer this question he compares earnings ratios in a sample of communist countries to a sample of noncommunist countries, on an economywide basis as well as within the manual trades. The group of noncommunist countries for which he has data include the United States, Canada, Australia, and Japan, which are clearly capitalist countries; France and Israel, which have mixed economies; and Belgium, Austria, Finland, West Germany, Norway, the Netherlands, and the United Kingdom, which have Social Democratic parties in power, espousing liberal versions of socialism.[1] Data was also included for Chile in 1964 which at the time was under Social Democratic leadership. It is not clear that the communist-noncommunist dichotomy is the correct one because the strength of market forces varies from country to country within both the noncommunist and communist groups for which data on female-male earnings are presented.

The data on earnings cited are for full-time, year-round workers, with thirty-eight observations from ten noncommunist countries and eight observations from three Eastern European communist countries (Czechoslovakia, Hungary, and Poland) used in the case of economywide ratios and forty-seven observations from eleven noncommunist countries and five observations from two Eastern European countries in the case of ratios for the manual trades.

The data used range over a wide number of years; the earliest observation is for 1926 in Austria and the most recent for 1975 in Japan, the United Kingdom, and Norway. It is unfortunate that so little data are available on an internationally comparable basis. But at the same time, it seems doubtful that data from such a wide range of years should be compared both because of radical changes that have taken place within economies in the growth process and because of improvements and changes in data collection over the last fifty years. Another question is why only particular years were chosen as observations for each country. In the case of the United States female-male earnings ratios are available for every year since 1955 and probably prior to that as well.[2]

In order to make full use of the data and to test for significant differences between the two groups, Moroney assumes that each of the earnings ratios is independent. This seems to be a reasonable assumption when comparing ratios across countries at a given point in time, but it is not always a reasonable assumption when using observations for different years within the same country. As Moroney has pointed out, among countries with large numbers of observations, the hypothesis of independence was definitely rejected in the case of the United Kingdom; in the case of the United States, although the hypothesis was not rejected, the years for which observations were chosen seems entirely arbitrary. The test could not be conducted in cases with fewer observations. If all observations are used, countries with more observations get a heavier weight in the average, and, therefore, the resulting average depends on whether countries for which relatively large numbers of observations are available have relatively high female-male earnings ratios or whether their ratios are relatively low.

Moroney points out the wide range of earnings ratios within the noncommunist group. He finds that on average the ratios in the English-speaking countries of the United States, the United Kingdom, Canada, and Australia are lower than the rest of his capitalistic group. These differences are large and statistically significant for the manual trades in both cases. The differences between the communist and noncommunist groups are almost as great as the differences between the communist and noncommunist countries.

These results cannot be interpreted as any kind of proof that women fare better under socialism than capitalism. Not only is the sample of countries being compared extremely small and diverse in terms of dates, but important questions arise about the comparability of earnings data across countries because of differences in statistical definitions, levels of economic development, and economic systems.

As Moroney himself says, definitions of full-time, year-round workers vary from country to country but generally include all workers working at least thirty hours per week and fifty weeks per year. In the United States data on average hours shows that women categorized as full-time employees work fewer hours on average than men categorized as full-time. This suggests that if average hours for men and women vary across countries, these earnings ratios will be noncomparable, and the biases are unclear.

Unfortunately data on male-female hourly wages are only available for noncommunist countries, but they do show significant variation across countries (table 7C-1). All the ratios are higher than the ratios quoted by Moroney because differences in hours of work have been controlled for. In addition, the ranking of countries is significantly affected, suggesting sharp differences in average hours between countries. I would warrant a guess that although comparable data for the communist countries would show an increase in the female-male wage ratio, the increase would not be as great as in the noncommunist group because differences between men and women in hours of work are likely to be smaller. If this guess is correct, then differences between the two groups of countries would be smaller than Moroney's data show.

In fact, it is puzzling to me why Moroney did not want to look at hourly wage ratios. He indicates that they were available for the Scandinavian countries, but he chose to use the data only in the case of Norway where he had information on average hours worked per week and could, therefore, translate the data into annual earnings. In the case of Norway a substantial increase from 1963-1973 in the hourly female-male ratio was exactly counterbalanced by a substantial decline in women's average hours of work. Should this be interpreted as an improvement in women's economic position or as no change? If one assumes that a decline in hours worked represents voluntary choice on the part

Table 7C-1
Female Hourly Wages in Manufacturing as a Percentage of Male Hourly Wages in Selected Non-Communist Countries, 1975

Country	*Ratio*
Denmark	0.84
Finland	0.73
France	0.87[a]
West Germany	0.72
Greece	0.70
Ireland	0.60
Netherlands	0.79
Norway	0.78
Switzerland	0.68
Sweden	0.85
United Kingdom	0.66
Australia	0.92

Source: International Labor Organization, *Yearbook of Labor Statistics (Geneva, 1976, table 19A).*
[a]Wage Ratio in nonagricultural employment.

of women, it seems that the rise in female-male wages represents an improved position. If, on the other hand, one believes that the patriarchal nuclear family structure and the class interests of capitalist are affecting women's work choices, then I suppose this decline in hours worked would be seen to negate the improvement in the wage ratio, leaving the relative economic status of the sexes unchanged. It would have been interesting to see more discussion of this issue because it clearly has a major impact on the ranking of countries' earnings ratios.

Another important question that arises in the cross-national comparison of earnings is the treatment of the agricultural sector. Agricultural employment varies considerably as a percentage of total employment within the group of countries compared. Agriculture is usually a sector within which average earnings are low, but, at least in case of the United States, it is the sector with the highest female-male earnings ratio. Also, the statistical definition of women's employment in the agricultural sector diverges sharply from country to country. Moroney has wisely recognized that economywide earnings ratios are particularly subject to criticism on this point and has included a table for earnings ratios for the manual trades as well. In all countries for which comparable data were available, the female-male earnings ratios for the manual trades were lower than those based on economywide averages, suggesting some systematic causes common to all countries. However, it would be more reassuring to the reader if some discussion had been included about the relative importance of agriculture in the economywide ratios and about the range of definitions of the manual trades in different countries.[3]

A final question relating to the comparability of earnings statistics has to do with the male-female age distribution in each country and the average difference between the sexes in labor market experience. In Eastern Europe and the Soviet Union this is particularly important because of the impact of World War II on the age-sex distribution. With women outnumbering men in the prime ages for the first ten to twenty years after the war, women of necessity worked more continuously in the labor market and accumulated valuable labor market experience. Therefore, one would expect countries who suffered large losses of male manpower during the war to show higher female-male earnings ratios, and this would be true whether the economic system was basically capitalist or socialist. Ideally, some kind of standardized earnings ratio would be preferable in which age-specific earnings across countries are weighted by the standard age distribution of a stable population. This has been done already by Durand in a cross-national study of labor force participation rates but would require considerably more data than are currently available in the case of earnings.[4]

The question still remains whether the communist-noncommunist distinction is the correct one given the question addressed in the paper. Moroney fairly states, "Many modern radicals deny that the bureaucratic systems of Eastern Europe are truly socialistic. They champion instead the participatory socialist economies of China and Cuba as models for expunging sex differentiation in the marketplace." Unfortunately, data on earnings ratios are not available for either of these countries, but data on broad occupational segregation exist in these countries with women in general more highly represented in the lower-paying sectors of the economy. Occupational segregation is seen to exist in all the communist and noncommunist countries and is not, therefore, the critical distinction between capitalist and socialist systems.

Recent research on U.S. earnings differentials suggests that a critical determinant of male-female wage differentials cross nationally could be the percentage of employment in the government sector. Smith has found that for the United States the female-male earnings ratio is significantly higher in the government sector than in the private sector, when all other determining factors are controlled for.[5] If government employment data exist on a comparable basis cross nationally, one would expect to find the United States at one end of the scale with the lowest percentage of employment and the Eastern European countries on the other end of the scale, with the Western European countries ranging widely in between. I would hypothesize that the female-male earnings ratio would be highly correlated with a variable measuring the percentage of employment in government or the percentage of GNP produced (including nationalized and government-regulated enterprises) across countries. The dramatic increase in the earnings ratio for the United Kingdom between 1972-1975 may be related to recent labor government tax and economic policies as well as to the rising strength of trade unions in those years.[6]

Smith finds discrimination against women less intense but still present in the public sector in the United States. In general, it is presumed that governments are committed to equalitarian policies in employment. However, they are not exempt from influences from the private sector because of pressures for comparability of wage structures and because of labor mobility between the two sectors. Therefore, if one believes that sex discrimination is engendered in a capitalistic environment, its impact on wage ratios would be a function of the share of total employment in the private sector. Obviously, however, this story is too simple because discrimination is not just specific to the private sector but may vary in intensity from one country's public sector to another, depending on many historical, social, and legal factors.

In fact, Moroney suggests that differences in the respective legal traditions between the English-speaking countries and the other noncommunist countries sampled may be an important explanatory factor. This is an interesting hypothesis but one that I cannot evaluate without more familiarity with the laws.

In conclusion, this is a fascinating topic and one well worth exploring. Unfortunately at this time the data included in Moroney's paper can only arouse our curiosity. Substantial data collection well beyond anything presented here will be required to push forward this research in the future. In the meanwhile, our thanks to Professor Moroney for provoking new interest in an underresearched and fascinating area.

Notes

1. This cross-national classification was recently published in an article "Socialism: Trials and Errors," *Time*, March 13, 1978.

2. U.S. Department of Labor, Employment Standards Administration, Women's Bureau, *Fact Sheet on the Earnings Gap,* 1975. The figures in this publication are not exactly the same as those used in Moroney's paper in the years prior to 1971. However, the definition of the ratio appears to be the same. In general, Moroney's ratios quoted for the United States are slightly lower than those published by the Women's Bureau.

3. A search through the *Current Population Reports* data used by Moroney in constructing the manual wage ratios for the United States did not reveal any separate manual trade classification, so it would be interesting to know which occupations were actually included. *Current Population Reports,* p. 60, no. 101, p. 143.

4. John Durand, *The Labor Force in Economic Development* (Princeton, N.J.: Princeton University Press, 1975).

5. Sharon P. Smith, *Equal Pay in the Public Sector: Fact or Fantasy* (Princeton, N.J.: Princeton University Press, 1977).

6. Sylvia Ann Hewlett, "Inflation and Inequality," *Journal of Economic Issues* 11, no. 2 (June 1977):353. Of course another problem with the data

compared is that they are on a pretax basis. If governments use the tax system as a form of income redistribution and treat men and women differently, this will affect the aftertax earnings ratio.

8 A Theory of Groups: Which Age, Sex, Ethnic, and Religious Groups are Relevant?

Lester C. Thurow

Should government economic policies focus on eliminating differences in economic outcomes among groups (black versus white, male versus female, the elderly versus the young), or should they focus on helping individuals whose economic performance is in some sense below society's norms of acceptability (the poor)? At the moment this is a fundamental ideological question facing the United States and most other Western industrialized countries. Both our political traditions and our economic traditions have historically focused attention on the individual. Individuals are awarded voting rights, and individuals are to have an equal opportunity to achieve economic success.

In this context the whole issue of group justice is often seen as illegitimate. Individual blacks may have been unfairly treated, but blacks have not been treated unfairly as a group. Consequently, remedies must come at the individual levels (a case-by-case fight against discrimination or remedial education programs for individuals) and not at a group level. Programs such as affirmative action or quotas that create group preferences are fought on the grounds that they are unfair even if everyone agrees that many or all members of the group to be helped have suffered from unfair treatment in the past.

This same tradition is seen within economic theory. The standard social welfare function is the individualistic social welfare function in which individual utilities (weighted or unweighted) appear as arguments. I am unaware of any major piece of economic analysis that has used group relative incomes as the right-hand arguments of a social welfare function. Neoclassical economics is at its heart an economics of the individual. Individuals organize into voluntary economic associations (the firm), but individuals earn and allocate income. Group welfare is, if anything, only the algebraic summation of the individual welfare of the members of the group. There are no involuntary groups. Individuals join groups only when groups raise individual welfare. No one assigns someone to a group to which he or she does not wish to belong.

At the same time our age is an age of group consciousness. Major income redistribution pressures exist not at the level of the individual (rich versus poor) but at the level of the group (black versus white, male versus female). These pressure groups basically argue that group parity is a fundamental component of the social welfare function and that an optimal distribution of income consists of more than an optimal distribution of income across individuals.

This chapter looks at the economic legitimacy of group measures of economic justice as opposed to individual measures of economic justice. While it focuses solely on economics, I am well aware that there are other arguments for being interested in the economic performance of groups. The most obvious interest springs from the political process. Democracies are designed to respond to the perceived needs of their citizens. If a group of citizens feels economically aggrieved—for example, the farmers—and are willing and able to band together to exert political power, economic policymaking will, and should, respond. Holding most major political groups in a state of relative contentment is a perfectly valid political function.

At the same time it is worth thinking about whether there is an economic case for looking at groups rather than individuals. Is the correct economic strategy to resist group measures of welfare and group redistribution programs whenever this is politically possible? Or do groups play a more positive role in economics? Whichever is correct, however, the issue is not simply semantics where nothing observable would change depending on how the decision is made. Suppose, for example, that society decided to eliminate poverty (as officially defined) using a negative income tax with a 50 percent marginal tax rate. Such a policy would significantly alter the distribution of income across individuals, but the median black household income would still be just 59 percent of that of the median white household—precisely what it is now without a public policy to eliminate poverty. Would we be willing to say that economic equity had been achieved since poverty had been eliminated?

I first look at the economic arguments for analyzing group economic performances and then consider what constitutes an economically legitimate group. There is a brief section on the current distribution of income among groups. Since I recently analyzed the economic performance of most major economic groups since World War II,[1] I shall not repeat that exercise but merely bring the picture up-to-date and present a static picture of where the different groups stand. Then I look at some of the implications of the previous analysis and data for public programs designed to alter the distribution of income among groups.

The Need for Group Analysis

Assume that society wishes to establish an economy that provides "equal opportunities" for individuals to be economically successful. How is society going to tell whether equal opportunity does or does not exist? In a deterministic world we could tell by seeing whether each individual reaches a level of economic performance consistent with his or her inputs (talents, efforts, human capital). Individuals could be identified as receiving less than equal treatment.

But the real world is highly stochastic and not deterministic. Since everyone is subject to a variety of good and bad random shocks, no one can tell whether any individual has been unfairly treated by looking at his or her income. You and I may have participated in the same economic lottery, but you may have won and I may have lost. My low income and your high income do not prove that I was unfairly treated relative to you. You were lucky and I was unlucky, but I was not unfairly treated and I did not suffer from discrimination or some systematic denial of equal opportunities.

Since the typical individual earnings function explains only 20 percent to 30 percent of the variance in individual earnings, we are obviously dealing in an area where the stochastic shocks (or unknown factors) are very large relative to the deterministic (or known) part of the system. The larger the stochastic portion of the system relative to the deterministic portion of the system, the less possible it is to identify individuals who have been unfairly treated. In the economic area no one can say that any individual has been subject to systematic discrimination as opposed to random bad luck. This judgment can be made only at the group level.

How do we determine whether discrimination or a denial or equal opportunity exists? The standard procedure is to estimate an earnings function that explains individual earnings based on the normal human capital factors (work effort, skills, education) and then to see whether the equation for one group of individuals differs statistically from that of another group of individuals. Essentially there are three tests for the denial of equal opportunity. If we were testing for the existence of equal opportunities among whites and blacks, we would look at earnings functions to see whether there were (1) a statistically significant negative dummy variable for blacks, (2) statistically significant differences in equation parameters, and (3) statistically significant differences in the input factors supplied. If the last were true, it would be necessary to investigate whether economic inputs were different because of some earlier denial of equal opportunity (blacks were not given an equal opportunity to acquire skills) or whether they differed because of voluntary behavior (blacks like leisure more than whites).

Using economic analysis it is impossible to determine whether any individual has suffered from the denial of equal opportunity. Within any group—no matter how privileged—there are individuals who have been denied equal opportunities and suffered from discrimination, but they have not been subject to a systematic denial of opportunities. Not being systematic, society may be concerned but is completely incapable of doing anything about random discrimination. It is simply one type of random good or bad luck that affects us all. A Polish-American may feel aggrieved and may have been denied equal opportunities, but Polish-Americans do not suffer from systematic denials of equal opportunity since their earnings functions do not meet the necessary tests. Conversely, within any group—no matter how underprivileged—there are individuals who have not suffered from a systematic denial of opportunities. In these cases the existence or nonexistence of equal opportunities is simply part of the random good or bad luck that affects us all.

All society can do is test whether the economic lottery played by whites is or is not statistically equivalent to the economic lottery played by blacks. It cannot tell whether any individual black or white has been treated equally.

Discrimination affects individuals, but it can be identified only at the group level. As a result it is not possible to determine whether the society is an equal opportunity society without collecting and analyzing economic data on groups.

But the measurement problem also creates a remedy problem. If it is impossible to identify individual discrimination, on whom should the remedies for systematic discrimination be focused? Basically the inability to identify anything except group discrimination creates an inability to focus remedies on anything other than the group. We can attempt to create an economy where everyone participates in the same economic lottery, but we cannot create an economy where each individual is treated equally. According to current earnings functions, 70 percent to 80 percent of the variance in individual earnings is caused by factors that are beyond the control of even perfect government economic policies. The economy treats different individuals unequally no matter what we do. Only groups can be treated equally.

The Use or Misuse of Group Characteristics

Suppose that you were the dean of a medical school charged with maximizing the number of doctors produced for some given medical school budget. In the process of carrying out this mandate you noticed that 99 percent of all male admissions completed medical school and that 99 percent of all male graduates became lifetime doctors but that the corresponding percentages for women were each 98 percent. As a consequence, each male admission represents 0.98 doctors and each female admission represents 0.96 doctors. Seeking to be efficient and obey your mandate to maximize the number of practicing doctors, you establish a male-only admissions policy.

In this case the dean of the medical school is practicing statistical discrimination. He is treating each group fairly based on the objective characteristics of the group, but he is unfairly treating 96 percent of all women because they would in fact have gone on to become practicing doctors. His problem is that he has no technique for identifying which 4 percent will fail to become practicing doctors, and therefore he expands a very small difference in objective characteristics (a difference of one percentage point in each of the two probabilities) into a zero-one decision rule that excludes all women. Is the dean acting fairly or unfairly, efficiently or inefficiently?

To be efficient at the macro level is to be unfair to individuals at the micro level. Where is the balance to be drawn? Wherever the balance is drawn, groups become important, since it is efficient for employers to open or close opportunities to individuals based on the groups to which employers assign them. But since employers of necessity use groups in their decision making, the state must of necessity become involved in the question whai constitutes a legitimate group or an illegitimate group. The option of prohibiting all decisions based on group characteristics simply is not possible, since the price of efficiency would be too high.

A controversy of just this type is currently raging in Massachusetts over automobile insurance rates. In the past these rates have been based on the age, sex, and geographic location of the driver and the associated actuarial data. The insurance commissioner of the state has recently shifted to a system that rates drivers based on the number of years they have had a license, their accident record, and their arrest record. Individuals pay very different insurance premiums under the two systems. Which is the right set of groups?

Ideally groups would be allowed only where all members of the group had the same characteristics, and thus a fair treatment of the group would be a fair treatment of each individual member of the group. Unfortunately, this situation almost never exists. A trade-off must be made between macro efficiency and micro justice. Since employers are interested only in macro efficiency, they make the trade-off in favor of efficiency and in favor of unfair individual treatment unless they are restrained from using certain group classification. As a result the state is forced to establish categories of illegitimate groups (sex, age, race). Our social desires for individual justice, at least to some extent, take precedence over our individual desires for efficiency.

Since we have both a desire for efficiency and a desire for individual justice, we have a dilemma. Individuals have to be judged based on group data, yet all systems of grouping result in the unfair treatment of some individuals. Thus we must establish how large differences in mean characteristics have to be before a particular set of groups is legitimate. Most of us would be unwilling to let the dean of the medical school exclude women on the basis of a 1 percentage point difference in objective probabilities, but what would our judgments be if the objective differences were 50 percentage points or 90 percentage points? At some point many of us might be willing to exclude women. Yet if we did this at any point we would be unfairly treating some individual female.

What this illustrates, however, is that every society has to have a theory of legitimate and illegitimate groups, when individuals can be judged on group data and when they cannot be judged on group data. A concern for group economic data and performance is unavoidable.

The Nature of the Social Welfare Function

While the individualistic social welfare function is widely used in economics, its adoption as the standard social welfare function is anything but axiomatic. Where did it come from? Why is it the right function? Basically it comes from our belief in democracy—everyone's wishes should count—and a much too narrow view of individual preferences. I have preferences about maximizing my own personal utility within the rules of the economic game as it is now played (private personal preferences), but I also have preferences about how the rules of the economic game should be structured (individual societal preferences). I may, for example, think that the 55-mile-per-hour speed limit is a good societal rule yet still drive at 75 miles per hour if that is the speed limit. If everyone else is driving at 75, I know that I am safer at 75 than I would be at 55 and that any energy savings I make by driving at 55 are so small as to not advance our society toward my goal of energy conservation. Similarly, I may think that an ideal economic game would limit the maximum amount of income or wealth that any individual can have yet still seek to exceed that limit in the economic game that is actually being played.

From this perspective there is nothing illegitimate about a social welfare function that includes the relative incomes of different groups as one of its arguments. If individual societal preferences are such that individuals think the relative performance of different groups is a legitimate part of social welfare, then the relative performance of different economic groups legitimately appears in the social welfare function. There is no logic that rules it out of order. From the perspective of neoclassical economics, there are no legitimate preferences.

Which Groups?

On first thought, mobility (or the lack of mobility) seems to be an easy way to eliminate any social concern about many groups. If an individual can easily leave any group, then individuals in that group cannot claim to be unfairly treated. The value of the group must exceed the costs of the group or they would not belong. They may receive less measurable income by being a member of the group, but their psychic income from being a member of the group must at least counterbalance the lower measurable income. It is precisely this argument that lies at the heart of the typically economic reaction that government should not have special programs to raise the money incomes of groups such as farmers. Farmers may have lower incomes than urban dwellers, but they could always cease to be farmers and become urban dwellers. Therefore farmers cannot be unfairly treated regardless of the relative income of farmers and regardless of the sources of this relative difference.

While this argument may sound reasonable to those of us who are not farmers, it is equally applicable to regions or religions. Technically it is just as easy, if not easier and less costly, to move from one region to another or from one religion to another. Yet most of us would not be willing to argue that one must change his or her religion to achieve economic parity. Why? What is the difference between changing one's occupation and one's religion? Individuals can certainly be just as psychologically committed to a particular occupation as they are to a particular religion.

For all practical purposes age, sex, and race are not changeable by the individual, but does this automatically lead to the conclusion that these categories cannot be used to make employment decisions? The age dimension is interesting, since we are evolving a very complicated set of social patterns that basically say that it is illegal to discriminate against individuals as they grow older but it is legal to discriminate in favor of individuals as they grow older (special provisions in the income tax laws, senior citizens discounts). Why is this pattern legitimate in the case of the elderly and illegitimate in the case of blacks? As a result, mobility does not seem to be a characteristic that helps us separate legitimate and illegitimate groups.

The stochasticity of the economy is one of the major factors leading to the need for group analysis. If the world were really deterministic, it would be possible to reduce the group to the level of one individual. Conversely, the more stochastic the world, the larger groups must be before meaningful economic analysis can occur. Given a world that is 20 percent to 30 percent deterministic, groups must obviously be very large. Significant differences in earnings functions cannot be found unless groups are large.

In addition, groups must be large enough so that there is every reason to believe that they contain the same potential distributions of inputs. Actual inputs into the economic process may differ due to discrimination and opportunities, but groups should be potentially identical in terms of ability, motivation, and the like. This obviously leads into theories of genetics, nurturing, and the endogeneity of motivation before one is able to establish legitimate groupings.

Given groups of sufficient size, it is presumably possible to eliminate some groups based on their inability to meet the earnings function test of a denial of equal opportunities. White ethnics are presumably not a source of social concern for this reason. Objectively they simply have not been denied equal economic opportunities on average even though some members of the group may have been denied opportunities.

This raises an interesting question: What are our social responsibilities to groups that meet the tests of being denied equal opportunities, or individuals who belong to such groups, who have achieved above-average economic performances? Many individual blacks have incomes above that of the average white. Is there a social responsibility to equalize the opportunities for blacks and whites to become millionaires, or do the social responsibilities focus only on those whose economic performance is below average? In Southeast Asia ethnic Chinese suffer from discrimination, yet they typically have achieved above-average economic performance despite these handicaps. If such a group existed in the United States, what would be our responsibilities to it? This is one of the main issues in a case such as the Bakke case. Is the appropriate focus of remedial attention on disadvantaged families (black or white) or on individuals who belong to groups that have suffered from systematic discrimination (rich or poor)? Presumably, if equal opportunity is really the goal, equalizing the proportions of black and white millionaires is just as much a part of achieving this goal as equalizing the proportions of blacks and whites in poverty.

Finally, there is a question about the economic dimension on which a denial of equal opportunities is to be determined. Equal opportunity may exist in one metric and not in another. Women, for example, may meet the earnings function test of being denied equal opportunities yet flunk a consumption function test of being denied equal opportunities. Their consumption standards may be equitable, yet their earnings standards inequitable. Which is the right dimension? From the point of view of conventional neoclassical economics—only consumption generates utility—the earnings function test is presumably illegitimate. Yet equal opportunity has traditionally been measured on an earnings dimension, not on a consumption dimension.

Creating Equal Opportunity for Individuals

Suppose that some group has been identified as suffering from a denial of equal opportunities. How is this situation to be corrected? Imagine a race in which some racers have been assigned a heavy weight to carry because they belong to some group. Because of this handicap the average runner with weights will be behind the average runner without weights, but some runners with weights will be ahead of some runners without weights. Now suppose that a magic wand were waved and the weights were lifted from the backs of all runners. If the two groups of runners were equal in ability, the mean difference between the weighted and unweighted groups would cease to expand, but those who suffered from the earlier discrimination would never catch up. If this is a race where parents who are ahead are able to hand the baton to their children, there is no equalization of the race even across generations. The race can be made into a fair race only if everyone is forced to start over at the same starting line, if those without weights are forced to carry weights until the differences in average group performances disappear, or if those who have been handicapped are given special privileges until they catch up.

Since it is not possible to stop the economy and redistribute human and physical capital equally, the only real choice is between handicapping those who benefited from the previous handicaps or giving special treatment to those who were hurt by the previous handicaps. Discrimination against someone is unfortunately discrimination in favor of someone else. The person gaining from the discrimination may not be the discriminator, but unfortunately he or she will have to pay part of the price of eliminating discrimination. But this means that society is forced to focus on whatever groups have been denied equal opportunities in the past and practice reverse discrimination.

An individualistic ethic is acceptable if society has never violated this individualistic ethic in the past, but it is unacceptable if society has not in fact lived up to its individualistic ethic in the past. To shift from a system of group discrimination to a system of individual performance is to perpetuate the effects of past discrimination into the present and the future. The need to practice discrimination (positive or negative) to eliminate the effects of past discriminations is in fact one of the unfortunate costs of past discrimination.

The Relative Economic Status of Different Groups

Race

If you look at household income data along ethnic lines, there are only three major groups with below-average incomes—blacks, Hispanics, and American Indians.[2] Of the almost 100 million white Americans who think of themselves as having an ethnic origin, every other group has an income that is above that of those Americans who think of themselves as native Americans.

The median black household had an income 59 percent as large as that of whites in 1976. Since the average black household is slightly larger than the average white household (3.15 people versus 2.81 people), per capita black household income is slightly smaller (58 percent), but the differences are not significant. On an earnings dimension blacks are slightly better off than household income numbers would indicate. The average black earns 60 percent as much as the average white and the average full-time full-year black worker earns 72 percent as much as the equivalent white. These higher earnings figures are offset by the fact that the average white household now has more earners than the average black household.

The median Hispanic household had an income 73 percent that of whites in 1976, but Spanish heritage households are substantially larger than white households (3.47 people versus 2.81 people), so that on a per capita basis Hispanic households have just 59 percent as much as whites and are in approximate parity with blacks. Black and Hispanic earning power is essentially the same, but more Hispanics are full-time full-year workers (50 percent versus 44 percent), so that Hispanic household incomes exceed that of blacks. Among Hispanics Mexican Americans are at the group average, Puerto Ricans are 25 percent below the group average, and Cubans are 18 percent above the group average.

American Indians are the forgotten minority in terms of statistical studies, but their median household income probably lies somewhere between 30 percent and 50 percent of that of whites.

Sex

Female-headed households have a median income just 45 percent that of male-headed households, but female households are much smaller (1.97 people versus 3.15 people), so that per capita female household income is 75 percent that of males. By race, white females do better than either blacks or Hispanics. White per capita female incomes are 80 percent that of males, blacks 57 percent that of males, and Hispanics 68 percent that of males. Women who work full-time full-year make 60 percent that of males who work full-time full-year. This percentage has remained constant since the data were first collected in 1939.

Farmers

In 1976 farm incomes were 90 percent of nonfarm incomes, but per capita household incomes were only 81 percent of those of nonfarmers. If, however, one uses the cost-of-living differences between farmers and nonfarmers to calculate their poverty lines, then farm incomes were 106 percent of nonfarm incomes and per capita farm incomes were 95 percent of nonfarm incomes. Farmers are essentially at parity even in a year with depressed agricultural prices.

Farmers are often talked about as if they are a low-income group since the Department of Agriculture is in the habit of comparing farm income from farming with urban incomes. This calculation ignores the fact that most farmers with low agricultural incomes supplement their farm incomes with off-farm income. In 1976 farmers earned $18 billion in net income from farming but $24 billion from nonfarming activities. To ignore nonfarm income is to ignore over half of farm income. Relative to the average, farmers are also substantially above average in terms of their ownership of physical wealth. In fact, they have over three times the wealth of the average nonfarmer.[3]

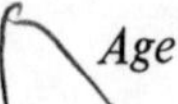

Age

The data in table 8-1 outline differences in household incomes by age of the family head. Household money incomes range from 132 percent of the national average for forty-five to fifty-five year-old families to 58 percent of the national average for families over sixty-five. On a per capita household income basis, however, the range is from 128 percent of the national average for fifty-five to sixty-four year-old household heads to 82 percent for fourteen to twenty-four year-old household heads. The elderly on a per capita basis have a higher income than all families below forty-five years of age. They are also substantially above average in terms of their ownership of physical wealth, with 36 percent more

Table 8-1
Household Income by Age, as Percentage of National Average

Age	*Household Income*	*Per Capita Household Income*
14-24	66	82
25-34	101	93
35-44	124	88
45-54	132	112
55-64	108	128
65+	58	94

assets than the average American.[4] As these data indicate, the social security system is to a great extent a transfer from the relatively poor to the relatively rich.

Regions

The data in table 8-2 indicate differences in household incomes by region. In addition to data on money incomes, the data are deflated by the intermediate cost-of-living budgets provided by the Bureau of Labor Statistics (BLS) to determine differences in real incomes as well as money incomes. On neither basis is it possible to argue that the United States has severe regional income inequalities. On a money basis the range is from 92 percent of the national average in the South to 108 percent of the national average in the West. On a real basis the range is from 97 percent of the national average in the Northeast to 103 percent of the national average in the West.

In contrast, however, there are very large differences in average household incomes among metropolitan areas. As shown in table 8-3, among the top twenty areas the range is from 94 percent of the national average in Philadelphia and Pittsburgh to 135 percent of the national average in Washington. On a real basis (once again deflating by the BLS intermediate cost-of-living budget for an

Table 8-2
Income by Region, as a Percentage of National Average

Region	*Household Income*	*Real Household Income*
Northeast	102	97
Northcentral	106	101
South	92	100
West	104	103

Table 8-3
Household Income by Metropolitan Area, as a Percentage of National Average

Area	*Household Income*	*Real Household Income*
Anaheim	113	114
Atlanta	100	110
Baltimore	108	108
Boston	101	85
Chicago	118	116
Cleveland	103	102
Dallas	119	131
Detroit	116	114
Houston	107	116
Los Angeles	98	99
Milwaukee	109	102
Minneapolis	119	114
Newark	106	91
New York	97	84
Philadelphia	94	90
Pittsburgh	94	98
San Francisco	113	107
Seattle	106	106
St. Louis	107	111
Washington, D.C.	135	130

urban family of four) the range is from 84 percent in New York to 131 percent in Dallas. A difference of 47 percent is significant in anyone's terminology.

Religion

While the U.S. government does not collect income data by religious preferences, it is possible to make an educated guess about religious income differences based on what we know about ethnic and regional income differences and the dominant religious preferences of these regions or ethnic groups. Ranked from highest to lowest income, the order is probably Jews, white ethnic Catholics, white ethnic Protestants, white native Protestants, Catholic Hispanics, black Protestants, and Catholic, Protestant, and native religion American Indians.

To some extent religious income differences are probably in the same position as chemical carcinogens. To the extent that we do not know of their existence they are not controversial, but if we were to actually know income differences by religion (as we now know of cancer-causing chemicals) they might very well be the subject of political controversy as they are in Northern Ireland.

Government Programs for Groups

If one looks at revealed social preferences, society certainly cannot claim to focus consistently on individuals rather than on groups. Affirmative action and quota programs for minorities and women are certainly on the defensive, but programs for the elderly and farmers both abound and are expanding. Demands for regional programs are expanding rapidly, but they are currently mired in controversy since it is not clear who is underdeveloped and since the variance in economic prosperity within any one region is clearly larger than the mean differences among regions. If one looks at actions, it is easy to conclude that society invokes the principle of individuality only when it comes to dealing with groups that have suffered from discrimination. In other cases it is willing to use the principle of group as opposed to individual welfare.

The differences are most extreme if one compares programs for farmers with those for minorities. Farmers on average are average in terms of income and are substantially above average in terms of wealth. Yet non-income-conditioned general price support programs are being expanded. These programs focus most of the income aid on those who produce the most output, and these are precisely the farmers with the highest income and wealth. Imagine the furor if someone were to seriously propose exactly the same program for blacks (a wage support program that would guarantee blacks income parity and give most of the benefits to wealthy blacks). It would be denounced as un-American from every rooftop.

Programs for the elderly are interesting, since they seem to embody every principle that those who argue against groups would oppose, yet they remain untouched by controversy. When one thinks about them in detail, it is hard to understand how they have escaped legal challenges. Senior citizen discounts (price discrimination) exists in both the public and the private sector. State and federal income tax laws have special provisions for the elderly. Only the elderly have national health insurance. These laws may be politically popular because we all know that sooner or later we will be elderly, but they clearly involve the grossest kinds of discrimination. Here again similar programs for minorities are unimaginable.

While there have been, are, and will be regional development programs, regional development is the clearest area for an individual rather than a group focus of attention. Regions have not suffered from discrimination, and the variance in income and opportunities within any region clearly dwarfs even the substantial differences in mean income across metropolitan areas. New York City may be the poorest large city in the United States in terms of real incomes, but it is also the home of the richest people in the United States. General aid to New York City would seem to be a perverse transfer.

It is not clear what will evolve from the rudimentary affirmative action programs that are now under attack in the courts, but the use of group criteria by discriminators in the past forces the state to use group criteria to eliminate the effects of discrimination in the present. To insist on an individual focus is to de facto insist that the effects of discrimination linger for a very long time after positive discrimination has ceased to exist.

Given that society is unwilling to be consistent and to use an individual focus when it comes to politically popular groups, it is easy to see the insistence on an individual focus for minorities as simply a more sophisticated version of the types of individual discrimination that have been outlawed in the past two decades.

Notes

1. Lester C. Thurow, "The Economic Progress of Minority Groups," *Challenge,* March-April 1976.

2. Unless otherwise specified, all the data in this section come from U.S. Bureau of the Census, *Current Population Reports: Consumer Income, Series P-60* (Washington, D.C.: U.S. Government Printing Office).

3. U.S. Federal Reserve Board, "Survey of Financial Characteristics of Consumers," *Federal Reserve Bulletin,* March 1964, p. 291.

4. Ibid.

Commentary

Martin Bronfenbrenner

Lester Thurow has made me worry and think about the inconsistencies and contradictions between the individualist and the groupist aspects of our poverty and redistribution policies. For this I am decidedly grateful, much as I dislike worrying and thinking. But when it comes to his conclusion–which way policy should move–we are on opposite sides. I remain the reactionary individualist, while Thurow goes all out for the particular groups he considers legitimate, which include women and blacks but not farmers and the aged. (His criteria for legitimacy impress me as unfair to the small minorities and likewise to those who have somehow overcome discrimination. While Benjamin Franklin thought that God helps those who help themselves, Lester Thurow believes that God helps those who don't or can't or won't do so.)

Our differences may be even more fundamental. Thurow wants to redistribute income all the way up and down the scale, somewhat à la John Rawls (1971). I am primarily against poverty, and I am willing to limit myself to three more modest and individualistic proposals in aid of the poor persons of all groups:

1. A social minimum income per person or family, along the lines suggested by Milton Friedman (1962 chap. 12) and augmented by James Tobin (1970). These will automatically aid the groups Thurow worried about, since they are overrepresented in the poverty strata of the personal income distribution.
2. A set of housing, health, and educational institutions such that income or wealth inequality makes less difference to economic opportunity than it still does. Here my text is R.H. Tawney's *Equality,* plus Tobin's "On Limiting the Domain of Inequality" 1970. What it means is that I do not care whether the rich have cars while the poor must ride the bus, provided that reasonably good bus service is available.
3. A set of fiscal institutions such that this minimum income and these institutions are financed along nonregressive and noninflationary lines. Here I am influenced by my former teacher Henry Simons and my former boss Carl Shoup.

We are not currently doing such a good job on these fronts to justify going forward toward overall redistribution of opportunity along the lines of Rawls or of Thurow. Thurow seems interested in having society perform redistributional matrix algebra before it has mastered the multiplication table, let alone the linear equation. So I would consign much of the detail of his proposal to science fiction or to close encounters of the *n*th kind.

For here-and-now policy, I should resolve the Thurow contradiction by minimizing groupist elements of policy rather than expanding them by affirmative action. Not that groupism is in any way illegitimate—it is not, and I have myself dabbled in interdependent utility functions—but the most important issue seems to me the inequality of individual income and wealth, especially the persistence of extreme poverty.

Since this puts Thurow and me on opposite sides of the affirmative action barricades, let me try to defend my position.

Despite Thurow's noteworthy attempt, I do not think we can tell ex ante which particular groups are legitimate in his sense. I wonder, for example, about the "closet" groups such as the homosexuals? What about the physically (and the mentally?) handicapped? What about the victims of crimes and torts? What about the addicts of alcohol and drugs? And so on and so on.

An obverse or reverse problem should also be remembered. When blacks, Hispanics, and women benefit from affirmative action, who can anticipate negative action in return? Surely one cannot realistically expect the costs to be spread evenly and equitably among the entire white, non-Hispanic, male population! It seems currently to be the Jews, sensitized by history, who anticipate playing the principal victim role. Others feel that Italian Americans or Slavic Americans will fall sooner and remain longer in the category of victims of discrimination. At any rate, the point should not be swept under the rug or entirely forgotten.

Thurow also seems less impressed with history than one might wish. Plenty of racial groups that neither of us would call discriminated against today were discriminated against at the turn of the century. How did they raise themselves from their disadvantaged positions? May there not be an important cost—Arthur Okun calls it the "leaky bucket" and George Stigler "Director's Law"—in spending money and hiring sociologists to do for people or groups today what they will do for themselves at less cost tomorrow? In pursuing this history I think special attention should be paid to the Asians, who have shared with the blacks and Chicanos the onus of American color prejudice—and have done better at overcoming or counteracting it.

I happen to hold an unscientific theory of racial integration. It is a two-stage theory. First one graduates from the street corner, the poolroom, or the Blackstone Rangers into skilled labor or white-collar status in one's own community, ghetto or otherwise. That is the first stage. Then one gains recognition, or one's children do, in the majority community. This recognition may easily involve integration to the extent of one's desires for integration. That is the second stage, but usually the first stage is the harder one.

One complaint against affirmative action is its concentration on the relatively easier second stage without doing much at the more difficult first stage. Within the Hispanic communities, middle-class Cubans in Miami seem to have gained more from affirmative action than peasant Chicanos in Texas. In the black community, again, the principal beneficiaries seem to be middle-class—the Martin Luther Kings, Julian Bonds, Andrew Youngs—rather than the "brothers on the block" in Bedford-Stuyvesant or the South Bronx. For the women, we academics have an example nearer home. The great gainers from affirmative action on campus seem to be well-trained faculty wives already in place in the right age groups with the right credentials, not the secretary behind her typewriter, nor the cleaning lady who comes in the evening.

One of my several debts to Thurow as a distributional statistician is for stressing the antiegalitarian effects of women's liberation, even without affirmative action, in permitting both members of advantaged couples—the Radcliffe wife of the Harvard doctor—to combine two highly desirable jobs within a single family group. Thurow makes allied points regarding aid to the farmers and the elderly—but is assistance for his "legitimate" groups significantly different?

And so, to conclude, I recognize that the Thurow contradiction is both neglected and important, but I would rather solve it for the present by retreat to individualism and the alleviation of poverty rather than by advance to groupism and equality of opportunity up and down the line. I have not mentioned medical school admissions and automobile insurance ratings, but my biases are all in favor of letting individual experience rebut group presumptions and prejudices as far and as soon as possible. To indicate what I mean: my late father served on the admissions committee of one well-known medical school and was faced year after year with precisely the Thurow problem—would women actually practice medicine if admitted? And I gather that particular medical school solved that problem on the individual basis of reverse discrimination—admitting plain Janes with poor marital prospects and rejecting glamor girls who seemed to have better ones. What was done with the Joan Robinsons and Bella Abzugs I did not think to inquire of my father during his lifetime, but I hope they were excluded too. (Does that make me a male chauvinist pig as well as a reactionary?)

References

Friedman, Milton. *Capitalism and Freedom* (Chicago: University of Chicago Press, 1962).

Rawls, John. *A Theory of Justice* (Cambridge, Mass.: Harvard University Press, 1971).

Tawney, Richard H. *Equality* (New York: Harcourt, Brace and Co., 1931).

Tobin, James. "On Limiting the Domain of Inequality," *Journal of Law and Economics,* 13 (1970):263-278.

Subject Index

About the Contributors

Martin Bronfenbrenner is Kenan Professor of Economics at Duke University. He received the Ph.D. in economics from the University of Chicago, but his professional interests span the disciplines of economics, sociology, political science, and psychology. His prodigious research scholarship includes *Income Distribution Theory* (University of Chicago Press, 1971).

Edgar Browning is professor of economics at the University of Virginia. He received the doctorate from Princeton University. His professional interests include public finance and the analysis of income distribution. He is the coauthor of a recent textbook in public finance. His research papers have appeared in the *American Economic Review,* the *Journal of Political Economy,* and other journals.

Janet G. Chapman is professor and chairperson of the Department of Economics, University of Pittsburgh. She received the Ph.D. from Columbia University. She is an authority on the Soviet economy, and has published numerous papers and books on Soviet labor markets and income distribution, including *Real Wages in Soviet Russia Since 1928* (Harvard University Press, 1963).

Robert Dalrymple is an economist with the Department of Health, Education, and Welfare. He received the Ph.D. from the University of Wisconsin.

Evsey D. Domar is Ford Professor of Economics at the Massachusetts Institute of Technology. He received the Ph.D. from Harvard University and has written extensively in the fields of economic theory and comparative economic systems. He is a Fellow of the American Academy of Arts and Sciences and the Econometric Society and the author of *Essays in the Theory of Economic Growth* (Oxford University Press, 1957).

Cynthia B. Lloyd is professor of economics at Barnard College. She received the doctorate from Columbia University. Her professional interests include the economic analysis of discrimination, especially discrimination toward women. She is the editor of *Sex, Discrimination, and the Division of Labor* (Columbia University Press, 1975).

Harold F. Lydall is professor at the Institute of Economics and Statistics, Oxford University. He was a Rhodes scholar and received the doctorate from Oxford. He is an authority in the fields of economic statistics and income distribution and the author of *The Structure of Earnings* (Oxford University Press, 1968).

Charles E. McLure is vice-president of the National Bureau of Economic Research. He received the Ph.D. from Princeton University and has written extensively in the field of public finance, particularly concerning the incidence of taxes. His papers have been published in the *Quarterly Journal of Economics,* the *Journal of Political Economy,* and other journals.

Joseph A. Pechman is director of the Economic Studies Program at the Brookings Institution. He received the Ph.D. from the University of Wisconsin and has written extensively in the field of public finance. He has published several books, most recently *Who Bears the Tax Burden?* (Brookings Institution, 1974).

Solomon Polachek is associate professor of economics at the University of North Carolina. He received the Ph.D. from Columbia University. His professional research has centered on the determinants of personal earnings, and he has published articles appearing in the *Journal of Political Economy,* the *International Economic Review,* and elsewhere.

Werner Pommerehne is lecturer in economics at the University of Zurich. He received the Ph.D. from the University of Konstanz and has published papers dealing with public goods and collective choice.

G. Randolph Rice is associate professor and chairperson of the Department of Economics, Louisiana State University. He received the Ph.D. from the University of Kentucky. His professional interests include regional economics and personal income distribution. He has published papers in the *Journal of Regional Science* and elsewhere.

Eugene Smolensky is professor and chairperson of the Department of Economics, University of Wisconsin. He received the doctorate from the University of Pennsylvania and has professional interests in macroeconomics, public finance, and income distribution. He is the coauthor of *Public Expenditures, Taxes, and the Distribution of Income* (Academic Press, 1977).

Lester C. Thurow is professor of economics at the Massachusetts Institute of Technology. He was a Rhodes scholar and received the Ph.D. from Harvard University. He is an authority in the fields of public finance and income distribution and is the author of *Generating Inequality* (Basic Books, 1975).

Jane Alison Weiss is assistant professor of sociology, University of Iowa. She received the Ph.D. from Stanford University. She is a specialist in comparative sociology and has a particular interest in the socioeconomic analysis of women's earnings and occupational mobility.

About the Editor

John R. Moroney is professor of economics at Tulane University. He received the Ph.D. from Duke University. His areas of professional interest include economic theory, monetary economics, econometrics, industrial organization, and natural resources. He is the author of *The Structure of Production in American Manufacturing* (University of North Carolina Press, 1972, and Oxford University Press, 1973).